Racial Conditions

Racial Conditions

Politics, Theory, Comparisons

Howard Winant

 University of Minnesota Press
Minneapolis
London

Chapter 2, "The Theoretical Status of the Concept of Race," reprinted in revised form from
Race, Identity, and Representation in Education, Warren Crichlow and Cameron McCarthy,
eds. (New York: Routledge, 1993); used with permission of the publisher. Chapter 6, "The
Los Angeles 'Race Riot' and Contemporary U.S. Politics," reprinted in revised form from
Reading Rodney King, Reading Urban Uprising, Robert Gooding-Williams, ed. (New York:
Routledge, 1993); used with permission of the publisher. Chapter 7, "Hard Lessons: Recent
Writing on Racial Politics," was previously published in *Socialist Review* 93, no. 2 (1993);
reprinted with permission of *Socialist Review.* Chapter 8, "Racial Formation and
Hegemony: Global and Local Developments," was previously published in *Racism,
Identity, Ethnicity,* Ali Rattansi and Sallie Westwood, eds. (New York: Basil Blackwell, 1994);
reprinted with permission of the publisher. Chapter 9, "Rethinking Race in Brazil,"
previously appeared in *Journal of Latin American Studies* 24, no. 1 (February 1992);
reprinted with permission of Cambridge University Press.

Published by the University of Minnesota Press
111 Third Avenue South, Suite 290, Minneapolis, MN 55401-2520.
Printed in the United States of America on acid-free paper

Second printing 1996

Library of Congress Cataloging-in-Publication Data

Winant, Howard.
    Racial conditions : politics, theory, comparsions / Howard Winant.
        p.   cm.
    Includes bibliographical references and index.
    ISBN 0-8166-2386-4 (hard cover : acid-free)
    ISBN 0-8166-2387-2 (pbk. : acid-free)
    1. Race relations.   2. United States—Race relations.
3. Brazil—Race relations.   I. Title
HT1521.W59   1994
305.8'00973—dc20   93-30445
                                                                              CIP

In appreciation of the work and struggle of Salman Rushdie,
tireless defender of the rights of minorities
and the cause of free expression.
May he regain complete liberty.

With gratitude to Deborah Haagens Winant,
who continues to sustain those she loves.

Não temos armas que vençam a opressão e jamais teremos, embora devamos lutar sempre que a nossa sobrevivência e a nossa honra tenha de ser defendida. Mas a nossa arma há de ser a cabeça, a cabeça de cada um e de todos, que não pode ser dominada e tem de afirmar-se. Nosso objetivo não é bem a igualdade, é mais a justiça, a liberdade, o orgulho, a dignidade, a boa convivência. Isto é uma luta que trespassará os séculos, porque os enemigos são muito fortes. A chibata continua, a pobreza aumenta, nada mudou. A Abolição não aboliu a escravidão, criou novos escravos. A República não aboliu a opressão, criou novos opressores. O povo não sabe de si, não tem consciência e tudo o que faz não é visto e somente lhe ensinam desprezo por si mesmo, por sua fala, por sua aparência, pelo que come, pelo que veste, pelo que é. Mas nós estamos fazendo essa revolução de pequenas e grandes batalhas, umas sangrentas, outras surdas, outras secretas, e é isto que eu faço. . . .

[We don't have enough weapons to overcome oppression and never will, although it's our duty to fight whenever our survival and our honor have to be defended. But our weapon must be the mind, each and everyone's mind, which must not be dominated and has to assert itself. Our objective is not really equality, rather it's justice, freedom, pride, dignity, good coexistence. This is a fight that will go across centuries, because our enemies are very strong. The bullwhip still prevails, poverty increases, nothing has changed. Emancipation didn't abolish slavery, it created new slaves. The Republic didn't abolish oppression, it created new oppressors. The people doesn't know about itself, has no conscience, nothing it does is seen, and all it is taught is contempt for itself, for its speech, for its appearance, for its food, for its clothing, for what it is. But we are making this revolution of small and great battles, some bloody, some muffled, some secret, and this is what I do. . . .]
—Joao Ubaldo Ribeiro, *An Invincible Memory*

Contents

Preface

This small book of essays has a large goal: to reconceptualize race at the end of the twentieth century. It is now ninety years since W. E. B. Du Bois, the nation's preeminent thinker on racial matters, formulated his famous maxim that "the problem of the twentieth century is the problem of the color-line" (1989 [1903]: 13). His words were prophetic, for race did emerge over the course of this bloody century as a crucial issue of culture and politics, as a defining dimension of social order and conflict all around the globe.

But the world Du Bois saw was very different from our own. At the turn of the twentieth century, the globe was carved up into the colonial empires of European powers. The United States—and practically every other multiracial society on earth—was a rigid caste society, a virtual racial dictatorship, a *herrenvolk* democracy. The nearly universal view of race was that it was a "natural" phenomenon, a biological essence, an immutable determinant of social distance and hierarchy. Eugenics was in full flower—the term had been coined in 1883 by Francis Galton, the cousin of Charles Darwin—and not only the halls of government but also the groves of academe resounded with debate on the most effective ways of preserving and extending the unquestioned superior traits of the white race. At the beginning of the twentieth century, only a few voices cried out in a seeming wilderness against the white supremacy so generally taken for granted. Thus, in identifying race as the problem of the age, Du Bois foretold dramatic changes indeed.

Nearly one hundred years later the situation has changed quite drastically. The far-flung colonial empires are gone, and their once haughty "mother countries" are declining powers. The twentieth century, despite its rivers of blood and orgies of hatred—racial and otherwise—has seen the rise of race to world center stage. Biologistic theories of race no longer retain even minimal credibility. Racial inequality, far from being perceived as "natural," is generally recognized as a form of injustice. Even the "ignoble and unhappy regime" (Marley 1976) of apartheid in South Africa—where racial difference was heretofore enshrined as the fundamental mark of caste—has been forced to undertake massive reforms. In the United States, a powerful movement for racial justice destroyed the system of racial segregation in the years after World War II, leaving a far more open—if still ambiguous and conflictual—political situation in its wake.

So, are things getting better or worse? The tremendous racial transformations of this century, I argue here, cannot be understood in the usual terms of plus and minus. Is race increasing or decreasing in significance on a world scale? Is country X more or less egalitarian than it was twenty years ago? Have the "life chances" of a black or indigenous person improved in country Y? In general, such questions cannot be answered with great assurance, because they do not address the contemporary complexities of race, the conflicting meanings and fragmented identities that characterize it today. In contrast to a century ago, the world today is more aware of race, more respectful of difference, even marginally more egalitarian. Yet how those putative improvements play in the streets of São Paulo or Detroit, and how they compare to the overall progress made since Du Bois penned *The Souls of Black Folk*—such questions remain open.

Thus, to understand race as a "problem" today means something very different than it did in 1903. When Du Bois wrote that famous line, he was appealing for the world's attention and demanding justice. Today, to speak of race as a "problem" is not to call attention to injustice but to propose to transcend race, to get beyond it, to eliminate it or at least drastically reduce its importance in sociopolitical terms. It is to seek a "solution"—intellectual, moral, or political—to the supposed incongruities of racial difference and inequality in ostensibly democratic and egalitarian societies.

What is wrong with "solving" the race "problem"? Why shouldn't we try to "get beyond" race? When a full account of the complexities of race remains far beyond our reach, such objectives are either foolish or dangerous, or both. Is it not rather disingenuous to contemplate "getting beyond" race when in almost every corner of the globe, dark skin still correlates with inequality? Since when has it been possible to make large-scale conflicts "go away"? What other major forms of human difference have been transcended recently? Class? Gender? Nationality? When we look with any degree of seriousness at the "problem" of race, we must recognize that it is not about to go away, not about to be "solved."

Indeed, rather than suggesting that race is a problem to be solved, I argue in this book that race is a condition of individual and collective identity, a permanent, though tremendously flexible, element of social structure. Race is a means of knowing and organizing the social world; it is subject to continual contestation and reinterpretation, but it is no more likely to disappear than other forms of human inequality and difference. Of course, racial inequality can be lessened, racial difference can be respected, but in no sense would such changes, though obviously desirable, get us "beyond" race.

More yet. Race is an epochal phenomenon that took on most of its importance as a result of the creation of the modern world. Although some forms of racial awareness preceded the rise of Europe, it was the European conquest of the Americas, Africa, and Asia and the introduction of the imperial forms of rule associated with capitalism that ushered in the consolidation of racial divisions in society. The five-hundred-year domination of the globe by Europe and its inheritors is the historical context in which racial concepts of difference have attained their present status as fundamental components of human identity and inequality. To imagine the end of race is thus to contemplate the liquidation of Western civilization.

Yet despite the racial holocausts that Europe authored from the navigators to the Nazis, the history of the West is not uniformly one of blood and hatred. As Du Bois knew, it is also a history of hybridity, of multiplicity, of reciprocity, and, ultimately, of the struggle for democracy. To rethink race is not only to recognize its permanence, but also to understand the essential test that it poses for any diverse society seeking to achieve a modicum of freedom. The two countries that occupy the bulk of this book's attention — the United States and Brazil — are perhaps the archetypal cases for this racial test of democracy. They are by far the most racially diverse democracies, and they share much racial history as well. Yet the organization of their respective racial orders, the role played by race as a fundamental principle of social organization within them, has been very different, almost opposite. They are the two great racial experiments of the West.

In the United States and Brazil, and in many other countries as well, the "solution" to the race "problem" is not transcendence but recognition, not denial of difference but respect for it, not coercion but democracy: more of it, better varieties of it, and the further extension of it into every realm of cultural, economic, and political life. That is the message of this book.

I got a lot of help in preparing these essays, a lot of encouragement, and a good deal of fierce criticism — the best kind of help. Over the past four years of writing, presenting, and revising these materials I have talked and corresponded with many people, more no doubt than I can remember or properly acknowledge. Of those, two friends, two brothers really, deserve special mention. Michael Omi of the University of California, Berkeley, has been my longtime collaborator and comrade. He is the coauthor of at least some version of three essays included here, chapters 2, 5, and 6, and the coparent (or codependent) of all my work on race. Michael Hanchard of the University of Texas, Austin, is my other great partner and critic. His fierce independence and critical intelligence have informed every page of this work.

Another key source of support has been the Rho Tau Gamma chapter of the Delaware Valley, whose members are Raphael Allen, Kimberly Benston, Eddie Glaude, Paul Jefferson, Wahneema Lubiano, Lucius Outlaw, Fasaha Traylor, and me. The mere existence of this group gives me encouragement, and its ferocious discussions have sustained me and supported this work in many ways.

Lisa Freeman of the University of Minnesota Press deserves special mention not only for her encouragement of the project, but also for her critical responses to the texts themselves.

Individuals with whom I have had the pleasure of dialogue or written exchanges about these essays include Amy Ansell, Lee D. Baker, Leslie Bary, Homi K. Bhabha, Nancy Board, Dain Borges, Maria Brandao, Heloisa Buarque de Holanda, Victor Bulmer-Thomas, Warren Crichlow, Marcy Darnovsky, Ann Ferguson, Charles (Chip) Gallagher, Robert Gooding-Williams, Stuart Hall, Carlos A. Hasenbalg, Martin Kilson, Paulo J. Krischke, Annette Lareau, David Lloyd, Peggy Lovell, Cameron McCarthy, Silvia Pedraza, Ali Rattansi, Debbie Rogow, Gay Seidman, Thomas Skidmore, Stephen Small, Dana Y. Takagi, Eddie Telles, Dan Tompkins, Peter van der Veer, Ronald Walters, Jerry G. Watts, Sallie Westwood, Alford Young, Jr., Iris Marion Young, and George Yúdice.

Beyond these whom I can list, there are many I cannot, undoubtedly because I have appropriated their ideas so completely that I no longer remember their original provenance. Responsibility for all errors, of course, remains with me alone.

Chapter 1

Introduction

Race shows no sign of declining significance. Quite the contrary: in a range of manifestations wider and wilder than the most fertile imaginations could have dreamed up, race continues to operate as a fundamental factor in political and cultural life all around the world. Its prevalence has proved puzzling for politicians, pundits, and professors alike.

Since the expectation of its transcendence, of its subsumption into some supposedly more fundamental form of social conflict, was all but universal, the continuity of race as a social fact confounds the entire political spectrum. At midcentury liberals anticipated that it would dissolve into matters of ethnicity, of culture—the more manageable and less consequential differences of customs, cuisine, and style. Marxists expected its supposed irrationalities to be overcome in a more enlightened consciousness—that of class. Nationalists sought to link racial difference to a redrawing of territorial boundaries, to the creation or resurrection of states in which the despised and colonized, the "natives" of the globe, could reclaim their majority status and their right to rule. The one twentieth-century political current that placed race per se at the center of its belief system—fascism—was defeated at midcentury, so the far right's version of race, with its politicized pathology of purity and blood, seemed to have been eliminated.

Today, at the end of the century, all these views are obsolete. Liberalism has surrendered to realpolitik. Marxism totters. Nationalisms of both left and right have capitulated to increasingly vapid and authoritarian romanticisms. Fascism has risen from its grave and reinstated its old victimology. And through it all, the racial dimensions of social life stubbornly refuse to disappear. It is a bit ironic that, long after the demise of the epoch-making practices that had originally placed it at the forefront of human awareness—such as the African slave trade and the various European seaborne empires—race should retain such a hold on our sense of self and society.

What *is* race, anyway? Biology is no longer destiny. "Natural" categories all stand revealed as deeply social and historical. Both the great chain of being and the imperialist chain have been broken in a hundred places. So what can this word—whose origins lie in eras and worldviews now remote to us—possibly *mean*? How can a concept with no scientific significance, a concept that is understood in such varied and often irrational ways, possess such force? Why, in so many varied settings all around the world, is race such an important source of meaning, identity, (dis)advantage, power, and powerlessness?

The answer to this question, I believe, is that race remains a fundamental organizing principle, a way of knowing and interpreting the social world. The meaning of race is utterly variable among different societies and over historical time. Yet in those *milieux* where, historically, race has been foundational—that is, in most if not all human societies—its centrality continues, even after the original reasons for invoking it have disappeared. This is but another way of saying that race is a significant dimension of *hegemony*, that it is deeply fused with the power, order, and indeed the meaning systems of every society in which it operates.

Consider the U.S. example. Well over a century since the abolition of racial slavery, and long after stable territorial boundaries were established through conquest, concepts of race remain deeply imbedded in every institution, every relationship, every psyche. This is true not only of such large-scale, macrosocial relationships as the distribution of wealth or income, or segregation in housing or education, but also of small-scale, microlevel relationships. Thus, as we watch the videotape of Rodney King being beaten by Los Angeles police officers, compare real estate prices in different metropolitan-area neighborhoods, select a radio channel to enjoy while we drive to work, size up a potential client, customer, neighbor, or teacher, stand in line at the unemployment office, or carry out a thousand other normal tasks, we are compelled to think racially, to use the racial categories and meaning systems into which we have been socialized. Despite exhortations both sincere and hypocritical, it is not possible or even desirable to be "color-blind." Not only is the social racialized, but the racial is socialized, such that identity itself is, so to speak, color-coded. Indeed, when one meets a person who is difficult to classify racially, the result is often a minicrisis of identity: not knowing to what race someone belongs is like not knowing to what sex the person belongs. For better or for worse, without a clear racial identity a North American is in danger of having no identity.

The problem, though, is that a clear racial identity does not, and cannot, exist. At the moment, the U.S. racial rules offer us a choice of five racial categories: white, black, brown, yellow, and red. Stripped of euphemism, these color categories, absurd as they are, define the racial universe. But of course, many people do not fit in anywhere. Where should we classify Arab-Americans, for example, or South Asians, or Brazilians? What about people with more than one salient racial characteristic, for example, black Puerto Ricans? Are they "African-American" or "Hispanic"? Such questions can be multiplied indefinitely. And although these details are drawn from a specifically U.S. context, a similar set of racial anomalies and contradictions could be adduced for most of the societies on the globe.

The continuing significance of race, though, does not ultimately lie in absurdities or anachronisms. Most basically, I believe, it consists in the permanence of human difference. The categories through which racial identities are understood, and the interpretations applied to them, may vary mightily from one period to another, and among distinct societies and cultures. Yet the social fact—in the Durkheimian sense—of racial difference persists.

If this is recognized, then the tasks that students of race must address are clear. We must strive to reinterpret the sociopolitical dynamics of race, to free the mind and heart as much as possible from the mistakes and shibboleths of the past. Just as in the nineteenth and early twentieth centuries the reduction of racial difference to biological phenomena, and the social Darwinism and eugenicism that flowed from it, had to be refuted (Barkan 1992), so too at the end of the twentieth century the reduction of racial difference to cultural, economic, or national phenomena must be opposed (Omi and Winant 1986). That is the analytical task, the imaginative task.

But there is also a political task. Bloodletting on a monumental scale, coercion unfathomed, has occurred in efforts to eradicate or to exploit racial difference. Nor are these offenses artifacts of earlier, more barbaric times; they remain in living memory, as testimony and admonition for us (Burleigh and Wippermann 1991; Kuper 1981; Mosse 1978). Because these things happened, we have incurred permanent social and political obligations to respect and preserve racial difference. Indeed, these commitments extend beyond race to human difference in general, for although race is a central form of difference, it is hardly the only one. Perhaps, though, race can be seen as *emblematic* of human difference, if only because of its flexibility and its deep interconnectedness with all forms of inequality and injustice.

With these general principles and commitments established, I shall now provide an overview of the problems addressed in this book. My main concern in Part I is to develop *racial theory*, by which I mean coherent explanatory accounts of significant racial phenomena. I have argued elsewhere that the meaning of race can only be understood as an evolving historical construct, that it can have no "objective" or unchanging interpretation (Omi and Winant 1986). This position, I suggest, is the culmination of the century-long struggle, already mentioned, to free the concept of race from the biologistic and deterministic frameworks in which it was located during the nineteenth century. Yet the discrediting of scientific racism does not of itself provide a new basis for racial theory. Rather, it casts the concept of race adrift in an exceptionally stormy sea.

In chapter 2, I undertake to steer the concept between the Scylla of a position that would dismiss it as a useless residuum of an earlier, benighted time, an "illusion" that we somehow must now learn to live without, and the Charybdis of a contrary view that, sometimes consciously but often unconsciously, reifies the concept as if it referred to something "objective." The effort to constitute the race concept theoretically as something neither apparitional nor tangible, as neither true nor false, so to speak, is a daunting task, but a necessary one. I suggest that, to be minimally effective from a theoretical point of view, the concept of race must incorporate at least three determinations that would definitively remove it from the biological to the social realm; these are the political, the global comparative, and the historicotemporal dimensions of race. In making this argument, I explicitly seek to foreshadow positions taken in subsequent chapters.

The next chapters undertake in various ways to develop these ideas. In chapters 3 and 4, I present a theoretical account of racial formation processes, focusing on the United States. Chapter 3 offers a model of the racial formation process in the contemporary United States that centers on the idea of racial *projects*. In this approach, the key element in racial formation is the link between signification and structure, between what race *means* in a particular discursive practice and how, based upon such interpretations, social structures are racially organized. The link between meaning and structure, discourse and institution, signification and organization, is made concrete in the notion of the racial project, and in my view is intrinsic and ineluctable. To interpret the meaning of race in a particular way at a given time is at least implicitly, but more often explicitly, to propose or defend a certain racial policy, a particular racialized social structure, a racial order. For instance, to argue for a "color-blind" conception of race in the United States today implies a strictly limited role for the state in racial policy, and therefore a certain acceptance of the legacy of the past in terms of the structure of racial inequality in the present. This example can be classified as a particular type of racial project in the present-day United States—a "neoconservative" one—and contrasted with others. By mapping the range of extant (and effective) racial projects in given historical contexts, we can analyze cases of racial formation in detail. In the contemporary United States, we can quite precisely document the emergence of racial hegemony, out of the ashes of earlier forms of racial domination, by using this approach.

When the focus is shifted from making an inventory of competing racial projects and assessing their interaction to looking at the evolution of racial projects over time, a different dimension of the racial formation process emerges. This is the link between the forms of racial rule and the construction of racial identities, which is the subject of chapter 4. Although it is often recognized that race was present and taken into account at the founding and in the construction of the United States, the logical next step—that of seeing the evolution of the society as a large-scale racial project in its own right—is rarely taken. But if we dump the more benign view that the racism written into the Constitution, and enacted in genocide, conquest, exclusion, and belated imperialism, was somehow aberrational, then a quite different view of U.S. history emerges. The United States is then seen to have been, over most of its history, a *herrenvolk* democracy, which is to say, a white (and male) dictatorship.

So the long nightmare of white supremacy constitutes the vast bulk of U.S. history. It was by no means unchanging or monolithic; indeed, the meaning of racial hierarchy underwent quite serious scrutiny, particularly in the aftermath of emancipation (Roediger 1991; Saxton 1990). There were of course fitful and partial awakenings, notably after the Civil War (Du Bois 1977 [1935]), yet on the whole it is difficult to characterize it as anything less than a sort of neofascism *avant la lettre*, at least from the perspective of its victims. Nor is it likely that today, a scant quarter century after the last legal vestiges of this racial dictatorship were destroyed, it could have lost all resonance in the minds and hearts of the U.S. populace.

It follows from this that our notions of racial identity, up to the present, have been deeply marked by the long period in which they were steeped in authoritarianism, terror, and violence, as well as in dogged resistance and determined struggles to survive. It follows too that the nation's commitment to democracy of the non-*herrenvolk* sort, and indeed to full citizenship for racially defined minorities, still remains tentative (Shklar 1991). The anxieties and uncertainties that pervade all racially defined identities today, that limit trust and reinforce desires for separation—even as U.S. society and culture become ever more hybridized—are the heritage of a democracy that is even yet unreconstructed.

These considerations shape the transition to Part II of the book, where the main focus is contemporary racial *politics*. Here I argue that in the United States, racial dictatorship and white supremacy were seriously weakened, though not destroyed, during the two decades following World War II. The enactment of civil rights legislation in the mid-1960s culminated a heroic struggle to eradicate the legal basis of racial inequality and signaled the end of *herrenvolk* democracy as state policy. Significant as this development was, however, it fell far short of dealing a deathblow to white supremacy in everyday life. Racial attitudes, practices, representations, and institutionalized inequalities were no doubt rendered more problematic by the civil rights "revolution," but they were hardly destroyed. What the civil rights movement accomplished was to replace racial domination with racial hegemony—a subject that also is addressed in chapter 3.

The more radical vision of the civil rights movement could not be achieved, so the movement split into moderate and militant factions. A deep chasm opened between those movement veterans who sought to minimize the salience of racial identity in the United States and those who insisted on its importance. In part as a response to such divisions, a *racial reaction* soon consolidated, determined to contain the movement's dream of an egalitarian society within more conservative and traditional political limits. The reaction too had its splits, most notably between neoconservatives, who sought to downplay the significance of race, and new rightists, who realized they could manipulate white racial fears for political gain. The result of these complex disagreements and battles was a decentered, *post-civil rights* racial order that remains transitional a quarter century after the civil rights reforms were enacted.

In the absence of an overt state commitment to white supremacy, explicit avowals of racism have been relegated to the margins of cultural and political discourse. Even KKK stalwarts claim to be antiracists today (J. Reed 1992). But the proliferation of racial projects on both the left and the right, the rise and fall of various forms of nationalism, both conservative and radical, both nonwhite and white (Walters 1987; A. Reed 1991; Van Deburg 1992), and, most significantly, the retreat undertaken by the Reagan and Bush administrations—under the influence of the new right—from even a moderate civil rights agenda, have led to massive ambiguities, ambivalences, and anxieties over race in the United States. In chapter 5, I discuss these conflicts, focusing on the changing meaning of race in the United

States and the shifting identities of all racially defined groups (including whites), in the post-civil rights period.

In chapter 6, I examine the 1992 "race riot" in Los Angeles. This momentous event provides a case study of virtually all the trends I have pinpointed in post-civil rights period racial dynamics; I consider it here under three broad rubrics. First, I suggest that a new, though only partial, convergence in mainstream racial politics was demonstrated in the way the Clinton and Bush presidential campaigns responded to the riot. Second, I argue that the riot demonstrated a host of changing tendencies in U.S. racial identities, including class cleavages among racial groups, significant conflicts among distinct racially identified minorities, and unexpected cross-racial alliances. Third, I consider the riot as a resistance phenomenon, a form of protest against state coercion.

Just as a riot can provide a "text" from which it is possible to "read" and interpret social and political developments (Darnton 1992), so too the appearance of a recent spate of books reassessing racial phenomena may be seen as something of an event, a symptom of the continuing and unresolved racial crisis that continues to engulf both the United States and much of the world. Chapter 7 is a broad review of recent works on racial theory and politics that have attempted to reinterpret the ongoing significance of race. The article begins close to home, with discussions of important recent analyses of race in the U.S. context; it then moves outward to bring in a more global perspective. Thus, I first focus on studies of black-white inequalities and conflicts in the United States; then I broaden the frame to look at works on race that take its emerging multipolarities into account—by examining other racially defined groups, the linkages between race and gender issues, and so on. Next I extend the discussion to include books on the postcolonial racial order and comparative studies on the "new racism" in the West. I conclude with some notes on the tasks of racial theory today.

These last points frame the transition to Part III, whose emphasis is the comparative sociology of race. Although U.S. conditions are by no means absent here, they are considered differently: as instances of broader global trends in racial politics and theory, and as elements useful for comparative analysis.

Chapter 8 is a longish essay that seeks to reset our analytical lenses on the dynamics of race and hegemony in global perspective. Here I develop more extensively themes first introduced in chapters 2 and 3, among them the racial dimensions of hegemony and the concept of racial projects. Drawing on Gramscian and poststructuralist reference points, I argue that race is a phenomenon whose meaning is pervasive throughout social and political life. In order effectively to deal with its centrality to systems of social order and signification across the globe, we must develop political and social theory that incorporates a nonreductionist conception of race. My effort here is to try to provide some of the tools and concepts necessary for such an effort.

I maintain that the concept of *hegemony* involves crucial racial dimensions, and that it must be stripped of its residual class determinism in order to deploy them more adequately. Once this is done, the concept becomes available to theorize both the global and local (and indeed the experiential) dimensions of race. Nor is the current centrality of race in the construction of hegemony an unprecedented phenomenon. The epochal process through which the contemporary global (dis)order — and its various local branches — developed was always thoroughly racialized. Imperialism, conquest, "world-system" — all these concepts carry racial freight. Thus, in this chapter I argue for a twofold approach to racial time: it has both a genealogical and a contingent aspect.

Having set these theoretical premises in place, I give an overview of the contemporary dimensions of racial formation, which — I argue — is linked in the contemporary world to both global and local forms of hegemony. I offer numerous examples at both levels in an effort to ground this position. Most centrally I argue that, as a worldwide phenomenon and in many distinct local cases, hegemony rests on the linkage between race- and class-based forms of rule.

In the final three chapters, the focus of the book shifts to the comparative sociology of race in Brazil and the United States. Chapters 9 and 10 apply the racial formation perspective to Brazilian materials, reinterpreting recent Brazilian racial theory (chapter 9) and employing Fanonian insights to explain the limits of Brazilian racial politics (chapter 10). Chapter 11 points out the increasing resemblance, if not convergence, between the racial dynamics of the two countries. The suggestion that race is becoming an increasingly global and interdependent phenomenon returns here in force.

Why Brazil? And, more broadly, why study the comparative sociology of race? To answer the first question it suffices simply to provide a few reference points: first, Brazil is the largest "black" country in the Americas, containing more people of recognizable African descent than all the other countries of the hemisphere combined.[1] After Nigeria, it is the world's "blackest" country. Second, Brazil shares with the United States not only a generally equivalent size and population, but also a similar set of origins in European colonization, Indian genocide, slavocracy, and extensive immigration. Third, though much is shared between the two countries, there are also useful contrasts: the United States is the preeminent nation-state on earth; Brazil, though it is possessed of tremendous resources and is a "developed" country in many respects, is a country of the "South"; many millions of its citizens indisputably qualify as members of "the wretched of the earth." Fourth and finally, there is a long-established tradition of comparison between Brazilian and U.S. racial dynamics, within which it is valuable to situate any effort at (re)interpretation. All of these factors make the comparison important, not only as a way of learning more about race in another country, but also as a way of thinking anew about one's own.

Let me strike a concluding note in answering the second question—why study the comparative sociology of race? Today it is no more possible to understand the dynamics of race without comparative reference points than it is to analyze them outside a historical framework. Though no national tradition can be assimilated to another, the world is knit together today by relationships of racial solidarity and conflict, just as it is by other forms of power and opposition. These relationships are increasingly complex; they are legatees of a brutal past; they are intertwined with every social struggle, and with the aspirations that abide in us all to control our own destiny and to live with dignity.

Not only that. We have met the "other" and (s)he is us. National societies, and the globe as a whole, are increasingly hybridized. National and transnational cultures make use of the widest possible range of elements to construct and reorganize identity in what seems a permanent bricolage. The cities of the "North"—New York, Los Angeles, Paris, London, Frankfurt—are black, brown, and yellow cities now. São Paulo and Monterrey, Lagos and Karachi communicate as well with New York and Tokyo as they do with their own hinterlands. Yet the signifiers and structures of race—however modified, however flexible—abide. We need our particularities more, not less, in a world grown ever more interrelated yet no less unequal or unjust.

The expectations of the past—of liberalism, Marxism, and nationalism—were that race would pass from the scene. Not only have those ideas proved false, but these very systems of ideas grow increasingly archaic. Since race endures, since it retains its significance in our politics, our culture, and our quotidian experience, and since this is the case not only in the United States but also around the world, the effort to comprehend its complexities, and to frame it as an issue of social justice, seems more worthwhile than ever.

PART I

Racial Theory

Chapter 2

The Theoretical Status of the Concept of Race

Race used to be a relatively intelligible concept; only recently have we seriously challenged its theoretical coherence. Today there are deep questions about what we actually mean by the term. But before (roughly) World War II, before the rise of nazism, before the end of the great European empires, and particularly before the decolonization of Africa, before the urbanization of the U.S. black population and the rise of the modern civil rights movement, race was still largely seen in Europe and North America (and elsewhere as well) as an essence, a natural phenomenon, whose meaning was fixed, as constant as a southern star.

In the earlier years of this century, only a handful of pioneers, people like W. E. B. Du Bois and Franz Boas, conceived of race in a more social and historical way. Other doubters included avant-garde racial theorists emerging from the intellectual ferment of the Harlem renaissance; black nationalists and pan-Africanists who sought to apply the rhetoric of national self-determination expressed at Versailles to the mother continent, and who returned from the battlefields of France to the wave of antiblack race riots that swept the United States in 1919; a few Marxists (whose perspectives had their own limitations); and to some extent the Chicago school of sociology led by Robert Ezra Park. But even these intellectuals and activists made incomplete breaks with essentialist notions of race, whether biologistic or otherwise deterministic.

That was then; this is now. Today the theory of race has been utterly transformed. The socially constructed status of the concept of race, which I have labeled the *racial formation* process, is widely recognized (Omi and Winant 1986), so much so that it is now often *conservatives* who argue that race is an illusion. The main task facing racial theory today, in fact, is no longer to critique the seemingly "natural" or "commonsense" concept of race—although that effort has not by any means been entirely completed. Rather, the central task is to focus attention on the *continuing significance and changing meaning of race*. It is to argue against the recent discovery of the illusory nature of race; against the supposed contemporary transcendence of race; against the widely reported death of the concept of race; and against the replacement of the category of race by other, supposedly more objective, categories like ethnicity, nationality, or class. All these initiatives are mistaken at best, and intellectually dishonest at worst.

In order to substantiate these assertions, we must first ask, what is race? Is it merely an illusion? An ideological construct utilized to manipulate, divide, and deceive? This position has been taken by many theorists, and activists as well, including many who have heroically served the cause of racial and social justice in the United States. Or is race something real, material, objective? This view too has its adherents, including both racial reactionaries and racial radicals.

In my view both of these approaches miss the boat. The concept of race is not an ideological construct, nor does it reflect an objective condition. Here I first reflect critically on these two opposed viewpoints on the contemporary theory of race. Then I offer an alternative perspective based on the approach of racial formation.

Race as an Ideological Construct

The assertion that race is an ideological construct—understood in the sense of a "false consciousness" that explains other "material" relationships in distorted fashion—seems highly problematic. This is the position taken by the prominent historian Barbara Fields in a well-known article, "Slavery, Race and Ideology in the United States of America."[1] Although Fields inveighs against various uses of the race concept, she directs her critical barbs most forcefully against historians who "invoke race as a historical explanation" (101).

According to Fields, the concept of race arose to meet an ideological need: its original effectiveness lay in its ability to reconcile freedom and slavery. The idea of race provided "the means of explaining slavery to people whose terrain was a republic founded on radical doctrines of liberty and natural rights" (114). But, Fields says, to argue that race—once

framed as a category in thought, an ideological explanation for certain distinct types of social inequality—"takes on a life of its own" in social relationships is to transform (or "reify") an illusion into a reality. Such a position could be sustained "only if *race* is defined as innate and natural
prejudice of color":

> Since race is not genetically programmed, racial prejudice cannot
> be genetically programmed either, but must arise historically. . . .
> The preferred solution is to suppose that, having arisen
> historically, race then ceases to be a historical phenomenon and
> becomes instead an external motor of history; according to the
> fatuous but widely repeated formula, it "takes on a life of its own."
> In other words, once historically acquired, race becomes
> hereditary. The shopworn metaphor thus offers camouflage for a
> latter-day version of Lamarckism. (101; emphasis original)

Thus, race is either an illusion that does ideological work or an objective biological fact. Since it is certainly not the latter, it must be the former.
No intermediate possibility—consider, for example, the Durkheimian notion of a "social fact"—is considered.

Some of this account—for example, the extended discussion of the origins of North American race thinking—can be accepted without major ob-
jection.[2] Furthermore, Fields effectively demonstrates the absurdity of
many commonly held ideas about race. But her position is so extreme that
at best it can only account for the *origins* of race thinking, and then only in
one social context. To examine how race thinking evolved from these origins, how it responded to changing sociocultural circumstances, is ruled
out. Why and how did race thinking survive after emancipation? Fields cannot answer, because the very perpetuation of the concept of race is ruled
out by her theoretical approach. As a relatively orthodox Marxist, Fields
could argue that changing "material conditions" continued to give rise to
changes in racial "ideology," except that even the limited autonomy this
would attach to the concept of race would exceed her standards. Race cannot take on a life of its own; it is a pure ideology, an illusion.

Fields simply skips from emancipation to the present, where she dispar-
ages opponents of "racism" for unwittingly perpetuating an illusory concept of race. In denunciatory terms, Fields concludes by arguing for abolition of the concept:

> Nothing handed down from the past could keep race alive if we
> did not constantly reinvent and re-ritualize it to fit our own
> terrain. If race lives on today, it can do so only because we
> continue to create and re-create it in our social life, continue to
> verify it, and thus continue to need a social vocabulary that will

allow us to make sense, not of what our ancestors did then, but of what we choose to do now. (118)

Fields is unclear about how "we" should jettison the ideological construct of race, and one can well understand why. By her own logic, racial ideologies cannot be abolished by acts of will. One can only marvel at the ease with which she distinguishes the bad old slavery days of the past from the present, when "we" anachronistically cling, as if for no reason, to the illusion that race retains any meaning. We foolishly throw up our hands and acquiesce in race thinking, rather than ... doing what? Denying the racially demarcated divisions in society? Training ourselves to be "color-blind"?[3]

I venture to say that only a historian (however eminent) could have written such an article. Why? Because at the least a sociologist would know W. I. Thomas's famous dictum that if people "define situations as real, they are real in their consequences" (Thomas and Thomas 1928: 572). Nor is Fields alone in claiming that racial ideology persists because people insist on thinking racially. Her position is espoused by many, on both the left and the right of racial debates.[4]

In any case, the view that race is a kind of false consciousness is held not only by intellectuals, based on both well-intentioned and ulterior motivations; it also has a commonsense character. One hears in casual discussion, for example, or in introductory social science classes, variations on the following statement: "I don't care if a person is black, white, or purple, I treat them exactly the same; a person's just a person to me ..." Furthermore, some of the integrationist aspirations of racial minority movements, especially the civil rights movement, invoke this sort of idea. Consider the famous line from the "I Have a Dream" speech, the line that made Shelby Steele's career: "that someday my four little children will be judged, not by the color of their skin, but by the content of their character."

The core criticisms of this "race as ideology" approach are two: first, it fails to recognize the salience a social construct can develop over half a millennium or more of diffusion, or should I say enforcement, as a fundamental principle of social organization and identity formation. The longevity of the race concept and the enormous number of effects race thinking (and race acting) has produced guarantee that race will remain a feature of social reality across the globe, and a fortiori in the United States, despite its lack of intrinsic or scientific merit (in the biological sense). Second, and related, this approach fails to recognize that at the level of experience, of everyday life, race is a relatively impermeable part of our identities. U.S. society is so thoroughly racialized that to be without racial identity is to be in danger of having no identity. To be raceless is akin to being genderless.

Indeed, when one cannot identify another's race, a microsociological crisis of interpretation results, something perhaps best interpreted in eth-nomethodological or Goffmanian terms. To complain about such a situation may be understandable, but it does not advance understanding.

Race as an Objective Condition

On the other side of the coin, it is clearly problematic to assign objectivity to the race concept. Such theoretical practice puts us in quite heterogeneous, and sometimes unsavory, company. Of course, the biologistic racial theories of the past do this: here I am thinking of such precursors of fascism as Gobineau and Chamberlain (Mosse 1978), of the eugenicists such as Lothrop Stoddard and Madison Grant, and of the "founding fathers" of scientific racism such as Agassiz, Broca, Terman, and Yerkes (Kevles 1985; Chase 1977). Indeed, an extensive legacy of this sort of thinking extends right up to the present. Stephen Jay Gould (1981) makes devastating critiques of such views.

But much liberal and even radical social science, though firmly committed to a social as opposed to a biological interpretation of race, nevertheless also slips into a kind of objectivism about racial identity and racial meaning. This is true because race is afforded an easy and unproblematic coherence all too frequently. Thus, to select only prominent examples, Daniel Moynihan, William Julius Wilson, Milton Gordon, and many other mainstream thinkers theorize race in terms that downplay its flexibility and historically contingent character. Even these major thinkers, whose explicit rejection of biologistic forms of racial theory would be unquestioned, fall prey to a kind of creeping objectivism of race. For in their analyses a modal explanatory approach emerges as follows: sociopolitical circumstances change over historical time, racially defined groups adapt or fail to adapt to these changes, achieving mobility or remaining mired in poverty, and so on. In this logic there is no reconceptualization of group identities, of the constantly shifting parameters through which race is thought about, group interests are assigned, statuses are ascribed, agency is attained, and roles are performed.

Contemporary racial theory, then, is often "objectivistic" about its fundamental category. Although abstractly acknowledged to be a sociohistorical construct, race *in practice* is often treated as an objective fact: one simply *is* one's race; in the contemporary United States, if we discard euphemisms, we have five color-based racial categories: black, white, brown, yellow, and red.

This is problematic, indeed ridiculous, in numerous ways. Nobody really belongs in these boxes; they are patently absurd reductions of human

no boxes

variation. But even accepting the nebulous "rules" of racial classification—
"hypodescent," and so forth[5]—many people do not fit anywhere: into what
categories should we place Turks, for example? People of mixed race?
South Asians? Objectivist treatments, lacking a critique of the *constructed*
character of racial meanings, also clash with experiential dimensions of the
issue. If one does not "act" black, or white, or whatever, that is just devi-
ance from the norm. There is in these approaches an insufficient appreciation of the *performative* aspect of race, as postmodernists might call it.[6]

To summarize the critique of this "race as objective condition" approach, then, it fails on three counts. First, it cannot grasp the processual
and relational character of racial identity and racial meaning. Second, it denies the historicity and social comprehensiveness of the race concept. And
third, it cannot account for the way actors, both individual and collective,
have to manage incoherent and conflictual racial meanings and identities
in everyday life. It has no concept, in short, of what Omi and I have labeled
racial formation.

Toward a Critical Theory of the Concept of Race

The foregoing clearly sets forth the agenda that any adequate theorization
of the race concept must fulfill. Such an approach must be theoretically
constructed so as to steer between the Scylla of "race as illusion" and the
Charybdis of "racial objectivism." Such a critical theory can be consistently
developed, I suggest, drawing upon the racial formation approach. Such a
theoretical formulation, too, must be explicitly historicist: it must recognize the importance of historical context and contingency in the framing of
racial categories and the social construction of racially defined experiences.

What would be the minimum conditions for the development of a critical, processual theory of race? I suggest three conditions for such a theory:

– It must apply to contemporary *political* relationships.

– It must apply in an increasingly *global* context.

– It must apply across *historical time*.

Let us address each of these points very briefly.

Contemporary Political Relationships. The meaning and salience
of race is forever being reconstituted in the present. Today such new relationships emerge chiefly at the point where some *counterhegemonic* or
postcolonial power is attained. At that point the meanings and the political
articulations of race proliferate.

Examples include the appearance of competing racial *projects*, by which I mean efforts to institutionalize racial meanings and identities in particular social structures: notably those of individual, family, community, and state. As egalitarian movements contend with racial "backlash" over sustained periods of time, as binary logics of racial antagonism (white/black, *ladino/indio,* settler/native, etc.) become more complex and decentered, political deployment of the concept of race comes to signal qualitatively new types of political domination, as well as new types of opposition.

Consider the U.S. example. In terms of domination, it is now possible to perpetuate racial domination without making any explicit reference to race at all. Subtextual or "coded" racial signifiers, or the mere denial of the continuing significance of race, may suffice. Similarly, in terms of opposition, it is now possible to resist racial domination in entirely new ways, particularly by limiting the reach and penetration of the political system into everyday life, by generating new identities, new collectivities, new (imagined) communities that are relatively less permeable to the hegemonic system.[7] Much of the rationale for Islamic currents among blacks in the United States, for the upsurge in black anti-Semitism, and to some extent for the Afrocentric phenomenon, can be found here. Thus the old choices—integration versus separatism, assimilation versus nationalism—are no longer the only options.

In the "underdeveloped" world, proliferation of so-called postcolonial phenomena also have significant racial dimensions, as the entire Fanonian tradition (merely to select one important theoretical current) makes clear. Crucial debates have now been occurring for a decade or more on the question of postcolonial subjectivity and identity, the insufficiency of the simple dualism of "Europe and its others," the subversive and parodic dimensions of political culture at and beyond the edges of the old imperial boundaries, and so forth.[8]

The Global Context of Race. The geography of race is becoming more complex. Once more easily seen in terms of imperial reach, in terms of colonization, conquest, and migration, racial space is becoming *globalized* and thus accessible to a new kind of comparative analysis. This only becomes possible now, at a historical moment when the distinction "developed/underdeveloped" has been definitively overcome. Obviously, by this I do not mean that now there are no disparities between North and South, rich and poor. Rather, I mean that the movement of capital and labor has internationalized all nations, all regions. Today we have reached the point where the empire strikes back,[9] as former (neo)colonial subjects, now redefined as "immigrants," challenge the majoritarian status of the formerly metropolitan group (the whites, the Europeans, the "Americans" or "French," etc.). Meanwhile, phenomena such as the rise of "diasporic"

diasporic

models of blackness, the creation of "panethnic"[10] communities of Latinos and Asians (in such countries as the United Kingdom and the United States), and the breakdown of borders in both Europe and North America all seem to be internationalizing and racializing previously national polities, cultures, and identities. To take just one example, popular culture now internationalizes racial awareness almost instantaneously, as reggae, rap, samba, and various African pop styles leap from continent to continent.

Because of these transformations, a global comparison of hegemonic social/political orders based on race becomes possible. I think that in a highly specified form, that is, not as mere reactions or simple negations of "Western" cultural/theoretical dominance, such notions as diasporic consciousness or racially informed standpoint epistemologies deserve more serious attention as efforts to express the contemporary globalization of racial space.[11] Furthermore, to understand such phenomena as the construction of new racial identities or in terms of the panethnicity dynamic is to recognize that the territorial reach of racial hegemony is now global.

The dissolution of the transparent racial identity of the formerly dominant group, that is to say, the advancing racialization of whites in Europe and the United States, must also be recognized as proceeding from the increasingly globalized dimensions of race. As previous assumptions erode, white identity loses its transparency, the easy elision with "racelessness" that accompanies racial domination. "Whiteness" becomes a matter of anxiety and concern.

The Emergence of Racial Time. Some final notes are in order in respect to the question of the epochal nature of racial time. Classical social theory had an Enlightenment-based view of time, a perspective that understood the emergence of modernity in terms of the rise of capitalism and the bourgeoisie. This view was by no means limited to Marxism. Weberian disenchantment and the rise of the Durkheimian division of labor also partake of this temporal substrate. Only rarely does the racial dimension of historical temporality appear in this body of thought, as, for example, in Marx's excoriation of the brutalities of "primitive accumulation":

> The discovery of gold and silver in America, the extirpation, enslavement, and entombment in mines of the aboriginal population, the beginning of the conquest and looting of the East Indies, the turning of Africa into a warren for the commercial hunting of blackskins, signalized the rosy dawn of the era of capitalist production. These idyllic proceedings are the chief momenta of primitive accumulation. On their heels treads the commercial war of the European nations with the globe for a theater. It begins with the revolt of the Netherlands from Spain,

assumes giant dimensions in England's AntiJacobin War, and is still going on in the opium wars with China, etc. (1967: 751)

Yet even Marx frequently legitimated such processes as the inevitable and ultimately beneficial birth pangs of classlessness—by way of the ceaselessly revolutionary bourgeoisie.

Today such teleological accounts seem hopelessly outmoded. Historical time could well be interpreted in terms of something like a racial *longue durée*: for has there not been an immense historical rupture represented by the rise of Europe, the onset of African enslavement, the *conquista*, and the subjugation of much of Asia? I take the point of much poststructural scholarship on these matters to be quite precisely an effort to explain "Western" or colonial time as a huge project demarcating human "difference," or more globally as Todorov, say, would argue, of framing partial collective identities in terms of externalized "others" (Todorov 1985). Just as, for example, the writers of the *Annales* school sought to locate the deep logic of historical time in the means by which material life was produced— diet, shoes, and so on[12]—so we might usefully think of a racial *longue durée* in which the slow inscription of phenotypical signification took place upon the human body, in and through conquest and enslavement, to be sure, but also as an enormous act of expression, of narration.

In short, just as the noise of the big bang still resonates through the universe, so the overdetermined construction of world "civilization" as a product of the rise of Europe and the subjugation of the rest of us still defines the race concept. Such speculative notes, of course, can be no more than provocations. Nor can I conclude this effort to reframe the agenda of racial theory with a neat summation. There was a long period— centuries—in which race was seen as a natural condition, an essence. This was succeeded although not entirely superseded by a shorter but potent way of thinking about race as subordinate to supposedly more concrete, "material" relationships; during that period, down to now, race was understood as an illusion, an excrescence. Perhaps now we are approaching the end of that racial epoch too.

To our dismay, we may have to give up our familiar ways of thinking about race once more. If so, there may also be some occasion for delight. For it may be possible to glimpse yet another view of race, in which the concept operates neither as a signifier of comprehensive identity nor of fundamental difference, both of which are patently absurd, but rather as a marker of the infinity of variations we humans hold as a common heritage and hope for the future.

Chapter 3

Where Culture Meets Structure: Race in the 1990s

The contemporary United States faces a pervasive crisis of race, a crisis no less severe than those the country has confronted in the past. The origins of the crisis are not particularly obscure: the cultural and political meaning of race, its significance in shaping the social structure, and its experiential or existential dimensions all remain profoundly unresolved as the United States approaches the end of the twentieth century. As a result, the society as a whole, and the population as individuals, suffer from confusion and anxiety about the issue (or complex of issues) we call race.

This should not be surprising. We may be more afflicted with anxiety and uncertainty over race than we are over any other social or political issue. Racial conflict is the very archetype of discord in North America, the primordial conflict that has in many ways structured all others. Time and time again what has been defined as "the race problem" has generated ferocious antagonisms: between slaves and masters, between natives and settlers, between new immigrants and established residents, and between workers divided by wage discrimination, by culture, even by psychosexual antagonisms (Roediger 1991). Time and time again this "problem" has been declared resolved, or perhaps supplanted by other supposedly more fundamental conflicts, only to blaze up anew. Tension and confusion in postwar racial politics and culture are merely the latest episode in this seemingly permanent drama.

The persistence of racial conflict, and of the anxiety and confusion that accompany it, has defied the predictions of most government officials, social critics, and movement leaders. Until quite recently, mainstream economists and Marxists, liberals and conservatives, ethnicity theorists and nationalists all expected the dissolution of race in some greater entity: free market or class struggle, cultural pluralism or nation-state. That race remains so central a factor both in the U.S. social structure and in the collective psyche, ought—at the very least—to inject a bit of humility into the discourses of all these sages.

Thus chastened, let us enter once more into the thickets of *racial theory*. No task is more urgent today. The mere fact that basic racial questions are at once so obvious and so obviously unanswered suggests how urgent is further theoretical work on race. Still, one must approach the effort modestly, for the concept of race in some ways is as large as social theory itself.

My strategy here is to examine contemporary U.S. racial dynamics from the standpoint of *racial formation theory*, an approach developed specifically to address the shifting meanings and power relationships inherent in race today. I begin with some basic propositions about racial formation. Then I look at recent U.S. racial history, which, I suggest, is in transition from a pattern of domination to one of *hegemony*. Next I discuss the range of contemporary racial projects, focusing on the contest for racial hegemony. Finally, I assess the system of racial hegemony in the 1990s.

Racial Formation Theory

Racial formation theory was developed as a response to postwar understandings of race, both mainstream and radical, that practiced reductionism. By this I mean the explanation of racial phenomena as manifestations of some other, supposedly more significant, social relationship. Examples of racial reductionism include treatments of racial dynamics as epiphenomena of class relationships, or as the result of "national oppression," or as variations on the ethnicity paradigm established in the early twentieth century, after successive waves of European immigration.

In contrast to these approaches, racial formation theory looks at race as a phenomenon whose meaning is contested throughout social life (Omi and Winant 1986). In this account race is both a constituent of the individual psyche and of relationships among individuals, and an irreducible component of collective identities and social structures.

Because race is not a "natural" attribute but a socially and historically constructed one, it becomes possible to analyze the processes by which racial meanings are attributed, and racial identities assigned, in a given society. These processes of "racial signification" are inherently discursive. They are variable, conflictual, and contested at every level of society, from the intrapsychic to the supranational. Inevitably, many interpretations of race, many racial discourses, exist at any given time. The political character of the racial formation process stems from this: elites, popular movements, state agencies, cultural and religious organizations, and intellectuals of all types develop *racial projects,* which interpret and reinterpret the meaning of race.

The theoretical concept of racial projects is a key element of racial formation theory. A *racial project is simultaneously an interpretation, repre-sentation, or explanation of racial dynamics and an effort to organize and distribute resources along particular racial lines.* Every project is therefore both a discursive and a cultural initiative, an attempt at racial signification and identity formation on the one hand, and a social structural initiative, an attempt at political mobilization and resource redistribution, on the other.

Interpreting the meaning of race is thus a multidimensional process in which competing "projects" intersect and clash. These projects are often explicitly, but always at least implicitly, political. Racial projects potentially draw both on phenomena that are "objective" or institutional and on those that are "subjective" or experiential. That such social structural phenomena as movements and parties, state institutions and policies, market processes, and so forth should be the source of political initiatives regarding race is hardly controversial. Racial formation theory, however, also finds the source of "projects" in less familiar social practices: in the manipulation and rearticulation of racial identities by their bearers, in the enunciation and transformation of racial "common sense," and in the various subversive, evasive, or parodic forms of racial opposition that closely resemble other forms of subordinated and postcolonial resistance (Scott 1985; Bhabha 1990a). In a later section of this essay I offer a "map," in table form, of contemporary U.S. racial projects.

Recent U.S. Racial History:
From Domination to Hegemony

From this theoretical vantage point, I propose now to examine, in what must necessarily be a fairly schematic account, the evolution of U.S. racial politics in the postwar period. To frame this account properly, let me present my key argument at the outset. The black movement upsurge of the 1950s and 1960s ended the epoch of racial domination and initiated the epoch of racial hegemony. The achievement of the movement was its initiation of sweeping political and cultural changes: it created new organizations, new political norms, new collective identities, new modalities of expression and representation; it challenged past racial practices and stereotypes; and it ushered in a vave of democratizing social reform, which ultimately extended well beyond the issue of race.

The Pre-Civil Rights Era. In the pre-civil rights era the U.S. racial order was maintained largely, though of course not exclusively, through *domination*. The most visible manifestations of this regime were all enforced by coercive means: segregation, racial exclusion, and physical violence culminating in extralegal terror. Periodic mob assaults on urban ghettos and barrios, deportations to Mexico in the Southwest, outright extermination and plunder of native peoples, anti-Asian pogroms, physical intimidation and murder by police, and of course the practice of lynching were all fairly characteristic of this epoch (McMillen 1989; Montejano 1987; Takaki 1990; Omi and Winant 1986: 73-74). It was not until well into the twentieth century, and even then only in certain areas where racially defined minorities had been able to establish themselves in large numbers and to initiate negotiations between the white establishment and minority elites, that a measure of "protection," and even patronage and political influence, were sometimes available. But even these gains were highly limited and fragile.

The Political Effects of the Black Movement. The black movement upsurge changed all that. It permitted the entry of millions of racial minority group members into the political process—first blacks, and later Latinos, Asian Americans, and Native Americans. It initiated a trajectory of reform that exposed the limits of all previously existing political orientations—conservative, liberal, and radical. With very few exceptions, all these currents had colluded with the denial of fundamental political rights to members of racially defined minorities.

The aftermath of this prodigious movement upsurge was a racial order in which *domination was replaced by hegemony*. Political mobilization along racial lines resulted in the enactment of reforms that dramatically restructured the racial order, reorganized state institutions, and initiated whole new realms of state activity. The achievement of the franchise, the establishment of limited but real avenues of economic and social mobility, the destruction of de jure segregation, the reform of immigration law, and the institution of a measure of state enforcement of civil rights were but a few of the movement's more dramatic accomplishments.

The Cultural Effects of the Black Movement. Furthermore, by transforming the meaning of race and the contours of racial politics, the racially based movements also transformed the meaning and contours of American culture. Indeed, they made identity, difference, the "personal,"

and language itself political issues in very new ways. They made mainstream society—that is, white people—take notice of "difference"; they
created awareness not only of different racial identities, but also of the
multiple differences inherent in U.S. culture and society. In short, the new
movements vastly expanded the terrain of politics and transfigured U.S.
culture.

Thus, where U.S. culture previously had been monolithic and stratified,
and indeed racially segregated ("race records," segregated media, etc.), it
now became far more polyvalent, far more complexly articulated. Without
being able to argue the point fully, I think it fair to assert that since the
mid-1950s—I am taking as a fairly arbitrary demarcating point the advent
of rock and roll—U.S. culture has adopted a far more pluralistic cast, With
respect to race, this means that genres of music, art, and language retain
their bases in particular communities while at the same time "crossing
over" with far greater regularity than was previously the case. Cultural differences coexist without requiring any overarching synthesis, yet partial
syntheses take place continually.[1]

This does not mean that a "cultural revolution," along the lines proposed by Harold Cruse in the 1960s, has been or even could be achieved
(Cruse 1968: 111-12). As in the political sphere, much of the increased
presence of "darker" visions and "other" voices in the cultural sphere is
the result of tokenism and co-optation. Pragmatic liberal practices advocat-
ing tolerance and diversity, rather than radical democratic practices celebrating difference, are the norm. Even granting all this, the present-day
proliferation of artistic and popular cultural forms with roots in racially
defined minority communities is quite astonishing when it is seen from a
historical and comparative vantage point; much has changed in a few
short decades. And this too must be judged an accomplishment of the
movement.

The Racial Reaction. The achievements and legacy of the black
movement were hardly greeted with universal acclaim. Various currents on
the right strongly objected to the extension of an egalitarian racial awareness into everyday, indeed personal, life. Strong opposition arose to confront the newfound assertiveness and proliferation of cultural difference
that the movement had fostered.

The very successes of the movement, however, set limits on the reaction
that succeeded it. Because such movement themes as equality, group identity, and difference could not simply be rolled back, it became necessary,
from the late 1960s onward, to rearticulate these ideas in a conservative
ideological framework of competition, individualism, and homogeneity. In
other words, since the movement's introduction of new political themes

could not be undone, opponents had to learn how to manage these political themes as well.

This is why today's political debates about racial inequality are dominated by charges of "reverse discrimination" and repudiation of "quotas," why demands for "community control" have reappeared in opposition to school desegregation, and why high government officials claim that we are moving toward a "color-blind society." Cultural debates are dominated by the right's *rejection* of difference and "otherness" (whether racial, gender-based, sexual, or anything else). The right's strong defense of "traditional values," of individualism, and of mainstream culture, its discourse about family, nation, our "proud heritage of freedom," and so forth betokens intense resistance to the very idea of a polyvalent racial culture. Many of the notes struck by the right in contemporary cultural debates over race are, shall we say, white notes. They reflect a deep-seated fear, perhaps unconscious and only occasionally expressed, of the racialized other who has plagued the European for so long.[2]

The "Decentering" of Racial Conflict. By the end of the 1960s the emancipatory effects of the black movement upsurge (and of its *sequelae* in other communities and constituencies) had been blunted by the racial reaction. Indeed, the dominant racial theory since World War II—ethnicity theory—which had once allied itself with the minority movements, reappeared as one of their chief theoretical antagonists: neoconservatism. Along with a reconstituted *far right*, the *new right* and *neoconservative* currents would emerge by the 1980s as three related but distinct right-wing racial projects.

Neoconservatism was largely an enterprise of intellectuals who sought to intervene in policy debates over race. Its chief concern was the threat to political and cultural traditions it discerned in racial minority demands for "group rights," or "equality of result." The *new right*, heir apparent of the 1960s backlash politics and the Wallace campaigns, was a far more grassroots movement, linked to the religious conservatism fostered by some sectors of Catholicism and Protestant televangelism; it was a key component of every Republican presidential victory from 1968 to 1988. The *far right* was a more motley crew, consisting of the traditional assortment of bigots and race baiters, but also newly possessed of a modernized wing. The latter emerged in the mid-1980s when Klan leader and Nazi David Duke decided to swap his robe for a sport coat, get a blow-dried haircut, and undergo extensive plastic surgery, both on his face and in his rhetoric.

On the left, the movement upsurge fell victim to its own success. In the effort to adapt to the new racial politics they themselves had created, racial movements lost their unity and raison d'être. Working within the newly reformed racial state was more possible, and confronting it more difficult, than during the preceding period. Opposition to the backward and coercive racial order of the South had permitted a tenuous alliance between moderate and radical currents of the movement, an alliance that the winning of civil rights reforms ruptured. The "triumph" of liberal democracy failed to placate radicals who sought not only rights, but power and resources as well. The conferring of rights did not appreciably change the circumstances of a black youth in North Philly or a *vato loco* in East Los Angeles. What was heralded as a great victory by liberals appeared to radicals as merely a more streamlined version of racial oppression.

By the late 1960s, then, the U.S. racial order had largely absorbed the challenge posed by the civil rights movement, responding effectively—from the standpoint of rule—with a series of reforms. At the same time it had largely insulated itself from the more radical of its racial challengers—for example, revolutionary Marxist and nationalist currents—by drawing upon traditional coercive means, but also by exploiting the ideological weaknesses inherent in these viewpoints.

Over the following two decades what remained of the movement evolved into two loosely knit racial projects, those of the *pragmatic liberals* and of the *radical democrats*. In the former group I include the surviving civil rights organizations, the liberal religious establishment, and the Democratic party. In the latter group I include "grass-roots" organizations that continue to function at the local level, cultural radicals and nationalist groups that have avoided mystical and demagogic pitfalls, and survivors of the debacle of the socialist left who have retained their antiracist commitments.

This spectrum of racial projects, running from right to left, characterizes the United States today. In contrast to the earlier postwar period, the political logic of race in the United States is now "decentered," because the racial formation process operates in the absence of a coherent conflict. Only a comprehensive challenge to the racial order as a whole could generate such coherence. This decenteredness reflects not only the incomplete and fragmented character of the available racial projects, but also the complexity of contemporary racial politics and culture. None of the extant racial projects seems capable of presenting a durable and comprehensive vision of race. None can realistically address in even a minimally adequate way *both* the volatility of racial expression, meaning, and identities on the one hand, *and* the in-depth racialization of the social structure and political system in the United States. Indeed, such a totalizing vision of race may no longer be possible.

This decentered racial situation reflects an unprecedented level of societal uncertainty about race. The various racial projects listed here are merely efforts to advance one or another current, one or another political agenda, in a society wracked by racial anxiety and conflict. They may compete in the effort to construct a new racial hegemony, but they do not offer any real prospect of clarifying or resolving ambivalent racial meanings or identities. Despite occasional appearances to the contrary, the right-wing racial projects have no more gained racial hegemony than have those of the left. Rather, the state, business, media, and religious and educational institutions appear permanently divided, riven, inconsistent, and uncertain about racial conflicts and issues, much as we as individuals are confused and ambivalent.

The System of Racial Hegemony: Contemporary U.S. Racial Projects

Hegemony is a system in which politics operates largely through the *incorporation* of oppositional currents in the prevailing system of rule, and culture operates largely through the *reinterpretation* of oppositional discourse in the prevailing framework of social expression, representation, and debate.[3] Of course, not everything in a hegemonic system works this way. For example, there is certainly plenty of room in contemporary U.S. racial politics and culture for exclusion, segregation, discrimination, malevolence, ignorance, and outright violence. Highlighting the hegemonic dimensions of present-day U.S. racial dynamics emphasizes the effects of several decades of racial formation processes and the qualitative shifts that have occurred in the meaning and structure of race since the movement upsurge of the 1960s.

Under hegemonic conditions, opposition and difference are not repressed, excluded, or silenced (at least not primarily). Rather, they are inserted, often after suitable modification, within a "modern" (or perhaps "postmodern") social order. Hegemony is therefore oxymoronic: it involves a splitting or doubling of opposition, which simultaneously wins and loses, gains entrance into the "halls of power" and is co-opted, "crosses over" into mainstream culture and is deprived of its critical content.

What is the logic of racial hegemony in the present-day United States? Today there can no longer be any single axis of racial domination and subordination. There can no longer be any explicitly segregationist politics, nor can there be forms of expressive culture reserved exclusively for whites.[4] Just as these once-powerful forms of racial domination have been eroded or even destroyed, so too has opposition to them. Racial hegemony has gradually evolved from this situation, which is a crisis of the movement legacy of the 1960s.

Racial Hegemony and Racial Projects. The evolution of racial hegemony means that the outmoded antinomy of racial domination and racial subordination has been replaced by a range of racial projects whose "formation and superseding" (Gramsci) constitutes the process of racial formation in the United States.

In the contemporary United States, racial formation proceeds, and racial hegemony is organized, through the interplay of these projects. Hegemony operates through the adoption by the state, the media, large corporations, and other key societal institutions of political initiatives and cultural narratives drawn from competing racial projects. Through the state and the major parties, for example, racial policies are worked out across the entire national political agenda. Thomas Byrne Edsall and Mary D. Edsall describe some of the items on the agenda:

> Considerations of race are now deeply imbedded in the strategy
> and tactics of politics, in competing concepts of the functions
> and responsibilities of government, and in each voter's conceptual
> structure of moral and partisan identity. Race helps define liberal
> and conservative ideologies, shapes the presidential coalitions
> of the Democratic and Republican parties, provides a harsh
> new dimension to concern over taxes and crime, drives a
> wedge through alliances of the working classes and the poor,
> and gives both momentum and vitality to the drive to establish a
> national majority inclined by income and demography to support
> policies benefiting the affluent and the upper middle class.
> (1991: 53)

Race provides a key cultural marker, a central signifier, in the reproduction and expression of identity, collectivity, language, and agency itself. Race generates an "inside" and an "outside" of society, and mediates the unclear border between these zones; all social space, from the territory of the intrapsychic to that of the U.S. "national character," is fair game for racial dilemmas, doubts, fears, and desires. The conceptualization and representation of these sentiments, whether they are articulated in a track by Public Enemy or a television commercial for Jesse Helms, are framed in one or more racial projects.

By the 1980s, then, the racial order consisted of a range of conflicting *racial projects*, each descended from the days of racial domination and movement opposition, each seeking to advance its own conception of the significance of race in contemporary U.S. society. At the core of each project was a particular articulation of the culture and structure of race, of racial discourse and racial politics. This range of projects, which together constitute racial hegemony, can be "mapped," somewhat schematically, as shown in table 1.

Table 1. Racial Hegemony in the United States (c. 1990)
CULTURE ← ARTICULATION → STRUCTURE

Project	Racial discourse: concept of identity, "difference" and the meaning of race	Political/programmatic agenda: orientation to the state, (in)equality, etc.
Far right	Represents race in terms of inherent, natural characteristics; rights and privileges assigned accordingly; traditional far right operates through terror; renovated far right organizes whites politically.	Open racial conflict; equality seen as a subversion of the "natural order"; the state is in the hands of the "race mixers." Whites need to form their own organizations, pressure the state for "white rights."
New right	Understands racial mobilization as a threat to "traditional values"; perceives racial meanings and identities as operating "subtextually"; engages in racial "coding"; articulates class and gender interests as racial.	Racial conflict focuses on the state; racial (in)equality determined by access to state institutions and relative political power.
Neoconservatism	Denies the salience of racial "difference," or argues that it is a vestige of the past, when invidious distinctions and practices had not yet been reformed; after the passage of civil rights laws, any collective articulation of racial "difference" amounts to "racism in reverse."	Conservative egalitarianism. Individualism, meritocracy, universalism. Rejection of any form of group rights; "color-blind" state.
Pragmatic liberalism	Racial identities serve to organize interests and channel political and cultural activities; as long as principles of pluralism and tolerance are upheld, a certain degree of group identity and racial mobilization can be accepted as the price of social peace.	Cultural and political pluralism; affirmative action as "goals, not quotas." State racial policy as moderating and eroding the legacy of discrimination.
Radical democracy	Racial difference accepted and celebrated; flexibility of racial identities; multiplicity and "decenteredness" of various forms of "difference," including race.	State racial policy as redistribution. Racial politics as part of "decentered" but interconnected pattern of "new social movements." Extension of democratic rights and of societal control over the state.

The linkage between culture and structure, which is at the core of the racial formation process, gives each project its coherence and unity. Indeed, once it is argued that the United States is inherently a "white man's country" (as in certain far right racial discourses), or that race is a spurious anachronism beneath the notice of the state (as in neoconservative positions), or that racial difference is a matter of "self-determination" (as in various radical democratic racial discourses), the appropriate political orientation, economic and social programs, and so forth follow quite naturally.

Racial Hegemony in the 1990s

Racial formation theory tells us that the racial order is in constant flux. Contested meanings and identities, conflict over political and economic resources, rivalries over territory and systems of cultural expression: these are the processes that continue to frame the complexities of race in the United States. Thus there is nothing eternal about the five racial projects outlined here. Indeed, they are presented somewhat schematically, in an effort to clarify divisions and antagonisms. In many respects the overlaps between these five projects are as significant as the distinctions between them.

This last point is quite important, since ultimately, as Gramsci argued, hegemony is constructed out of differing social forces welded together in what he called a "historical bloc." For there are clear grounds for potential polarization in the five-part typology developed here: if racial hegemony today is in flux and divided among many initiatives, tomorrow it may be bifurcated among left and right currents.

Furthermore, the racial dimensions of political conflict and cultural representation are becoming ever more central as we approach the end of the twentieth century. Racial hegemony is converging in important respects with overall societal hegemony. In this situation the political and cultural currents that most effectively establish the link between racial "difference" and social inequality will win the contest for hegemony in the United States.

The right enjoys considerable privileges in this situation. Besides the institutional advantages realized during the Reagan and Bush years, right-wing racial projects have been able to portray minority racial identities, and minority insistence on the continuing significance of race and racism, as anachronistic, pernicious, and unfair. Left racial projects have only intermittently and partially succeeded in countering these views (as in the Jackson campaigns), and often appear mired in outmoded conceptions and proposals.

Indeed, at present throughout U.S. society, including in racially defined minority communities and on the left, there is an unwillingness to enter into discussions about race. This reluctance is not illogical: it is born of fear and bitter experience. But it is also politically dangerous. As the projects of the right advance a view of race that links difference and diversity to national weakness, economic decline, and widespread racist fears (Walters 1987), those on the left cannot refuse to debate the contemporary meaning of race and the programmatic alternatives before us. Such issues as the relationship among minority middle classes and "underclasses," the relevance of nationalist and integrationist traditions today, and, perhaps most centrally, the relationship between race and class must be extensively discussed in an atmosphere where dogma and orthodoxy are effectively resisted.

Race and Class. *In the contemporary United States, hegemony is determined by the articulation of race and class*. The ability of the right to represent class issues in racial terms is central to the current pattern of conservative racial hegemony. All three rightist projects—those of the far right, the new right, and the neoconservatives—partake of this logic. Conservative/reactionary politics today *disguises* class issues in racial terms. In so doing it builds on a thematic current that is as deep and wide as U.S. history itself. This theme can be called divide and conquer, dual/split labor markets, white-skin privilege, Eurocentrism, immigrant exclusion, or internal colonialism. Its clearest name is racism.

Conversely, any challenge to this current, any counterhegemonic initiative, must be *explicitly race-conscious* in its approach to issues of class or fall victim to the same hegemonic strategies that have doomed so many other progressive political initiatives. Traditional left politics have consistently failed to do this; they have steadily refused to afford race the centrality it receives on the right. Rather, left politics—both moderate and radical—has been steeped in class reductionism. In the particular conditions of U.S. politics, the subordination of race to class has never been viable; it is less logical in the contemporary period than ever before.

Making race consciousness explicit and central to class politics means recognizing the irreducibility of race in U.S. political and cultural life and thinking about class, inequality, and redistribution in ways that take racial divisions and conflicts into primary account. How might the racial projects of the left articulate the relationship of race and class? A full answer to this question must await large-scale political and cultural experimentation, but a more limited and schematic response is already possible.

First, such approaches cannot be mere inversions—whether innocent or cynical—of the new right uses of racial coding, nor of the neoconservative strategic denial of the significance of race. Left racial projects must affirm the ongoing reality of racial "difference" in U.S. cultural and political life. Indeed, in their radical democratic aspects at least, they must go further and create (or recreate) a recognition of racial difference that goes well beyond mere tolerance. One of the striking features of the contemporary racial situation is that many examples of such an appreciation exist in cultural life and in everyday experience—in music and art, sexual relationships, educational and religious settings, the media—without finding any political articulation at all.

Additionally, a radical democratic articulation of race and class must acknowledge that racial minority status still serves as a negative marker, a stigma, in the class formation process. Although significant minority middle classes have arisen since the 1960s, dark skin still correlates with poverty.[5] Class position is in many respects *racially assigned* in the United States.

It follows from this that radical democratic challengers should reopen the question of discrimination as a racial process with class consequences. The reactionary redefinition of the nature of racial discrimination (in the "reverse discrimination" arguments of the 1970s and 1980s) as something that only happens to individuals and thus is disconnected from history and from any preponderant collective logic in the present conveniently suppresses the fact that discrimination drives all wages down.

Linking race and class in a manner that does not reduce race to class involves a *democratic challenge* to the fundamental authoritarianism of the right. It involves rethinking *populism* and the economic and cultural logics of *equality and fairness*. As a mass politics with strong themes of social injustice, exclusion, and resentment, U.S. populism has traditionally been directed at one of two main targets: on the one hand, at big business, the conglomerates, the trusts; on the other hand, at racial minorities, the blacks, the "yellow peril," and so on.

Efforts to reconstruct the far right racial project along populist lines are indicative of the latter tendency. David Duke ran for president in 1988 on the ticket of the "Populist party," which was exhumed in the mid-1980s almost a century after its heyday of free silver, agrarian revolt, and southern lynching. This time around, the scapegoating of blacks is particularly central.

To counter this approach, a left populism will be needed. One such set of proposals, whose advocates have included William Julius Wilson and Orlando Patterson, involves the resuscitation of class-based New Deal policies (extensive public investment and job creation, expansion of the welfare state in a social democratic direction) combined with "race-specific" measures where discrimination per se is the issue (Wilson 1987; Patterson 1979). Until recently, this sort of proposal would have appeared totally utopian, given the lethargy of the Democratic party, the perpetual fiscal crisis of the state, the absence of a strong and independent minority movement, and the political profits available to Republicans who played the racist card ("quotas," Willie Horton, etc.) in the 1980s. The 1992 electoral victory of Bill Clinton on a populist platform raised some hopes for more left-leaning initiatives, based on cuts in defense spending, a program of social invest- ment, and the new president's promises to improve education and expand access to health care. On race, however, Clinton's orientation borrowed ex- tensively from the right. He directed his attention almost exclusively to- ward the suburbs, and proved far more attentive to the needs of the middle class than to those of the poor. No significant effort to push Clinton's pop- ulism to the left has yet appeared.

If there is to be any progressive initiative, such left populist currents will have to be combined with an ethical thrust, as Cornel West has recently argued (West 1991). In this view, social justice in all its forms—class-based, race-based, and gender-based—is achieved only through a combined po- litical and moral vision. This suggests that the pragmatic liberal and radical democratic projects can learn from the right, just as the racial reaction learned from the minority movements of the 1960s.

In order to overcome right-wing populism's racist politics of resent- ment, notions of *equality and fairness* must be rethought in the combined light of race and class (and gender). Thinking of discrimination in terms of the restriction of the individual's rights and opportunities—in a "color- blind" way as the right-wing projects would have us do—becomes a lot more logical in a state committed to social and class justice. In a situation of tight labor markets such as the one Wilson proposes, the problem of "reverse discrimination" would be far less conflictual than it is in a situa- tion where the gap between rich and poor is widening and middle-income people's "life chances" are eroding. Thus, linking race and class justice concerns would facilitate efforts to overcome historic patterns of racial dis- crimination without unduly threatening whites (Ezorsky 1991).

Similarly, the right-wing appeal to racial fears requires careful scrutiny. The right must employ the "politics of resentment" in this process; at a minimum, it must articulate these resentments and fears in "coded" racial terms, such as "quotas." David Duke, Lee Atwater, and Jesse Helms offered an authoritarian and exclusive program: to protect whites against non- whites, against people they do not trust or understand. This authoritarian politics is open to a *democratic challenge*: it can be rearticulated as inclu- sion, not exclusion. Jesse Jackson demonstrated this with his rhetoric of "common ground" and his talk of "adding another patch to the quilt." By accepting and celebrating racial, gender, and sexual "difference" within a plural community, by offering and accepting a place under the "quilt," such a program reaffirms the themes mentioned earlier: equality, fairness, social justice, and an ethical society.

Racial hegemony is being reconstituted as overall hegemony; unfortunately, it is the right that is largely responsible for this trend and that stands to benefit the most from it. The task now is to provide an alternative, emancipatory account of the virtues of racial difference and racial diversity, and to reconstruct the links between the fate of racially defined minorities and the fate of U.S. society as a whole.

Chapter 4

Dictatorship, Democracy, and Difference: The Historical Construction of Racial Identity

Introduction: The Sources of Racial Identity

The paradox of racial identity is that it is simultaneously an utter illusion and an obvious truth. Whatever those of us in the United States—and in many other countries as well—might wish to be the case, we live in a racialized society, a society in which race is engraved upon our beings and perceptions, upon our identities. Indeed, our ability to recognize race is so finely tuned, so ingrained, that it has become a "second nature." And with the development of this ability comes a *naturalizing* of race itself: if racial identity is so recognizable, so palpable, so immediately obvious, then in practical terms at least—irrespective of what one might believe about race—it becomes "real." The sociological dictum that if people "define situations as real, they are real in their consequences" has its truth (Thomas and Thomas 1928).

Yet at the same time, this "reality" is illusory, illogical, unspecifiable beyond the most superficial terms. When we seek to delineate the principles underlying racial categorization, we encounter tremendous obstacles. Not only ordinary individuals but even specialists cannot present a convincing rationale for distinguishing among human groups by physical characteristics. Our "second nature," our "common sense" about race, it turns out, is deeply uncertain, almost mythical.

37

Consider: in the United States, hybridity is universal; most blacks have "white blood," and many millions of whites have "black blood." Latinos, Native Americans, Asians, and blacks, as well as whites, have centuries-long histories of contact with one another; colonial rule, enslavement, and migration have dubious merits, but they are all effective "race mixers" (F. J. Davis 1991; Forbes 1988). Of course, even to speak in these terms, of "blood," "mixture," or "hybridity," even to use such categories as "Asian" or "Latino," one must enter deeply into the complexities of racial discourse. Such language reveals at once the sociohistorical imbeddedness of all racial categories. For these are merely current North American designations, and hardly unproblematic ones at that. They are not in any sense "true" or original self-descriptions of the human groups they name. Nor could any language be found that would avoid such a situation.

Thus, race may be real, but it is also a construct. Race may be present, even permanent, in U.S. society, but what we mean by race is by no means obvious, despite any appearances to the contrary. We may not be able to do without race, now or in the future, but we are always changing the "nature" of race, and of the various racial meanings and categories through which we identify ourselves.

These ideas would have seemed strange, if not incomprehensible, until a few years ago. The "naturalness" of race was taken for granted for a very long time. Indeed, from colonial days until World War II, biologistic notions of race were the ruling ideas in the United States. While not fixed and unchanging, biologism itself was not fundamentally challenged until the early twentieth century, and did not undergo substantial modification until quite recently. It is only since World War II, and most importantly since the rise of the modern civil rights movement, that the idea of equality— however fuzzy—has been coupled with notions of race in an accepted, commonsensical way. But debate over such issues as what equality might mean, how it might be achieved, and who is responsible for achieving it obviously continues.

Thus, the noise generated by the disruption of the U.S. racial order, by the postwar politicization of race, by the resistance on the part of racially defined minorities to policies of systematic inequality, conquest, and exclusion is still reverberating quite strongly. It takes the form of fierce debate about racial policies, a subject that continues to attract significant attention, both scholarly and popular. But less intensively examined is the anxiety and confusion over racial identity—experienced both by racial minorities and by the white majority—that derives from the same sources: the political struggles that transformed but did not destroy the long-standing racism built into U.S. society.

This is an effort to explore that terrain, to consider some of the forces now at play in the construction of contemporary racial identity. I examine the logic of racial identity as it has evolved in the United States, from the aftermath of the Civil War to the present. I emphasize four basic themes: First, in the United States there has always and necessarily been a deep relationship between nonwhite and white identities. Second, until about the end of World War II, the United States was a *herrenvolk* democracy, a de facto racial dictatorship constituted by the denial of basic democratic rights to racially defined minorities (and to women, though that is not my focus here). Third, movement-based democratic challenge to this increasingly atavistic racial order necessarily transformed all U.S. racial identities in the process of reducing, though not eliminating, white supremacy. Fourth, in the aftermath of that ruptural moment, in the present, post-civil rights era, racial identity is experienced at unprecedented levels of tension, for it can be neither fully affirmed nor denied. Finally, in a brief conclusion entitled "Toward Racial Democracy," I offer some notes on the contemporary politics of racial identity.

While this chapter is intended as an overview of the historical processes through which racial identity developed in the United States, it makes no attempt to be comprehensive. I pursue what I consider to be central political and cultural themes in the construction of the racial present out of the past. I ignore others. Indeed, it could not be otherwise with a topic of this size. The relational and increasingly complex nature of racial identity and the centrality of a conception of identity to the ongoing struggle for racial democracy and social justice continue to preoccupy us today. The forces now at play in the construction of contemporary racial identity are descended from a past that we ignore or misinterpret at our peril.

Historical Racialization

By now it is a commonplace to note the centrality of racial slavery in the development of notions of freedom and democracy in the United States (Morrison 1992a; Fields 1990; D. Davis 1975; Fredrickson, 1987). The racialization of these political categories (and their genderization as well) was already well codified by the time the United States was founded. Similarly, arguments about the connections between race and class may be traced back to the contradictory relationship between enslaved and "free" labor. The classical Marxian position that "labor cannot emancipate itself in the white skin where in the black it is branded" (Marx 1967: 301) unquestionably recognized an important truth, and one that resulted in considerable support among white workers for the cause of the North in the U.S. Civil War. Yet, despite their occasionally enthusiastic support for emancipation, these workers were determined to maintain the separate and elevated status the designation "white" bestowed upon them. Why?[2]

It is not enough to argue that whites were protecting their jobs and higher wage levels, though this is of course significant. This analysis (which I have criticized elsewhere) relies too much on economic factors. The "split labor market" cannot be seen as operating in a vacuum, or as automatically determining political orientation, cultural reference points, or notions of identity (Omi and Winant 1986: 30-37). As several decades of crucial work in social history and social theory have taught us, "interests" are never obvious, never objective, never simply given. They are always mediated by politics, culture, subjectivity; they are always constructed.

So it is not surprising that race was already present in the way *white* workers recognized themselves in the nineteenth century. Why else would they have been more threatened by emancipated black labor (or conquered Mexican labor or immigrant Asian labor) than by the flood of European immigrants in the later nineteenth century? Why else would they have adopted—with a few noble but short-lived exceptions—racially exclusive forms of organization? Their class identity was itself racialized, and the class formation process that took shape in this situation drew not only upon fears of economic competition—wage cutting and even replacement by nonwhite labor—but also upon larger fears of a political, cultural, and even sexual nature. Such ideas were deeply imbedded in nineteenth-century biologistic notions of race.

White workers defined themselves through various cultural forms— notably minstrelsy—accepting the disciplinary regime of industry, "hardening" themselves against any weakness (perceived as effeminate), and against the idleness and ease they associated with blacks, the sunny southland, and so forth. Minstrelsy enacted and commented upon a generalized social process: the racial constitution of working-class identity. This *racializing* process worked to organize both resentment and desire in the service of an essentially tragic but noble whiteness that was constantly threatened by "weakness" and "longings" no amount of discipline could ever fully dispel. Such was the legacy for whites of enslavement and emancipation. The consequence was *herrenvolk* democracy and a system of racial difference as monolithic—because of its deep psychological imbeddedness in the working class—as any in the world.

Parallel processes occurred in other spheres of nineteenth-century U.S. race relations. In the Southwest, for example, where the issue was *conquest*, not enslavement,[3] the construction of Anglo and Mexicano racial identities was a prolonged and occasionally violent process. As David Montejano writes:

In the "liberated" and annexed territories, Anglos and Mexicans
stood as conquerors and conquered, victors and vanquished, a
distinction as fundamental as any sociological sign of privilege and
rank. How could it have been otherwise after a war? (1987: 5)

From the end of the war with Mexico onward the region underwent a
lengthy transition from ranching to commercial agriculture (and ultimately
to industrialization), all undertaken under the heavy legacies of conquest,
the defeat of the South in the Civil War, and the Mexican revolution. Locally
this brought about a varied combination of antidemocratic forms of rule,
not only incorporating coercive labor systems and widespread discrimination, but also creating what Montejano defines as a "race situation": "a situation where ethnic or national prejudice provided a basis for separation
and control" (1987: 82). The system of racial rule in the Southwest was certainly coercive and arbitrary, but retained a distinctiveness and paternalism
that derived from the semicolonial status of the area—in which a white
settler minority ruled over a racialized "native" majority—and from the
presence of the border.

After the conquest, the native Spanish-speaking *Tejanos* outnumbered
the white settlers and resisted land usurpations and other indignities in the
"Cortina Wars" (1859-60, 1873-75) and the El Paso "Salt War" (1877), as
well as in innumerable skirmishes. Eventually terms of accommodation
developed (though not for decades in some areas). The resulting arrange-
ment involved de facto segregation, a recognition of citizenship rights
combined with significant disenfranchisement of ordinary Mexicanos, and
a limited conciliation among the Anglo and Mexicano elites. While perhaps
less harsh than the repressive regime of the Deep South, this system was
nevertheless of the *herrenvolk* variety.[4]

On the West Coast, exclusion also provided the basis for coercive racial
control, crystallizing a complex pattern of white fears and exploitation of
Asians.[5] Asian subordination was distinct from that of blacks or Mexicans,
since it distinguished among racialized groups on a national basis. Great
variation also existed among particular locales[6] and over historical time:
Filipinos, for example, were subject to anti-Asian racism but were less easily excluded, since the Philippines were a U.S. territory after 1898 (Takaki
1990: 331). The chief motivation for exclusionist policies was demands
made by white workers, but here too the construction of working-class
identity and political collectivity were intensively racialized. The labor historian Selig Perlman suggested some of the ferocity and complexity of this
process when he wrote:

The political issue after 1877 was racial, not financial, and the
weapon was not merely the ballot but also "direct action"—

violence. The anti-Chinese agitation in California, culminating as it did in the Exclusion Law passed by Congress in 1882, was doubtless the most important single factor in the history of American labor, for without it the entire country might have been overrun by Mongolian [*sic*] labor and the labor movement might have become a conflict of races instead of one of classes. (1950: 52)

As this passage makes clear, the labor movement *did* in fact become a conflict of races. Nor was there ever a chance that Asians might immigrate in the numbers that Europeans did; Perlman reflects some of the fears his white working-class subjects felt.

In fact, exclusionary policies merely formalized the anti-Asian mobilization—chiefly based in the labor movement—that had been building on the West Coast for decades. The various laws and policies aimed at restricting immigration—the 1882 Act (renewed in 1892 and made permanent in 1907), the "Gentlemen's Agreement" of 1907 sharply restricting Japanese immigration, and the 1924 immigration law—were only the most prominent anti-Asian measures. Restrictions on citizenship, marriage, land ownership, and legal rights in general had little to do with immigration, and everything to do with widespread fears of the "yellow peril." Anti-Asian agitation also had a *herrenvolk*ish character that went far beyond labor-market competition. It relentlessly emphasized the *alien* qualities of Asians, their necessary and presumably permanent incompatibility with the North American (i.e., white) way of life. As early as 1854, in *People v. Hall,* the California Supreme Court articulated these concepts in quintessential form:

> The anomalous spectacle of a distinct people, living in our community, recognizing no laws of this State except through necessity, bringing with them their prejudices and national feuds, in which they indulge in open violation of the law; whose mendacity is proverbial; a race of people whom nature has marked as inferior, and who are incapable of progress or intellectual development beyond a certain point, as their history has shown; differing in language, customs, color, and physical conformation; *between whom and ourselves nature has placed an impassable difference*, is now presented, and for them is claimed, not only the right to swear away the life of a citizen, but the further privilege of participating with us in administering the affairs of our Government. (excerpted in Daniels and Kitano 1970; emphasis added)

At times anti-Asian agitators stressed degeneracy and disease, or harped on sexual fears. For example, such themes as opium use, prostitution, and "white slavery" were constantly invoked in anti-Chinese propaganda. Here is a certain parallelism with the construction of whiteness as antiblackness in the same historical epoch. While the particular arguments of anti-Asian rhetoric varied, the underlying theme of otherness was always present. The Asian immigrant was seen as irremediably alien, the "stranger from a distant shore," whose acceptance in the United States was almost unimaginable (Takaki 1990; Saxton 1971; Lyman 1970).

Constructing the Present

Enslavement, conquest, and exclusion, then, were the chief means through which U.S. society was racialized beginning with its colonial origins. Racialization varied over time, across regions, and in respect to particular groups. But it was always present, always crucial to the construction of what Saxton calls "the white republic." Racialization can be understood in many ways: as a repertoire of coercive social practices driven by desires and fears, as a framework for class formation, or as an ideology for nation building and territorial expansion, to name but a few.

Here I wish to emphasize the political consequences of racialization: beyond class formation, beyond territorial expansion, beyond the biologism that informed the building of a *herrenvolk* society, racialization organized a basic U.S. social structure: it established the overall contours, as well as the particular political and cultural legacies, of subordination and resistance. It restricted or even eliminated the political terrain upon which racially defined groups could mobilize within civil society, thus constituting these groups as outside civil society. It denied the existence of commonalities among whites and nonwhites—such as shared economic activities, shared rights as citizens, even on occasion shared humanity—thus constructing race in terms of all-embracing social difference. Racialization, then, also tended to homogenize distinctions among those whose difference from whites was considered the only crucial component of their identities. Over time, then, this white versus other concept of difference created not particular and unchanging racial identities—for these are always in flux—but the potentiality, the social structures, indeed the necessity of universally racialized identities in the United States. Elsewhere Omi and I have described this process, drawing on Gramsci, as *racial war of maneuver*: a conflict between disenfranchised and systematically subordinated groups, whose principal efforts are devoted to self-preservation and resistance, and a dictatorial and comprehensively dominant power.[7]

Paradoxically, white institutionalization of racial difference; white refusal to grant such basic democratic rights as citizenship, access to the legal

v I : organization resultant of white discriminatory policies

system, and access to the vote; and white resistance to the participation by racially defined minorities in civil society permitted—and indeed demanded—the organization and consolidation of excluded communities of color. Because it had so comprehensively externalized its racial others, *herrenvolk* democracy helped constitute their resistance and opposition. It set the stage for its own destruction because, over centuries, whites forced nonwhites to forge their own identities, to suppress their differences, and to unite outside the high walls of a supposedly democratic society whose rights and privileges were systematically restricted on the basis of race.

Disruption of Identity

It would be too optimistic to assert that at some point the walls came tumbling down. Indeed, in many respects the racial walls remain impenetrably thick today. Yet clearly with emancipation, with the consolidation—at often terrible costs—of racially identified communities whose permanent presence on these shores was no longer in serious doubt, with the development of racial *war of maneuver* the preconditions of the political movements of our own time had been created. The pioneering movement, of course, was the black movement.

The modern civil rights movement was a long time coming. Born from black churches and the NAACP; born from the nationalism that from Delany through Washington and Garvey to Malcolm had sustained black people in their isolation from democracy; born from the pens of W. E. B. Du Bois, Langston Hughes, Richard Wright, and countless others; born from legal assaults on the edifice of segregation; born from black colleges and "movement halfway houses" (Morris 1984); born from A. Phillip Randolph's Pullman Porters and from radical commitments to integration in the CIO; born from black women's death-defying opposition to lynching; born from the great migrations northward that accompanied the world wars; and born from the wars themselves and the hypocrisy they exposed of a United States willing to crusade for democracy abroad while murdering it at home, the modern civil rights movement gradually extricated black people from the political ghetto to which they had been confined.[8]

Then, beginning in the 1950s, the modern civil rights movement took off, and far more comprehensive struggle began. The movement transformed the American political universe, creating new organizations, new collective identities, and new political norms; challenging past racial practices and stereotypes; and ushering in a wave of democratizing social reform. This transformation, which at first affected blacks, but soon touched Latinos, Asian Americans, and Native Americans as well, permitted the entry of millions of racial minority group members into the political process.

It set off the "second wave" of feminism, a new anti-imperialism and anti-war movement, movements for gay and disabled people's rights, and even for environmental protection. The black movement deeply affected whites as well, challenging often unconscious beliefs in white supremacy and demanding new and more respectful forms of behavior in relation to non-whites.

These changes can be understood as the eruption of a racial *war of position*, supplanting the war of maneuver that had largely shaped previous racial conflict in the United States. Gramsci understands war of position as political and cultural conflict, undertaken under conditions in which subordinated groups have attained some foothold, some rights, within civil society; thus they have the leverage, the ability to press some claims on the state (Omi and Winant 1986: 74-75).

In transforming the meaning of race and the contours of racial politics, the movement shifted the rules of participation and organizing principles of American politics itself. It made identity, difference, the "personal," and language itself political issues in very new ways.[9] By the mid-1960s, popular support for the main principles of the "civil rights revolution" had been secured, and legislation had been passed.

Yet this triumph was partial and contradictory. The movement agenda had been accepted, but only in its most moderate form. A significant distance remained between the formal acknowledgment by Congress or the Supreme Court of black *rights* to equal justice, education, housing, or employment and the actual *achievement* of those rights. The unity of the movement eroded rapidly as its mainstream liberal supporters—and most of its white adherents—congratulated themselves on their victory. But many movement activists—and much of its black membership—wondered how much change civil rights could bring, absent significant redistribution of income and major efforts to eradicate poverty. They wanted not only rights, but also the power and resources to achieve dramatic social change; they demanded not simply abstract and often unrealizable opportunities, but also concrete results.

Perhaps most important, movement moderates sought to downplay the significance of racial identity, while movement radicals tried to reemphasize it. The debate over identity focused in crucial ways on black views of whites: would they be able to move beyond their own racism, their own dependence, often unconscious, on the privileges conferred by white skin in the United States? Was American democracy, in the familiar dichotomy articulated by Martin and Malcolm respectively, a dream or a nightmare?

These divisions between moderates and radicals, over matters not only of policy but also of identity, were the inheritance of centuries-long conflicts in the U.S. social structure. They reflected the submerged but still powerful legacy of American *apartheid*, of the tradition of *herrenvolk* democracy, of the institutionalization of racial categories at the base of North American society. Simultaneously, they epitomized the unraveling of these structures, the impossibility of sustaining a racial dictatorship, and the potential for an even more serious explosion of racially based movement opposition if serious reforms were not undertaken. Such ferocious divisions, rooted in the framework of U.S. society and history, could hardly be resolved by the movement; they could only be mirrored within it. They would continue to sunder not only the black movement but all racially based movements in the post-civil rights period. They would continue to divide racial identities—*all* identities, including those of whites—from the 1970s onward.

In the aftermath of the civil rights reforms the forces of racial reaction also had to regroup. They could no longer sustain an implacable resistance to black demands for basic social rights, for such a posture risked their marginalization at the far right of the political spectrum. On the other hand, although white supremacy had certainly been shaken, it had not been destroyed. The cultural framework that supported it—the racial subjectivities, representations, and cognitive capacities of the U.S. populace—had not been comprehensively transformed. So the racial right, like its movement antagonists, was divided.

The nascent *new right* recognized that white supremacy was not dead, but only wounded. It therefore attempted to tap into repressed but still strong currents of racism in order to counter the black movement's egalitarian thrust. Born in the campaigns of George Wallace and Richard Nixon's 1968 "southern strategy," the new right developed a new subtextual approach to politics, which involved "coding" white resentments of blacks, and later of other minorities, women, and gays.

Another approach was developed by the *neoconservatives,* former liberals who had been affiliated with the moderate wing of the civil rights movement, but were disaffected by its post-1965 nationalist and class-based radicalisms. Marked by their white ethnicity, by their experience as the children of immigrants, and in particular by their youthful leftism and their struggles against anti-Semitism (many key neoconservatives were Jews), neoconservative thinkers and politicians had made visceral commitments to what they saw as the core political culture of the United States: pluralism, consensus, gradualism, and centrism. They subscribed to an ethnicity-based model of race, derived quite consciously from the "immigrant analogy" (Omi and Winant 1986: 16-17; Blauner 1972: 51-81). Their opposition to the outright institutionalized prejudice of Jim Crow, which temporarily allied them with the pre-1965 civil rights movement, thus had very different sources than that of their erstwhile movement allies. The idea of white supremacy as an abiding presence in American life was anathema to the neoconservatives, for it called into question their idealized view of U.S. political culture.

Neoconservatives abhorred the arguments of black militants—as typified in Malcolm's "I don't see any American democracy. All I see is American hypocrisy." In a striking way, they reproduced the fearful and compensatory allegiance to whiteness exhibited in the late-nineteenth-century United States. Just as many whites in the nineteenth century had opposed slavery but resisted a comprehensive reorganization of their privileged status vis-à-vis emancipated blacks, so too the neoconservatives opposed overt discrimination but resisted an in-depth confrontation with the enduring benefits that race conferred on whites. Thus they sought to confine the egalitarian upsurge, to reinterpret movement ideas more narrowly and individualistically, and to channel them in more conservative directions. Their views aligned them with the white ethnics whose integration into mainstream American society resulted in conservative politics and a sense of "optional" ethnicity (more on this later), amounting in practice to a denial of the significance of race in American life.

Thus the racial reaction too was beset by divisions, in this case between the new right and neoconservatives. These conflicts were probably not as deep as those confronting the civil rights movement and its post-1965 successors, but they were nevertheless real. Should the legacy of racial dictatorship and white supremacy, of *herrenvolk* democracy, be exploited or suppressed? Should the state uphold the civil rights legacy or undermine it? Should whites be mobilized *qua* whites—in defense of their racial privilege—or should the erosion of that privilege be anticipated or even encouraged? These questions sharply problematized white identities in the post-civil rights period and created serious difficulties for nonwhites as well.[10]

Tension Rules, OK?

The racial sea change wrought by the movement was incomplete; it was immediately challenged by "backlash" and a resurgent racial right, and the movement was itself split between moderates and radicals. Therefore, the meaning of race in the United States, and the ongoing significance of race for North American identities, remained as problematic as ever, as the civil rights legacy was drawn and quartered, beginning in the late 1960s and with ever greater success in the following two decades. The tugging and hauling, the escalating contestation over the meaning of race, resulted in ever more disrupted and contradictory notions of racial identity. The significance of race (declining or increasing?), the interpretation of racial equality (color-blind or color-conscious?), the institutionalization of racial justice (reverse discrimination or affirmative action?), and the very categories—black, white, Latino/Hispanic, Asian American, and Native American—employed to classify racial groups were all called into question as they emerged from the civil rights "victory" of the mid-1960s.

In the post-civil rights period, what did it mean to be "black"? One was no longer, in general, a "Negro." This term had once been asserted with pride as a token of independence and resistance to racism, but in the era of black power it was tainted by its long association with the old-line civil rights organizations such as the NAACP and the Urban League, groups that came to be seen as co-opted, even as "Toms." The reassertion of the term "black," then, symbolized race consciousness and pride.[11] Black psychologists noted a "negro-to-black conversion experience" (Cross 1991). Indeed, in the wake of the black power revolt, debates over what constituted a "true" black identity expanded vigorously into every area of social and cultural life: language, skin color, taste, family life, and patterns of consumption all became testing grounds of blackness. Prescribing criteria for identity formation became one of the chief preoccupations of so-called cultural nationalism (Van Deburg 1992; Baraka 1972). Radical nationalisms could not consolidate themselves politically, however, though they continued to exercise important cultural influences. Nationalism appeared to thrive only in the conservative framework of the Nation of Islam.

The decline of the organized black movement in the 1970s and the wholesale assaults against the welfare state initiated by Ronald Reagan during the 1980s created a black community sharply divided along class lines. A small but relatively secure black middle class, a "coping stratum" of black workers increasingly threatened by deindustrialization and the erosion of public services, and a marginalized sector dubbed "the urban underclass" by William Julius Wilson (1987) and others, offered three quite different models of identity, and indeed embodied three disparate sets of interests.

Middle-class blacks were unable and unwilling fully to integrate, and they still faced significant levels of discrimination; yet the range of opportunities available to them would have been unimaginable only a few years before. The dilemmas of racial identification thus hit them with special force.[12] Sharply distinguished from the professionalized and upwardly mobile middle class was the "coping stratum" of working-class blacks, who struggled to survive the continuing threats of declining neighborhoods, worsening schools, and eroding employment markets.[13] Meanwhile, the desolation of the poor increased steadily, interrupted only by periodic revivals of victim blaming (Murray 1984; Sleeper 1990; Kaus 1992).

Although divided by status, these sectors were united by a residual racial solidarity, rooted both in the complex web of social ties—provided by family, work, religion, and so on—and in the recognition that white supremacy and racial inequality were far from dead. But without question black experience in the post-civil rights period was characterized by greater division than the community had ever known before.

Although I have no wish to extol the merits of racial segregation or the racist ethos of the *herrenvolk* democracy that preceded World War II, it is undeniable that the black community in those years experienced a certain *organic* interrelatedness—especially in the urban context (Drake and Cayton 1962)—that the winning of civil rights reforms tended to erode. The significance of disrupted black identity is complex, even contradictory. On the one hand, the emergence of diverse and even conflicting voices in the black community is welcome, for it reflects real changes in the direction of mobility and democratization. On the other hand, the persistence of racism, of white supremacy, and of glaring racial inequality demands a level of concerted action that division and discord tend to preclude.

In the post-civil rights period, what did it mean to be "yellow" or "brown"? The civil rights reforms had tremendous demographic and political effects on racialized groups of Asian and Latin American origins. The reforms included the 1965 passage of a new immigration act that abolished many overtly racist features of the 1924 law. As a result, these communities began to grow rapidly. Politically, the black movement—and the victories it won—exerted a substantial influence upon Asians and Latinos, sparking substantial *panethnic* currents. Previously isolated in enclaves based on language and national origin, Koreans, Filipinos, Japanese, and Chinese underwent a substantial racialization process from the late 1960s onward, emerging as "Asian Americans" (Espiritu 1992). Thenceforward, the racism they had previously experienced as separate groups would be seen in a more common light, although the conflicts among these groups did not entirely abate. Similar shifts overtook Mexicans, Puerto Ricans, Central Americans, and even Cubans as the "Latino" and "Hispanic" categories were popularized. The destruction of formal segregation in Texas had a profound impact on Mexican-Americans there, while the brief rise of militant black nationalism greatly influenced the development of *Chicanismo* throughout the Southwest,[14] as well as affecting Puerto Rican groups in the Northeast.

But for both Asian Americans and Latinos this new racial identity was fraught with contradictions. Apart from long-standing antagonisms among particular groups—between, for example, Cubans and Puerto Ricans, or Koreans and Japanese—significant class- and gender-based conflicts existed as well. Tendencies among long-established residents to disparage and sometimes exploit immigrants who are "fresh off the boat," or for group ties to attenuate as social mobility increases, suggest the centrality of class in immigrant life (Portes and Bach 1985; Takaki 1990). The liberating possibilities encountered by immigrating women, and their willingness to settle in the United States (often greater than their husbands') rather than to return to their countries of origin, suggest the centrality of gender in immigrant life (Grasmuck and Pessar 1991).

Knit together by "racial lumping" and by a series of common political concerns — in the Asian American case continuing anti-Asian violence[15] and recession-driven increases in prejudice, in the Latino case hostility to immigrants, the "English only" movement, and so on (Miles 1992; Coleman 1993) — these groups were also uncomfortable with the new terms in which their identities were racialized. Japanese Americans, and all Asian Americans by extension, were faced with hostility they had not experienced since World War II as Japanese economic competition revived working-class anti-Asian prejudice and new talk of exclusion, for example in the universities (Takagi 1993). At the same time Asian Americans were held up as "model minorities," and their accomplishments were used (and often distorted) to justify neoconservative racial politics and policies. The realization that racism can stigmatize one not only as inferior but also as superior was startling.

Some parallel tensions erupted among Latinos and blacks, who often were pitted against each other in local electoral contests (particularly in California and Texas, but also in other areas), and in struggles for influence over such city and county agencies as school systems and police departments. Many of Latin American descent resisted the very categories "Latino" and "Hispanic," in recognition of the sharp disparities between the racial order in their countries of origin (or of their parents' origin) and the system of racial classification in the United States (Oboler, forthcoming). When they returned the 1990 census questionnaire, for example, many Puerto Ricans checked the box marked "Other" rather than selecting a "Hispanic" category (Rodriguez 1990).

Thus Asian Americans and Latinos found themselves frequently caught between the past and the future. Old forms of racism resurfaced to confront them, and it was sometimes intimated that they lacked the rights of whites — as in the controversy over Asian admissions to universities. Yet at the same time their newly panethnicized identities brought them face to face with challenges that were quite distinct from anything they had faced in the past. Some examples of these challenges were the dubious gift of neoconservative support, the antagonism of blacks, and the tendencies toward dilution of specific ethnic/national identity in a racialized category created by a combination of "lumping" and political exigency.

In the post-civil rights period, what did it mean to be "white"? This is a difficult question. Recent research shows the components of classical white *ethnicity* to be in inexorable decline. Large-scale European immigration is a thing of the past (although contemporary upheavals in Eastern Europe may slow this tendency); while urban ethnic enclaves continue to exist in many major cities, suburbanization and gentrification are taking their toll. Communal forms of white ethnic identity are eroded not only by marriage outside the group but also by the very situation that generates it: heterogeneous contact in schools, workplaces, neighborhoods, religious settings, and so forth.

The result of these trends is the development of a new, catch-all category, the "European-American."[16] This designation may seem merely a synonym for "white," but according to the best recent studies, it incorporates not only a residual commitment to racial "status honor,"[17] but also a certain set of cultural tools allowing the bearers to identify with American individualism and with the ideology of opportunity so basic to U.S. culture.

Ironically, retention of some ethnic identification becomes more important as the communal supports for ethnicity erode. According to Waters, the quest for an ethnic identity helps counteract the experience of homogenization that accompanies white middle-class existence, which is often culturally deracinated. The vacuity of suburban life, combined with the tendency to change residences and jobs frequently, robs many whites of their sense of cultural identity. "Symbolic ethnicity" revitalizes and individualizes one's sense of self.[18] But because ethnicity remains largely symbolic for whites, it is fundamentally different from race. This is a point whites frequently do not understand:

> Americans who have a symbolic ethnicity continue to think of ethnicity—as well as race—as being biologically rooted. They enjoy many choices themselves, but they continue to ascribe identities to others—especially those they can identify by skin color. Thus a person with a black skin who had some Irish ancestry would have to work very hard to present him or herself as Irish—and in many important ways he/she would be denied that option. ... Thus respondents exhibit contradictory ideas about minorities in American society. They are clear that there is a fundamental difference between a white ethnic and a black person when the issue is intermarriage in their own families. On the other hand, they do not understand why blacks seem to make such a big deal about their ethnicity. They see an equivalence between the African-American and, say, the Polish-American heritages. (Waters 1990: 167)

The ability to *choose* one's degree of ethnicity, and often even the particular ethnic group with which one will identify, is vouchsafed in contemporary white identities. But nonwhites have very limited options in this regard. One's ethnicity—Haitian black, Detroit black, Dominican, Mexican, Korean, Chinese—may be a crucial factor in one's life, salient in ways that were discarded decades ago by the ancestors of a hybridized Irish-Scots-Italian-American. Yet the latter enjoys easy access to an ethnic particularity that for the former is still a luxury, due to the "racial lumping" that almost universally characterizes the United States.

At bottom, white identity is undergoing a crisis that is deeply political. The destruction of the communal bases of white ethnicity is far advanced, yet whiteness remains a significant source of "status honor." This white privilege—a relic of years of *herrenvolk* democracy—has been called into question in the post-civil rights period, yet is far from destroyed. The result has been significant anxiety and a drift to the right, a tendency that modern, more subtle race baiters have found it easy to manipulate.

Although it is too early to draw any firm conclusions, the rightist drift in white identity politics may have reached a limit. The election of Bill Clinton with strong suburban support, with the backing of both working-class whites and racially identified minority voters, may presage the next cycle of U.S. politics at the national level. Certainly such a coalition would have to make some concessions to the racial sensibilities of those whites who practice a "symbolic ethnicity." Indeed, Clinton already did so in conducting a campaign relentlessly focused on the "middle class" and its needs. But there are other whites out there too, who have committed themselves to integrated neighborhoods, churches, and schools; recognized the overlaps between racism, sexism, homophobia, and anti-Semitism; and generally struggled to resist the temptations of racial privilege. Millions of white women and gays understand something about the ongoing realities of discrimination, for example. White identities remain uneven and contested: white ethnics are not uniformly "Reagan Democrats"; even conservative whites may be antiracist; class and gender play important parts in determining racial attitudes; and other factors such as age, work experience, and neighborhood are also involved. The question is whether the new administration will recognize the volatility of contemporary white identities, and not assume their neoconservative consolidation. One hopes that Clinton will have the courage of the egalitarian convictions he claims.

Toward Racial Democracy

Not since the aftermath of the Civil War, and possibly not since Europeans first landed on these shores, has racial identity has been more uncertain and contested. The contest is a truly epochal one whose origins are simultaneously age-old and contemporary.

Over the past few decades, after preparatory labors lasting a century and more, a fundamental challenge was finally posed to the long tradition of racial dictatorship, of *herrenvolk* democracy, in the United States. This challenge, and the reaction to it, deeply disrupted the sense of racial identity, of what it means to be black, white, Latino, Asian American, or Native American. Initiated by the civil rights movement but not limited to blacks—indeed, not limited to racially defined minorities—this challenge sought to open up the floodgates of democracy and social justice, to sweep away the legacy of white male privilege. It was only partially successful. It achieved many political reforms, and it significantly reshaped social and cultural life, but it did not accomplish the destruction of white supremacy. Nor could it have, for such a thoroughgoing social change is the work of many years; the struggle continues.

Nor could the movement have succeeded for another reason: it was itself deeply divided over the meaning of race. The movement's limitations created openings for racial reaction, which fashioned its defense of white supremacy as a conservative egalitarianism, sometimes upholding a vision of a "color-blind" society, sometimes blatantly manipulating racial fears. Thus, for roughly two decades (say, 1970 to 1990), the disruption of racial identities did not result in the upsurge of democracy desired by the movement. Rather, it increased racial tensions, both in U.S. society at large and among (and within) racially defined groups. Such tensions combined advances and setbacks, progress and defeats, for the cause of racial democracy and for democracy in general.

The task today is to reignite the movement toward greater democracy. To achieve that is not the work of a book, but I would like to offer one suggestion, to contribute one idea, to that effort, as a concluding thought based on the analysis offered here. It is this: *racial democracy involves the democratization of racial identity.* What this means above all is that open discussion is needed about the commonalities and differences that exist not only among distinct racially defined groups but also within each group. As I have argued, divisions within each group are greater today than ever before, yet this does not in any way place U.S. society "beyond" race. Events like the Los Angeles riots and the Thomas-Hill hearings demonstrate the significance of class- and gender-based differences for contemporary racial identities and the fallacies of invoking criteria of "racial authenticity" in making political or ethical judgments about individuals or events (West 1992; Omi and Winant 1993). But they also demonstrate the persistence and adaptability of racism.

Nearly a century ago Du Bois analyzed "double consciousness" as a basic tension in black identity produced by the painful but ineluctable presence within black subjectivity of white attitudes and prejudices. Today we may reasonably extend this insight to propose the existence of a "multiple consciousness" through which most North Americans necessarily experience their racial identities. Their sense of themselves and each other as racially identified persons and groups always involves not only external differentiation (I am different from another), but also internal differentiation (I contain differences within myself). This is a crucial lesson of the post-civil rights period in U.S. history. The ongoing transformation and increasingly complex construction of racial identities in the contemporary United States is an accomplished fact. The big question is how this perception is to be interpreted politically. Will it take the form of increasing distrust and defensive mobilization of difference and division? Will it revert to a blame-the-victim mentality that frankly or subtly exculpates the beneficiaries of white privilege from responsibility for the fate of the underprivileged? Will it, conversely, blame "whitey" for every defect and problem experienced in racially defined minority communities? Will it be manifested in efforts to police the boundaries of racial identity and to deny voice and rights to those who do not meet increasingly archaic criteria of racial authenticity?

Or will a future politics of race take the form of democratic solidarity, granting equal access to all the institutions of society, recognizing differences, and carrying out the commitment made so long ago to rid this nation of the last vestiges of racial dictatorship?

PART II

Racial Politics

Chapter 5

Contesting the Meaning of Race
in the Post-Civil Rights Period

There were two senior proms in May 1991 at the Brother Rice High School, a Catholic college preparatory academy in Chicago—an official one that was virtually all white and, for the first time, an alternative, all-black prom.

Popular music, in this instance, provided the rallying point for racial consciousness and self-segregation. The trouble began when a white prom committee announced that the playlist for the music to be featured at the prom would be based on the input of all the members of the senior class. Each student would list his or her three favorite songs, and the top vote getters would be played. While this procedure was ostensibly democratic, African-American students (who constituted 12 percent of the student body) complained that their preferences would be effectively shut out in a system of majority rule—tracks by Public Enemy would be overwhelmed by those of Guns N' Roses.

But parity was not the only issue. One African-American senior noted that even if they got half the requests, he and his friends would still be unhappy since "we would have sat down during their songs and they would have sat down during ours." So the African-American students organized their own prom against the wishes of school administrators, who disavowed the prom and barred the use of the Brother Rice name. The principal of the school, Brother Michael Segvich, said, "There is only one prom this year at Brother Rice. [The black prom] is something we don't want. I think it has to do with racism" (Wilkerson 1991).

Ah yes, but "racism" on whose part? The controversy over two proms raises a host of questions regarding the relationship of majority and minority cultures, fairness and representation, and (in the immortal words of soul singer Aretha Franklin) "who's zoomin' who." In essence, issues that debate the very meaning of racial integration and equality in American life.

While educational institutions have been formally integrated for decades, we are nonetheless witnessing a growing "balkanization" among students of different racial backgrounds, and a parallel increase in racial conflict and tension. Such difficulties are by no means confined to the schools. The workplace, neighborhoods, the health care industry, the media, and political parties are equally sites of conflicts regarding issues of racial organization and composition. Despite legal guarantees of equality and access, race continues to be a fundamental organizing principle of individual identity and collective action. The "continuing significance of race" results in part from the *contested meaning* of race—and of terms like "equality," "difference," and "racism"—in the post-civil rights period.

More than twenty-five years since the passage of key pieces of federal legislation outlawing racial discrimination in jobs, public accommodations, immigration policy, and voting rights, we remain consumed by political and cultural attempts to define and redefine the meaning of race for institutional life and individual identity. Discrimination's scope and meaning are still debated, legislated, and litigated. "Self-segregation" in daily practice and institutional life is both denounced and defended. While an overwhelming majority of whites favors egalitarian principles, according to survey data, only a minority supports state attempts to ensure equality (Schuman et al. 1985).

Despite the civil rights movement's profound impact on racial attitudes and institutional arrangements, in the post-civil rights period the issue of race remains more controversial than ever. Why is this so? I would argue that specific patterns of *racialization* that create new racial subjects and significantly transform existing ones have emerged. Far from declining in significance, the racial dimensions of political and social life have expanded.

Racialization

Over the past several decades, we have witnessed attempts from across the political spectrum to define the appropriate meaning of race in institutional life and to establish coherent racial identities based on that meaning.[1] In my view, such objectives were, and continue to be, unattainable. This is because race, a preeminently social construct, is inherently subject to contestation; its meaning is intrinsically unstable.

From a *racial formation* perspective (Omi and Winant 1986), race is understood as a fluid, unstable, and "decentered" complex of social meanings constantly being transformed by political conflict. Race both shapes the individual psyche and "colors" relationships among individuals on the one hand, and furnishes an irreducible component of collective identities and social structures on the other.

Employing this approach, I argue that it is necessary to interpret the meaning of race not in terms of definitions, but in terms of racial formation processes. Chief among these processes is the construction of racial identity and meaning that I call racialization.

The concept of racialization signifies the extension of racial meaning to a previously racially unclassified relationship, social practice, or group.[2] A historical example would be the consolidation of the racial category of *black* in the United States from Africans whose specific identity was Mande, Akan, Ovimbundu, or Ibo, among others. Parallel to this, as Winthrop Jordan (1977 [1968]) observes, was the evolution of the term *white* as a crucial form of self-identity for Europeans, who had earlier thought of themselves under such categories as *Christian*, *English*, and *free*.

As Lieberson and Waters (1988) note, racial/ethnic groups should not be viewed as static categories, but "as products of labeling and identification processes that change and evolve over time." They suggest "a continuous process of combining and recombining" in which "groups appear and disappear" (252). In line with this approach, I utilize the concept of racialization to argue that race and racial meanings have been significantly transformed by the civil rights movement. In its wake, North Americans have witnessed state and policy reforms (such as affirmative action), demographic changes (influenced in large part by the "liberalization" of immigration policy), and dramatic shifts in sociocultural understandings of race and racism.

In the post-civil rights period, new forms and expressions of racialization have unfolded. These include the emergence and consolidation of new racial categories, the appearance of differences and divisions within previously well defined racial groups, and the phenomenon of groups confronting previously unexamined questions regarding their racial identity and status. In the sections that follow, I examine in turn three key examples of these tendencies: the development of new racial subjects as a result of panethnic consciousness; the increasing significance of class for African-Americans; and the crisis of white identity.

Panethnicity and the Development of New Racial Subjects

In the post-civil rights period, groups whose previous national or ethnic identities were quite distinct have become consolidated into a single racial category.

Prior to the late 1960s, for example, there were no "Asian Americans." In the wake of the civil rights movement, distinct Asian ethnic groups, primarily Chinese, Japanese, Filipino, and Korean Americans, began to frame and assert their common identity as Asian Americans. This political label reflected the similarity of treatment that these groups historically encountered at the hands of state institutions and the dominant culture at large. Different Asian ethnic groups had been subject to exclusionary immigration laws, restrictive naturalization laws, labor market segregation, and patterns of ghettoization by a polity and culture that treated all Asians as alike.

The *racialization* of Asian Americans involved muting the profound cultural and linguistic differences, and minimizing the significant historical antagonisms, that had existed among the distinct nationalities and ethnic groups of Asian origin. In spite of enormous diversity, Asian American activists found this new political label a crucial rallying point for raising political consciousness about the problems of Asian ethnic communities and for asserting demands on state institutions.

The racialization of Asian ethnic groups was paralleled by the racialization of other groups, notably Latinos and Native Americans. Such panethnic activism was inspired by the civil rights movement and anticolonial nationalist movements in Asia, Africa, and Latin America. Somewhat ironically, the very movements that sought an end to racial discrimination at home and colonial rule abroad also fostered an increased political awareness among formerly fragmented ethnic groups that they constituted a larger, racially defined entity.

David Lopez and Yen Espiritu (1990) define panethnicity as "the development of bridging organizations and solidarities among subgroups of ethnic collectivities that are often seen as homogeneous by outsiders" (198). Such a development, they claim, is a crucial feature of ethnic change — "supplanting both assimilation and ethnic particularism as the direction of change for racial/ethnic minorities" (198). Lopez and Espiritu suggest that panethnic formations are not merely "alliances of convenience" but are shaped by an ensemble of cultural factors such as common language and religion, and by structural factors such as race, class, generation, and geographical concentration. They do conclude, however, that a specific concept of race is fundamental to the construction of panethnicity, since "those ... groups that, from an outsider's point of view, are most racially homogeneous are also the groups with the greatest panethnic development" (219-20).

The rise of panethnicity is a process of racialization that is driven by a dynamic relationship between the specific group being racialized and the state. The elites representing such groups find it advantageous to make political demands by using the numbers and resources that panethnic formations can mobilize. The state, in turn, can more easily manage claims by recognizing and responding to large blocs as opposed to dealing with the specific claims of a plethora of ethnically defined interest groups. Conflicts often occur over the precise definition and boundaries of various racially defined groups and their adequate representation in census counts, reapportionment debates, and group-specific social programs (scholarships, bilingual education, etc.).

Panethnic consciousness and organization are, to a large extent, contextually and strategically determined. There are times when it is advantageous to be in a panethnic bloc, and times when it is desirable to mobilize along particular ethnic lines. Therefore, *inclusionary* and *exclusionary* politics are involved in panethnicity, as racial and ethnic boundaries and definitions are contested.

Two examples illustrate the situational nature of this dynamic. In an attempt to boost their political clout and benefits from land trust arrangements, native Hawaiians voted four to one in January 1990 to expand the definition of their people to anyone with a drop of Hawaiian "blood." Previously, only those with at least 50 percent Hawaiian "blood" were eligible for certain benefits (Essoyan 1990). By contrast, in June 1991 in San Francisco, Chinese American architects and engineers protested the inclusion of Asian Indians under the city's minority business enterprise law. Citing a Supreme Court ruling that requires cities to define narrowly which groups had suffered discrimination in order to justify specific affirmative action programs, Chinese Americans contended that Asian Indians should not be considered "Asian" (Chung 1991). At stake were obvious economic benefits accruing to designated "minority" businesses.

The post-civil rights period has witnessed the rise of panethnicity as a phenomenon of racialization. Groups that were previously self-defined in terms of specific ethnic background, and that were marginalized by the seemingly more central dynamic of black/white relations, began to confront their own racial identity and status in a political environment of heightened racial consciousness and mobilization.

Panethnicity will continue to be an enduring feature of political life as we enter the next century. The dramatically changing demographic landscape, the transformation of global, regional, and sectoral economies, and the contested nature of political power all conspire to insure a role for panethnic identity, consciousness, and political organization in the foresee-able future.

The Increasing Significance of Class

According to law professor Roy Brooks, "Deep class stratification within African-American society is without a doubt the most significant development in the 'American dilemma' since the civil rights movement of the 1960s" (Brooks 1990: xi). Few analysts today would take issue with him. When William Julius Wilson argued in 1978, however, that the contemporary life chances of individual African-Americans "have more to do with their economic class position than with their day-to-day encounters with whites" (1980: 1), he created a storm of debate about the relative importance of race and class in American life.

Since then, many scholars have emphasized the primacy of nonracial factors, particularly class variables, in shaping African-American life chances in the post-civil rights period. Thomas Sowell (1983), for example, asserts that differences in racial/ethnic group economic performance are solely a function of the group's human capital, and not a function of societywide discrimination. Wilson himself, in *The Truly Disadvantaged* (1987), argues that the impersonal forces of the market economy explain more about the current impoverishment of the inner city African-American poor than analyses relying on notions of racial discrimination. While he does not dismiss the effects of historical racial discrimination, he concludes that capital is "color-blind," and that the large-scale demographic, economic, and political changes that have negatively affected the ghetto have little to do with race.

Stressing the role of class in shaping the African-American experience is nothing new. As pioneering studies by Du Bois (1967 [1899]) and Frazier (1957) have demonstrated, class antagonisms within the African-American community have a venerable history. Socioeconomic homogeneity has never existed in any racially defined community. So are class divisions any more significant today than they were in the past?

I think the answer is yes. Previous conflicts between the "black bourgeoisie" and the "black masses" took place in a context of nearly complete segregation. However much these two sectors of the community viewed each other with suspicion and mistrust, they were forced to live together, and frequently to ally against the system of white supremacy. But the civil rights movement created a new context for racialization. With the passage of civil rights reforms, patterns of racial segregation in a range of institutional arenas were severely challenged.

Thus, twenty-five years after the enactment of major civil rights reforms, the African-American community is both the beneficiary and the victim of its own success. A community once knitted together by survival imperatives in a segregated society and bound up by internal "thick" relationships of intracommunal labor, commerce, residence, and religion has now been divided, and this division has occurred primarily along *class* lines.

African-Americans who could take advantage of the slow but real lowering of racial barriers in education, employment, and housing have been able to achieve an unprecedented degree of upward mobility since the late 1960s (Freeman 1976). This does not mean that they are shielded from discriminatory acts or that they have abandoned their identification as "black." But it does mean that they are living in a far more integrated world and that racial identity and racism no longer determine their fates or futures as inexorably as before (Landry 1987). At the same time, capital flight and fiscal crisis have further impoverished low-skilled and undereducated African-Americans, leading to the much-publicized dilemma of the "underclass," or "ghetto poor" (Wilson 1991).

The result of these transformations, therefore, is the *differential racialization* of African-Americans along the lines of class. Such differentiation has important consequences for individual identity, collective consciousness, and political organization. For the African-American middle class, for example, it generates profound ambivalence about racial identity. As Dr. Alvin Poussaint notes:

> There's a lot of pressure on the black middle class to stay black.
> . . . It's kind of a contradiction. Your kids are living in an integrated
> community, and you want them to feel part of the community,
> participating equally in it. Then you feel very ambivalent about it
> psychologically, when they do. (Garreau 1987)

Nor are middle-class African-Americans shielded from discriminatory treatment by virtue of their class position. In a study of antiblack discrimination in public places, Joe R. Feagin found that African-American shoppers were subject to excessive surveillance and frequently received curt and discourteous services from clerks: "No matter how affluent and influential, a black person cannot escape the stigma of being black, even while relaxing or shopping" (Feagin 1991: 107; see also Williams 1991).

Poussaint and Feagin suggest that racial identity is still conflictual, and racial discrimination is still problematic, for all strata of the African-American community. Such analyses also reveal, however, that the effects of these conflicts and problems vary widely by class. The middle-class ambivalence about racial identity described by Poussaint contrasts sharply with the bitter frustration and pervasive violence through which impoverished ghetto youth experience their blackness (Eric B. and Rakim 1990). The sites and types of discriminatory acts, and the range of available responses to them, obviously differ by class. Yet in other instances, the malevolent attention that police devote to African-Americans reveals a frightening uniformity across all classes; such is the judgment of the Christopher Commission report on the Los Angeles Police Department (Dunne 1991).

The "increasing significance of class" does not, therefore, suggest a "declining significance of race." In the wake of civil rights reforms, distinct paths of opportunity created a modicum of upward mobility for the African-American middle class, but did little or nothing to improve conditions for the ghetto poor. Despite this dramatic transformation, African-Americans remain a preeminently racialized group in politics, cultural representation, and social life. They are not, however, racialized in a uniform and homogeneous manner.

Such a perspective is important since much of the race versus class debate suffers from the imposition of rigid categories and analyses that tend to degenerate into dogmatic assertions of the primacy of one category over the other. Wouldn't a more fruitful mode of inquiry seek to account for the impact of class transformation within a social order still highly structured by race? We need a way, in other words, to grasp the increasing significance of class for African-Americans and other racially defined groups that does not deny the centrality of race in the formation of identity and everyday experience.

The Crisis of the White Identity

It is an unremarkable observation that we are increasingly becoming a multiracial society. The dramatic increase in "minority" populations in the United States renders much of the very language of race relations obsolete and incongruous. By 2003, whites are expected make up less than 50 percent of the population of California, for example, and the demographics of the workplace and the campus are changing faster than those of the general state population (Institute for the Study of Social Change 1990).

The prospect that whites may not constitute a clear majority nor exercise unquestioned racial domination in various institutional settings has led to a *crisis of white identity*. As previous assumptions erode, white identity loses its transparency, the easy elision with "racelessness" that has accompanied racial dominance since the end of the Reconstruction period in 1877. Today the very meaning of "whiteness" has become a matter of anxiety and concern. In this respect, whites have been racialized in the post-civil rights era.[3]

During the 1970s, as the influence of the civil rights movement waned, there was a backlash against the institutionalization of civil rights reforms and to the political realignments set in motion in the 1960s. Resistance to affirmative action programs grew among whites who felt that it was they, and not racially defined minorities, who were discriminated against by state policies ostensibly designed to promote racial equality in the schools, the workplace, and other institutional settings. As one respondent noted in *The Report on Democratic Defection,* the "average American white guy" gets a "raw deal" from the government because "Blacks get advantages, Hispanics get advantages, Orientals get advantages. Everybody but the white male race gets advantages now" (Greenberg 1985: 70). The idea that white racial identification could be a *handicap* is unprecedented. In the aftermath of the civil rights era, though, the nature of whiteness has become more controversial than at any time in this century.

One response to the civil rights challenge was to assert the primacy of ethnicity over race. In this account, there was no such thing as a homogeneous white majority. Many whites were really minorities in their own right, "unmeltable" ethnic minorities (Novak 1972). More recent research, however, suggests that most whites do not experience their ethnicity as a definitive aspect of their social identity. They perceive it dimly and irregularly, picking and choosing among its varied strands to exercise, as Mary Waters (1990) suggests, an "ethnic option." The specifically ethnic components of white identity are fast receding with each generation's additional remove from the old country. Unable to speak the language of their immigrant forebears, uncommitted to ethnic endogamy, and often unaware of their ancestors' traditions (if in fact they can still identify their ancestors as, say, Polish or Scots, rather than a combination of four or five European — and non-European! — groups), whites undergo a racializing panethnicity as "Euro-Americans" (Alba 1990).

The "twilight of white ethnicity" in a racially defined, and increasingly polarized, environment means that white racial identity will grow in salience. The racialization process for whites is very evident on university campuses, as white students encounter a heightened awareness of race that calls their own identity into question. Students quoted in a recent study on racial diversity (Institute for the Study of Social Change 1990) conducted at the University of California at Berkeley illustrate the new conflictual nature of white identity:

> Many whites don't feel like they have an ethnic identity at all and I pretty much feel that way too. It's not something that bothers me tremendously but I think that maybe I could be missing

something that other people have, that I am not experiencing.
(52)

Being white means that you're less likely to get financial aid. . . . It
means that there are all sorts of tutoring groups and special
programs that you can't get into, because you're not a minority. (50)

If you want to go with the stereotypes, Asians are the smart
people, the Blacks are great athletes, what is white? We're just
here. We're the oppressors of the nation. (52)

Here we see many of the themes and dilemmas of white identity in the
post-civil rights period: the anomic absence of a clear culture and identity,
the perceived disadvantages of being white with respect to the distribution
of resources, and the stigma experienced in thinking of one's group—even
somewhat facetiously—as the "oppressors of the nation."

How will white identity be interpreted at the turn of the twenty-first century? What political and ideological elements will be invoked in the refash-
ioning of whiteness? Already, far right political actors such as David Duke
actively seek to organize whites to defend their supposedly threatened racial privileges, all in the name of equality. Such racist populism is not all
that distinct from the demagogic use of the code word *quotas* by Jesse
Helms and George Bush to attract white votes.

On the other hand, white resentments cannot be wholly dismissed; they
are not solely the result of racist demagogy or a last-gasp attempt to retain
some vestige of racial privilege. Such sentiments also express loyalty to an idealized and seemingly threatened civic culture in which *individual equality* was
enshrined as a core democratic principle. That culture was never guaranteed
to most whites, much less to nonwhites, but it was certainly espoused, across
the political and cultural spectrum, as a central ideal. At present it seems to
many Americans to be a receding ideal, obscured by hypocrisy and greed. The
future avoidance of racial polarization will depend on resuscitating and reart-
iculating that vision, combining it with a heightened awareness of race to demand greater social justice for all.

Whites have not been immune to the process of racialization. Racial mobilization in the post-civil rights era has not been limited to "people of
color," and whites have had to consider the racial implications of an order
that formally disavows "white privilege." The changing demographic
scene, global economic competition, and the perception that America has
fallen from grace have provoked a profound crisis of white identity. What
direction this takes politically depends to a great extent on the way racial
difference and social inequality are interpreted in the years ahead. There
are many sources of "common ground"—to use Jesse Jackson's phrase—

across the lines of race. Those lines are increasingly porous and flexible, but they are not about to disappear. On the other hand, the racial right has proved adept at drawing political capital from its exploitation of white fears, and these cannot be expected to diminish dramatically in the years ahead. The politics of whiteness, in short, remains unresolved.

Conclusion: The Challenges to Racial "Common Sense"

The civil rights movement challenged long-standing racial understandings and oppressive racial practices, ushering in a period of desegregation efforts, equal opportunity mandates, and other state reforms. Various forms of racial discrimination — in the labor market, in housing, in public accommodations, and in marriage laws — were overthrown in this process. But, despite these tremendous accomplishments, patterns of institutional discrimination proved to be quite obstinate, and the precise meaning of race, in politics and law as well as in everyday life, remained undefined. The ambiguity of race in the post-civil rights period has now reached the point where any hint of *race consciousness* is viewed suspiciously as an expression of *racism*.[4]

Ironically, the present situation is a legacy of the civil rights movement. While the movement cannot be seen as a homogeneous or monolithic entity, it contained from its very inception an irresoluble dilemma regarding racial consciousness and identity and their meaning for social and political life. On the one hand, the movement sought an end to racial inequality by advancing a vision of an integrated, "color-blind" society. On the other, it simultaneously sought to increase the level of racial identification among African-Americans and other people of color. This contradictory stance was structured not only by movement ideology and strategy, but also by its conflictual and accommodative relationship to the state.

Different currents within the civil rights movement sought to synthesize the two movement objectives, arguing that integration and the politics of racial difference could coexist. All such attempts — ranging from cultural pluralism through neo-Marxism to various forms of nationalism — were ultimately unsuccessful. The two horns of the movement dilemma apparently could not be articulated in a single comprehensive political and cultural outlook.

As a result, the issues of racial equality and identity were later vulnerable to *re*articulation from political projects on the right (Omi and Winant 1987). These have ranged from "white racial nationalism" (Walters 1987) to neoconservative critiques of affirmative action and other "color-conscious" remedies. Despite their clear ability to mobilize sectors of the white electorate, the arguments of the right have been no more successful than those of the left in establishing a new understanding of the relationship between racial equality and racial identity. The right's failure to resolve the dilemma has led to continuing controversies surrounding the role race plays, or should play, in various institutional arenas and in U.S. society as a whole.

Neither the civil rights movement nor the racial reaction, therefore, have been able to advance and consolidate a new racial *common sense*—a general conception of the role of race, if any, in a good and just society. But both political forces have succeeded in weakening or even demolishing the system of racial categories, meanings, and institutions that they opposed. The repressive racial order of legally sanctioned segregation has been overthrown, but no clear and consensual racial order has been consolidated in its place.

The paradoxical result of all this has been that, far from decreasing, the significance of race in American life has expanded, and the racial dimensions of politics and culture have proliferated. The process of *racialization* continues apace. New racial identities and meanings continue to be created as a result of panethnic linkages. Differentiation within racially identified communities continues as a result of the partial but significant reforms wrought by the civil rights movement. And to the extent that the "complexion" of U.S. society changes and widespread shifts in patterns of racial inequality and the rules of racial difference actually occur, whites too experience the contradictions and conflicts of racial identification.

Debates about the meaning of racial equality, the nature of racial identity, and the role of the state with respect to race will deepen and intensify in the immediate future. From the senior prom in Chicago to the disputed nomination of Clarence Thomas to the Supreme Court, racialization continues.

Chapter 6

The Los Angeles "Race Riot" and Contemporary U.S. Politics

The charred buildings were still smoking when George Bush arrived in Los Angeles for a whirlwind tour of the South-Central area. Speaking on May 8, 1992, at the Challenger Boys' and Girls' Club in the heart of the riot zone, the president sought to explain the previous week's events:

> Things aren't right in too many cities across our country, and we must not return to the status quo. Not here, not in any city where the system perpetuates failure and hatred and poverty and despair. (Bush 1992)

At first, such remarks may seem startling. Had the devastation Bush witnessed suddenly transformed him into a critic of institutional racism and corporate capitalism? When he referred to "the system," was the president thinking of the relegation of millions of racially stigmatized poor to the torpor and despair of ghettos? Was he alluding to the widespread acceptance of this warehousing as an apparent condition for the prosperity of the elite, and for the survival of a suburban and largely white middle class? Did he have new plans to reverse the withdrawal of already meager public benefits and services from the inner cities? Was he contemplating ending the brutal police occupation and surveillance of the ghettos out of a new-found respect for human and civil rights?

Hardly. Bush had something quite different in mind. He argued that the federal government had spent as much as $3 trillion over twenty-five years in an attempt to address poverty and racism, all with little success. We must now, he said, face some "unpleasant realities." First and foremost among these was the realization that "liberal" social welfare programs had not resolved the problem of poverty. In fact, he argued, such programs fostered dependence on the state, nurtured irresponsible personal behavior, and led to the overall deterioration of inner-city communities.

How then to address the needs of the urban ghettos and barrios? What new policy alternative would the administration launch to confront the deterioration, the destruction, the despair? Bush concluded his address with an outline of the broad features of his approach:

> [My] belief [is] that we must start with a set of principles and policies that foster personal responsibility, that refocus entitlement programs to serve those who are most needy, and increase the effectiveness of government services through competition and through choice. (Bush 1992)

Thus the administration echoed neoconservative analysts who argue that poverty results from moral failure, lack of personal responsibility, and dependence on the welfare state.[1] He renewed the traditional distinction between the deserving and undeserving poor, between those who had a just claim on public resources and those who needed discipline, not material support (Katz 1989; Polanyi 1957 [1944]). While he revived the 1960s denunciations of "rioting for fun and profit," the president offered a rehash of "trickle down" policy recommendations like subsidized enterprise zones and privatization of public housing.

Not to be outdone by Republican criticisms of the poor, Democratic presidential candidate Bill Clinton adopted a more pragmatic version of the same rhetoric. While he was perfectly willing to criticize the Reagan and Bush administrations for neglecting the inner cities and manipulating racial fears, Clinton too argued that many 1960s programs have not worked and suggested that in the future government programs must "demand greater responsibility" from the poor (Brownstein 1992: A8).

Within the Clinton camp, a host of political sages linked to the Democratic Leadership Council and the *New Republic* expatiated on the duties of family and community, preaching like television evangelists to nonwhite women about proper child rearing and the values of the work ethic. As E. J. Dionne informs us:

> Values such as taking responsibility for one's family, struggling to be self-reliant, remembering that the communities of which we

are a part have a right to expect something of us are neither left
nor right. (1991)

Other Democratic "wise men" like Mickey Kaus and Laurence Mead
joined neoconservative analyst Charles Murray in urging the elimination of
welfare *tout court*. In place of AFDC they would substitute various combinations of market discipline and authoritarian workfare. As Kaus put it:

> There are good reasons why people hate welfare, because welfare
> provides an economic substitute for work. It's a bad thing with
> bad social consequences. People have always hated welfare and
> people have always been right. (*Tikkun* 1992: 75)

Nor has this "tough love" approach been confined to Democratic policy
papers and party platforms. In New Jersey, for example, liberal governor
Jim Florio lent his support to a new law that denies increased benefits to
mothers who bear additional children while they are on welfare.

Thus have we come, so it seems, full circle. Poverty and discrimination,
seen in the past as problems requiring state action, are now seen as the
results of state activity. What was once the solution (activist social policies)
has now become the problem (dependence), and what was once the problem (the lash of poverty) has now become the solution (market forces).

Surely this dramatic analytical inversion is indicative of broader changes
in racial ideology and politics in the post-civil rights era. Slowly during the
1970s, and more rapidly during the Reagan-Bush years, the tables
turned—in matters of race—from benign to malign neglect. In the aftermath of the great racial transformations of the 1960s, the state and the major political parties professed a sincere interest in racial equality and in
genuine pluralism. More recently we have seen the triumph of race bait-
ing, racially coded appeals for votes, and victim blaming.

Out of this situation, out of this cesspool of combined brutality and neglect in racial matters, came the explosion of April 30-May 2, 1992, in Los
Angeles. The massive disturbance occurred on the eve of the most important presidential campaign in decades, threatening to recast the election
into a debate about race, social inequality, and urban decay (Apple 1992:
Y9). The riot took an unprecedented form. Unconfined to a concentrated
ghetto territory, unrestricted to a racially homogeneous group, the riot re-
asserted what may be the sole significant power that remains in the hands
of the marginalized and oppressed—the power to disrupt.

By riveting attention on the failed Reagan-Bush strategy to use race as
the lever to displace the U.S. political spectrum to the right, the Los Angeles
riot marks an end to the rightward drift in U.S. racial politics in general.
There remains, however, a significant gap between the lessons the riot has

to teach and the ability of the U.S. political system to learn them. The political process has indeed shifted to the right over the past decades. As a result, Americans are poorer, less politically engaged and effectual, and culturally more benighted. All of these transformations have been wrought, to a significant extent, by the adroit deployment of racial politics. Their reversal, their transcendence, cannot occur overnight.

What does the Los Angeles riot tell us about racial politics in the United States? Above all else, it serves as an immanent critique of the mainstream political process, of the political convergence that dominates national politics today. It demonstrates the continuing significance, and the continuing complexity, of race in American life. And it shows the ineffectiveness of any authoritarian strategy, whether neoconservatism or pragmatic liberalism, in addressing the problems of inequality in America.

This chapter examines three interrelated questions. The first of these is *the new convergence in mainstream racial politics*. Here the argument is that George Bush's self-righteous call to repudiate the legacy of the 1960s bears more than a passing resemblance to a new Democratic drive to de-emphasize race and play better in the suburbs. This new convergence in mainstream racial politics continues the 1980s legacy of the marginalization of racially defined minority constituencies. Furthermore, the intersection of mainstream right and mainstream left takes place in a symbolic manner. As political rhetorics joust over the merits of their moralisms, they fail to address the complexities of race in the ways they are experienced, represented culturally, and structured into politics. The Los Angeles riot challenged these manipulative approaches to race. It drew attention to the continuing presence of race in the social structures and meaning systems that organize the U.S. social order and identify its members.

This context frames a second theme, which is *the nature and varieties of racial identity today*. A quarter century after the civil rights movement's peak, the meaning of race and the nature of racial identity have become far more uncertain, far more ambivalent, than they were in earlier periods of U.S. history.[2] The Los Angeles riot testifies to the complexity of contemporary racial dynamics. Despite various depictions to the contrary, the riot was not a black, but rather a multiracial, affair. It involved significant antagonisms between racially defined minority groups, most notably between blacks and Koreans. It also involved substantial class conflicts within particular racially defined groups. What do these splits and conflicts signify?

The third theme is the phenomenon of *resistance to state coercion*. The riot was sparked, as so often has happened in the past, by police violence and impunity, but at a deeper level it was a response to impoverishment and neglect. The suffering of a society subjected to a drawn-out process of regressive economic restructuring, increasing authoritarianism, and an increasingly vapid discourse about "values" is concentrated among the racially defined minorities of the ghettos and barrios. The riot represented an act of defiance, a somewhat desperate effort to respond to the impoverishment not only of the ghetto poor, but of U.S. society as a whole. As such it sets certain limits on the state's ability to enforce and extend the human suffering concentrated at the "lower depths" of our society.

Convergent Racial Politics

In the United States, understanding of the meaning of race is forged in large measure through the political system. Debates over state policy and political party affiliation, and media coverage of important racial events such as the Rodney King incident and the Los Angeles riot, inculcate in the general public a "commonsense" or hegemonic conception of the significance of race. Historically, racial "common sense" has fluctuated wildly. Beliefs about equality, about the nature of racial difference, and indeed about what constitutes a race have shifted dramatically over time. In the post-World War II period, and even more so in the post-civil rights era, conflict over the significance of race has been continuous and vituperative.

Today's "common sense" about race is more a product of past controversies than an accurate rendering of present circumstances or actual experience. Just as the riots were multiracial events despite the political and media efforts to paint them in terms of black insurrection and white law and order, so too is experience "racialized" in ever more complex fashion. Class differences fissure racially defined groups, creating far different stakes for middle-class Latinos in Silver Lake, for example, than for those in Pico-Union, a poor neighborhood that includes many Central American refugees and undocumented workers. Blacks in Baldwin Hills are not powerless and desperate; their situation is quite distinct from that of blacks in Compton.

Yet part of the continuing reality of racism revealed in the riot lies precisely in the incomprehension, and indeed the willful ignorance, that the political process demonstrates when racial issues are at stake. The system is intellectually limited: it can only "think" one thought at a time. Either the riot is the product of the failed 1960s policies and the dependence and sloth they induced in their unfortunate victims, as Bush would have it, or it is a result of the greedy and regressive domestic policies pursued by the Reagan and Bush administrations, as Bush's critics would suggest. Faced with a choice between these two positions, one would obviously select the latter, but this limited choice, between what I have elsewhere labeled the racial projects of neoconservatism and pragmatic liberalism, leaves a lot to be desired (Winant, forthcoming).

Here is the present situation: on the right wing of the mainstream, and firmly linked to the Republican party, is the neoconservative project; on the left wing of the mainstream, and equally firmly rooted in the Democratic party, is the pragmatic liberal project. Neither view is uniformly held; certainly there are outriders in both parties. But within the mainstream, the battle over what is to be the hegemonic view of race is joined—perhaps more intensely than at any other moment in decades—between the neoconservative and pragmatic liberal projects. As a result of the persistent racialization of politics in the United States, the stakes are high. In 1992, the prize was the presidency and the future direction of domestic policy. Yet, also because of the persistent racialization of politics in the United States, neither neoconservatives nor pragmatic liberals are able to address issues of race and poverty in a sufficiently comprehensive way. Racial "common sense," whether of the mainstream right or the mainstream left, therefore persists in its failure.

The impoverished racial "common sense" of 1992, and the convergence between the neoconservative and pragmatic liberal racial projects, was dictated by a political logic in which the major parties competed for the suburban—largely white—vote. The situation is dramatically delineated by Thomas and Mary Edsall in their book *Chain Reaction* (1992). The Edsalls describe how race became a powerful "wedge issue" that fractured the traditional liberal coalition. Since 1965, they assert, whites have found less and less reason to carry the burden of redressing social grievances. Working-class and middle-class whites have been directly affected, the Edsalls claim, by school integration, preferential hiring, and higher taxes to fund group-specific programs. The result of all this has been massive defections from the Democratic party and the consolidation of a conservative Republican majority.

Dramatic new patterns of segregation have emerged as whites have moved to the suburbs surrounding the declining cities, many of which have majority black and Latino populations. The nation, the Edsalls claim, is moving steadily toward a national politics that will be dominated by the suburban vote. The suburbs allow white middle-class voters to meet their own communities' needs by taxing themselves for direct services (e.g., schools, libraries, police) while denying resources to the increasingly poor and nonwhite cities. Appeals to the middle class's "fiscal conservatism" and "communitarian" impulses thus have a hidden racial agenda: to prevent white tax dollars from going into programs to benefit racial minorities and the poor. The Edsalls argue:

What all this suggests is that a politics of suburban hegemony will come to characterize presidential elections. With a majority of the electorate equipped to address its own needs through local government, not only will urban blacks become increasingly isolated by city-county boundaries, but support for the federal government, a primary driving force behind black advancement, is likely to diminish. (1991: 231)

Here is the reasoning that underlies Bush's neoconservative appeal to "personal responsibility." Beneath all the color-blind rhetoric, not only of Bush but of his academic intelligence agents Kristol, Glazer, Murray, and Sowell, lies a strong belief that racial inequality is an effect of other, non-racial factors. Because its origins lie in differentiated human capacities, racial inequality can never be overcome through politics.[3] The distance between this view and blaming the victim is short.

Confronting this neoconservative racial project is a pragmatic liberal project advanced by the newly "centrist" Democratic party under Bill Clinton. This project takes a leaf from the neoconservative book in its attempt to deemphasize race and accept some of the "personal responsibility" logic. It seeks, however, to reinvigorate the coalition that, from the 1930s to the 1960s, united minority and white workers under the New Deal and Great Society banners. The pragmatic liberals draw heavily on the work of sociologist William Julius Wilson, who has acted as an adviser to Clinton.[4]

Wilson believes that Clinton assembled a "remarkable biracial coalition" by promoting programs that unite, as opposed to divide, racial minorities (particularly blacks) and whites. In doing so, Wilson says, Clinton destroyed the myths that blacks respond only to race-specific issues, and that whites, particularly the poor and working class, will not support a candidate heavily favored by blacks:

> If the message emphasizes issues and programs that concern the families of all racial and ethnic groups, whites will see their mutual interests and join in a coalition with minorities to elect a progressive candidate. (Wilson 1992: A15)

This belief flows from Wilson's analysis in *The Truly Disadvantaged* (1987). There he argues that the impersonal forces of the market economy explain more about the current impoverishment of the inner-city African-American poor than any analysis relying on notions of racial discrimination. While Wilson does not dismiss the effects of historical racial discrimination, his conclusion is that capital is "color-blind," and that the large-scale demographic, economic, and political changes that have negatively affected the ghetto have little to do with race. Therefore, "group-specific" policies, emanating from the reforms of the civil rights era, cannot improve the situation experienced by the African-American "underclass." Wilson thus calls for "universal programs," rather than group-targeted ones, to halt the deterioration of inner-city communities:

> The hidden agenda is to improve the life chances of groups such as the ghetto underclass by emphasizing programs in which the more advantaged groups of all races can positively relate. (Wilson 1987: 120)

This "hidden agenda," of course, justifies a pragmatic attempt to woo white middle-class voters. Their needs—for more and better jobs, access to education and health care, and reductions in drug trafficking and crime—can be linked to those of the minority poor if the "wedge issue" of race can be blunted. Hence the "convergence" between neoconservative and pragmatic liberal approaches to racial policy. The overlap is not total: there is a good deal more room for race baiting, and for sheer neglect of the cities, on the neoconservative side, while pragmatic liberals are willing to consider certain "group-specific measures" that neoconservatives reject out of hand.[5] Yet both the neoconservatives and the pragmatic liberals share the conviction that racial matters, and racial minority constituencies, should receive less attention in the political process. The "dirty little secret" of continued racial hostility, segregation, and discrimination of all sorts is not to be politically addressed. Not now, and not in the foreseeable future.

Ambivalent Racial Identities

Even during "normal" times, when no racially significant riots or other crises loom, the contours and significance of racial identity are complex and delicate matters. The idea that we know what it means to be, say, black, Latino, or white is quite untenable. There are multiple difficulties involved in racial identification. Among these are, first, the sociocultural variability and conflict involved in defining racial categories; second, the significance, for a given individual or group, of membership in a particular racial category; and third, the ability of individuals and groups to make judgments about the racial identities of others. Beyond these experiential factors lie structural ones. Some examples include the deployment of shifting and often hidden racial criteria in stratification and discrimination, spatial patterns of inequality, and the mobilization of racial signifiers in politics, both explicitly and covertly.

Long-standing disputes exist in each of these general areas. For instance, consider the continuous discussion that takes place among blacks (and in scholarship about blacks) on the subject of "what's in a name." Who are "blacks"? Are they "Africans"? "Negroes"? What is the significance of color in identifying them, as well as others? The vicissitudes of naming this racialized group have a history as long as the presence of Africans in the Western Hemisphere; this debate is coterminous with North American black writing itself (Gates 1992, 1986a; Hanchard 1990; F. J. Davis 1991). Similar conundrums have preoccupied Latino/Hispanic, Native American, and Asian American groups, as well as those who study them.[6] More recently, the white category has become problematic as well, as an increased remoteness from the "ethnicizing" experience of immigration has created more and more "unhyphenated" whites, whose group identity more and more coincides with their race (Lieberson and Waters 1988; Waters 1990; Alba 1990).

A monumental event like the Los Angeles riot not only reasserts collective racial interests; it also recasts racial group identities. I have already noted that the riot was a "multicultural" one: blacks, Latinos, and whites were all seriously engaged in looting and burning. There were few reports of Asian American participation; rather, Asians—and particularly Koreans—appeared to be the rioters' chief victims. Black hostility was especially directed at Korean merchants (Rutten 1992; Kim and Yang 1992).

The riot acted as a pressure cooker, intensifying and revealing the ambivalences, fault lines, and polarizations that characterize U.S. racial identities today. The complex patterns it disclosed cannot possibly be examined in depth here; intensive primary and archival research will be needed to understand them fully. Here I can only point out a few intriguing instances of these variations.

Geography. The riot was not spatially confined, as had been its most obvious precedent, the Watts uprising of 1965. Although it began in a black ghetto neighborhood near Watts, it quickly spread out, particularly toward the north. Intense looting and arson took place in Koreatown, whose very location—between the black South-Central area and Hollywood—signifies the "middleman minority" and "buffer" roles played by Korean merchants.[7] Without question, the Korean American community was the most severely damaged by the riots. More dispersed incidents took place, however, as far north as Santa Monica Boulevard. Although police response was conspicuously limited or even nonexistent in the early phases of the riot, the downtown area was afforded significant protection. This, plus an informal truce between black and Chicano gangs (and more broadly between the two communities), kept the riot from spreading significantly to the east, while to the west and south targets were limited.[8]

Class. These geographical patterns, the concentrated attack on Korean merchants whose economic role placed them in a very exposed position, and extensive nonblack participation in the looting and burning all suggest that class factors, as well as racial ones, were significantly in play during the riot. It will not come as news that the riot was a response to poverty: looting is not generally a middle-class pastime. The novelty lies in the way the riot made visible the partial fissures and fault lines that now exist within minority racial communities and even within individual racial identities. At the same time, the riot demonstrated the unity—partial but real—that links the urban poor regardless of race. Its effect was to *attenuate racial identities in favor of class identities* for those low-income people who were involved in the rioting or closely linked to it.

The riot also had a profound effect on those minorities who were not poor, and who by and large did not participate. Hatred and distrust of the police were extremely strong in the black and Latino communities, as many better-off residents—some of them celebrities such as Wesley Snipes—recalled police mistreatment they had received. Since the immediate cause of the riot was the Rodney King verdict (discussed in greater depth later), and since the behavior of the police during the riot itself was a mysterious and undoubtedly exacerbating factor, the tendency of middle-class blacks and Latinos to identify with the rioters was increased. Thus the effect of the riot was to *attenuate class identities in favor of racial ones* for those middle-class minorities who were by and large not involved in the actual disturbances. Many members of this latter group actually made their way to the riot zone in the later stages or immediate aftermath of the disturbances, to express their solidarity, perhaps, to check on the safety of relatives or friends, or simply to experience and thereby clarify their ambivalence and uncertainty at having "made it" out of the ghetto or barrio.

Intragroup Cleavages. The riot demonstrated the cleavages that underlie such panethnic racialized identities as "Latino/Hispanic" or "Asian American." Among the former group, a key division between documented and undocumented people, long visible on other cultural and political terrains, was intensified during the riots. This fault line intersected another division, that between Mexican-Americans/Chicanos and Central Americans, to produce a complex pattern of antagonisms in the Latino community. The Los Angeles police arrested more than twenty-seven hundred Latinos during the riot, the majority for looting, but many for curfew violations as well. This number represented about half of all the arrests made, incidentally; more Latinos were arrested than blacks. Of this number, more than twelve hundred "were found to be 'without papers,' and were turned over—in violation of city policy—to the Immigration and Naturalization Service for deportation" (Rutten 1992: 53). More than three hundred Central American refugees were in this number, and more than six hundred Latinos were deported;[9] with typical ignorance and bigotry, police chief Daryl Gates singled out Central Americans as "participating in this riot in a very, very significant way" (*Los Angeles Times* 1992: A7).

The wholesale assault on Korean merchants dramatically intensified existing political splits among Asian Americans. Generally aligned with the Democratic party and officially supportive of civil rights and antidiscrimination initiatives, Asian American communities have long harbored inner racial antagonisms. Class divides many groups both from other Asians and internally. Solidly middle-class Japanese Americans, largely working class Filipinos, generally low-income Southeast Asians, Chinese Americans, and Korean Americans whose class position varies significantly—all these come into conflict where economic and political issues are concerned. In addition, there are significant parallels with Latino/Hispanic divisions over issues of assimilation and integration: long-established residents may disdain those who are "fresh off the boat." By and large, Asian Americans abhorred the rioting, even where they were not its direct victims. Yet there was also substantial sympathy with the plight of the impoverished inner city. At a rally held on May 2, 1992, in Koreatown there were numerous calls for peace between blacks and Koreans, while "several elderly Korean men left the parade route to shake the hands of Latinos and African-Americans who were watching" (Chang and Krikorian 1992: A3). Signs demanded "Justice for Rodney King," quite a remarkable slogan given the past week's experience (Rutten 1992: 53).

Intergroup Cleavages. Black-Korean tensions have been widespread for years, reflecting patterns of antagonism between low-income communities and the "middleman minority" entrepreneurs who provide their services. Such arrangements have a worldwide similarity, extending to Chinese in Malaysia, East Indians in Africa, and so on. For Koreans operating businesses in the ghetto, as for Jews before them, high personal risks (for example, of robbery and arson) are offset by low rents and reduced competition. To black ghetto residents, these businesses appear to offer inferior products at high prices; their owners and employees (often family members) appear to customers as fearful and hostile. The mere presence of these businesses seems to crowd out potential black-owned competitors. Black-led boycotts of Korean grocers have occurred from coast to coast, and gunplay has been widespread on these premises. Robberies, as well as shootings of suspected shoplifters, are common. One such case, that of the killing of fifteen-year-old Latasha Harlins by a Los Angeles Korean American grocer in early 1991 and the subsequent handing down of a suspended sentence, served as an immediate prelude to the rioters' assaults on Korean merchants.

In contrast to other Asian Americans (and to other racial minorities generally), the Korean community had maintained a low profile in Los Angeles politics, running almost no candidates for local office, mounting few public protests about its underrepresentation. Nor had Mayor Tom Bradley acted to mediate black-Korean disputes as had, for example, David Dinkins in New York. A big factor in Bradley's base has traditionally been what Mike Davis calls "the inner circle of Southside ministers and cronies" (M. Davis 1990: 309),[10] which included a number of figures actively promoting grocery boycotts. Thus, when the riots came, the mayor and Chief Gates did little to defend Koreatown itself, not to mention Korean businesses in South-Central. Armed Korean men soon mounted the rooftops of many establishments and organized neighborhood patrols.

The Nature and Limits of State Coercion

The proximate cause of the riot, of course, was the acquittal of the Los Angeles Police Department (LAPD) officers who had brutally beaten motorist Rodney King. I can add little to the journalistic accounts that have saturated the nation (and the world) about the beating and the trial. The beating itself—this must be recognized—was a routine event that would have attracted no attention had not witness George Holliday captured it on videotape. The farcical acquittal was based on many factors: political toadying and miscalculation in the Los Angeles County district attorney's office,[11] a botched courtroom strategy that wound up identifying the jury with the defendants,[12] and, probably most important, a change of venue to all-white Simi Valley. "Of the 8,300 officers on the LAPD, a staggering 2,000 of them live in Simi" (Cooper and Goldin 1992: 39).

But the riot was more than an emphatic rejection of a single verdict; it was a protest against the systematic aggressions to which poor and nonwhite residents of Los Angeles are routinely subjected, especially if they are black.[13] The police are simply the most visible reminder of subordinate status. Certainly the LAPD enforces that status (or, more properly, the complex combination of statuses that constitute racial identity) quite crudely and brutally. But however it acts on the street, the LAPD's combination of neglect and violence pales in comparison with the state's overall repertoire. If we measure brutality in terms of human costs—in lives destroyed, communities savaged, pain inflicted—then surely the denial of jobs, education, health care, drug treatment, and housing is far more serious brutality than any number of police beatings. So, rather than stew about a miscarriage of justice, it is more valuable to reframe the riot as an eruption of anger against the coercive powers of the state.

Over the past two decades a massive restructuring of U.S. society has taken place. The changes involved have been manifold: they have included a regressive redistribution of income and a decline in real wages; a signif-

icant shift to the ideological right in terms of public discourse; and an increase in the use of coercion on the part of the state. It is not necessary to
consider these shifts only in racial terms to recognize their profound nature. They include, for example, the increasingly repressive atmosphere
experienced by unions (especially those daring to exercise their rights to
strike or organize), and the increased state commitment—beginning under Carter but greatly augmented under Reagan and Bush—to the denial
of women's rights, notably reproductive rights.

Coercive state power has been extensively involved in this restructuring. Obviously, not everyone has been subjected to the same coercive powers. For most of the U.S. citizenry, it has not been necessary to apply
authoritarian measures in order to effect the desired changes. The socio-
economic condition and political power of the majority of the labor
force—the middle class, the skilled work force—could in general be allowed to erode rather than being directly assaulted. There were exceptions: the PATCO strike, for example. But these were relatively unusual.

Where racial minorities were concerned, however, this pattern was re-
versed. Here the exceptions were those "coping strata," in Martin Kilson's
term (Kilson and Cotingham 1991), those exemplary groups that had
against all odds achieved a sometimes precarious but relatively stable economic position. For the majority of blacks and Latino/Hispanics, for Native
Americans and many Asian Americans, however, this restructuring has
largely been a disaster. It has been carried out in many respects at their
economic expense, it has been rationalized by discussions of their supposed defects, and it has been enforced by an intensity of repression not
seen in the United States since the 1960s.

Thus the underfunding of schools and the restriction of educational opportunities, the flight of less-skilled employment from the cities to the
maquilas and their equivalents around the world, the growth of underground and illegal economies dealing in drugs and illegally sweated labor,
all of this has become a way of life in the ghettos and barrios of the United
States. The creation of a "third world within" has been a corollary of the
reactionary restructuring I am describing.

Most central to this new authoritarianism has been a sustained attack on
the welfare state. Although the primary victims of this attack are minority
women and children,[14] these are but the cannon fodder for a larger assault
on the bargaining power of working- and middle-class people in the economy, and on the political power of the majority of the population in the
electoral process (Piven and Cloward 1982; Phillips 1991). Economic restructuring, political repression, ideological rationalization—in respect to
supposedly unfair taxes, lax morals, and a propensity toward violence—all
these elements come together in the assault on the welfare state.

And while this stew has been prepared largely in the Republican—which is to say neoconservative—kitchen, it is being eagerly lapped up by many "moderate" Democrats as well. One has only to examine the *New Republic* or consider the latest moralizing by Jim Sleeper or Mickey Kaus to find its pragmatic liberal incarnation (Sleeper 1990; Kaus 1992).

What, then, generates a riot, even of a "new kind" like that of Los Angeles? Without question, there must be a spark, there must be an outrage. But there also must be a rage, and rage is not born in a moment. The kind of rage that created the Los Angeles riot was a political sentiment: nobody cares about me, about us; nobody offers us a chance; there is no hope for us in this system; it's built on our despair. Such ideas are hardly misguided. Indeed, their widespread acceptance reflects the fact that the price of American decline is the creation of a stratum of society with nothing left to lose. Having no other, more acceptable, political means at their disposal, the urban poor resort to what Orlando Patterson (1979) has called their "counter-leviathan power." This power—to disrupt, to frighten, to resist, to limit the coercive powers of the state even at great cost and risk—retains its effectiveness.

Conclusion

The Los Angeles riot signaled the limits of the reactionary racial politics practiced during the Reagan-Bush years. More eloquently than any blue ribbon report or policy tract, the riot made the case for a new social policy. The uprising demonstrated the need to reverse the decay of U.S. cities, and the declining economy linked to the urban crisis. Both the Republican and Democratic parties rushed to apply their policy prescriptions to the nation's urban wounds. Some version of the immediate needs highlighted by the uprising—jobs, education, and investment in the urban environment—was compatible with the political agenda being framed by both the Republican and Democratic candidates in their 1992 electoral campaigns.

For the neoconservatives clustered around Republican campaign headquarters, these were the natural issues of a "traditional values" campaign, one that would emphasize privatization of welfare state programs, incentives for inner-city investment, and school choice. To the neoconservatives, the riot's message was the failure of the welfare state; this was, they thought, a tune that would play very well among surburban, middle-class, white voters. It was a political formula that could build on white resentments, on the coded racial appeals of the Reagan-Bush years, while still claiming to believe in racial equality. As in years past, neoconservative racial politics could work by denying the significance of race.

The riot's message for the pragmatic liberals grouped in the Democratic camp was only somewhat different. To them, the fires of Los Angeles helped justify a more activist social policy, greater state investment in job creation, education, infrastructure, and so on, precisely because these were not "group-specific" measures. Jobs, education, and increased social investment were justifiable demands now because whites who were not poor, and who did not live in the central cities, wanted them as well. For the pragmatic liberals, then, a promise to return to the more activist policies of the welfare state would be successful if it principally addressed the needs of suburban, middle-class, white voters. Of course, it would not hurt to mouth some platitudes about the scourge of racism, but the crucial thing was to reach the suburbs with the message that the middle class, and not the low-income minorities who supposedly sucked up all the taxes, were to be the chief beneficiaries of liberal largesse. To this end, appropriate moralizing about "personal responsibility" and "family values" had to be inserted into Democratic party discourse. Thus, for the first time, liberals would adopt the "code word" strategy previously associated with the Republican right; in order to win back the white suburbanites, they too claimed the right to blame the victim, to disparage the "dependence" of welfare mothers. For their own reasons but with some of the same authoritarian rhetoric employed by the neoconservatives, the pragmatic liberals too denied the significance of race.

There were two ironic elements to this situation. The first irony was that, as the riot had demonstrated, racial matters had attained a complexity and variety that both these political formulas were incapable of addressing. Coded racial appeals to whites made less sense in the context of a multiracial riot. Despite the best efforts of politicians and media mouthpieces, the Los Angeles riot was not simply a black affair. Unlike Watts's in 1965, the flashpoint of this riot—the Rodney King beating and its sequel, the Simi Valley trial and acquittal—had been witnessed by millions. Few doubted that an injustice had been committed. This riot occurred in a post-civil rights era America, one substantially leavened by the presence of middle-class blacks and Latino/Hispanics, few of whom leaped to the defense of the LAPD or the state in general, particularly when the issue was repression directed at racial minorities. A situation in which blacks, Latinos, and whites were the rioters and blacks, Latinos, whites, and Asians were the victims of the violence generated a certain amount of explanatory difficulty, except perhaps where compassion for Korean merchants was concerned. When even they—surely the most unambiguous class of "riot victims" visible on the nightly news—revealed themselves as having some sympathy for the impoverished inner-city dwellers, how could the official story cope?

The second irony was that it was the very destruction of the welfare state that had jeopardized the interests and egalitarian aspirations not only of racially defined minorities, but those of the middle class as well. Whatever short-term benefits they had gained by moving to the suburbs and voting against the "tax and spend" social programs excoriated by the Republicans, the white middle class now stood to lose because an eviscerated welfare state meant lousy schools, inferior and costly health care, eroding infrastructure, and, worst of all, declining wages, capital flight, and unemployment! The Republican formula for electoral victory—driving a wedge between suburb and city, between white and racial minority voters—had worked well enough as long as the burdens of economic decline and political powerlessness could be shifted onto the shoulders of racial minorities. When general economic decline spread from the ghettos and barrios to the suburbs, and when the flames of Los Angeles demonstrated the limits of any further assaults on the inner cities, "universal programs" (Wilson 1987: 163) suddenly regained their attractiveness. Finally, it took the riot to drive home the point that middle-class anxieties about crime and drugs and taxes were pretty minimal in comparison to the fears a full-blown urban uprising could unleash. The middle class heard a clear message in the riot, one that was as old as the nation: if we do not hang together, we shall surely hang separately.

Chapter 7

Hard Lessons: Recent Writing on Racial Politics

The subject, once again, is race. The meaning of that term remains as elusive and paradoxical as ever. A staple of common sense, a word that we live by, "race" retains its profound ambiguities and contradictions, its uncertainty, and, most deeply, its power. Racial inequality still structures the social world, assigning varied "life chances" to winners and losers distinguished only by their color. Racial difference still acts as an all-purpose social signifier, designating attributes of taste and style, attaching symbols of pleasure and danger, hope and fear, to our physical bodies.

Yet race is also changing constantly. In the past, the meaning of the concept was taken for granted in ways that would be impossible today. Certainly, critical reflection on the concept of race always existed. But from the time the race concept attained world-historic importance about half a millennium ago to quite recently, that critique has been a largely marginal one. Even the great racial upheavals of the past, such as the U.S. Civil War, did not expunge the biologistic cast of much race thinking. In the past, questions of racial identity, racial meaning, the role of race in history, and the relationship between race and justice were at times debated; they were even at times the source of bloody conflicts. But they were probably never as complicated as they are today. Never before has race—as a social structure, a set of attitudes, beliefs, and emotional identifications—attained the level of societywide attention that it now demands. Never before has the task of theorizing race been as complex, as daunting, as it is today.

Nor is theorizing enough. Here lies an even greater difficulty. We would like to move beyond theory to practice, to participate meaningfully in the transformation of the inequities, the assaults, the power plays, the misunderstandings, and the sufferings to which the term "racial injustice" is attached. We know too—controversial assertion here—that these desires for coherent thought and meaningful action cannot be realized simply, by any nostrum or formula prescribing a "color-blind" or other similarly nonsensical "solution." For race is not a matter of color alone, nor is it something one can be blind to, nor indeed is it a "problem" that can be solved. It is more like a way of life, a way of being, in which we must learn to act consciously, usefully, and justly. Knowing these things, what can we do?

If indeed we know these things today, or intuit them, it is a result of hard lessons. In the United States, the past half century has been a continuing course in "race relations." Many loathsome social practices and modes of thought have been destroyed during this period, as radical movements, sustained critical interrogation, and the eventual mobilization of the powers of the state were trained upon them. But in this process the "racial progress" that has been won has also been cast into doubt. The early visions of harmony and community evoked by civil rights leaders have come to appear rather simplistic. Dreams of a raceless society are now cited—often disingenuously—by the right. Hopes for integration have been tempered. The militant rhetoric of movement radicals has also encountered obstacles: inchoate goals, a tendency toward demagogy, and persistent sexism and homophobia have tarnished racial radicalism's earlier luster. Finally, the state has proved an unreliable partner in the cause of racial justice; policies framed throughout its various branches—from the Supreme Court to the Census Bureau, from city councils to state legislatures—have chipped away at the dream of racial justice. The presence of Republican administrations from 1968 to 1992 (interrupted only by the Carter interlude), administrations sustained in large measure by their commitment to foot-dragging if not outright reaction in racial policy, certainly has not helped matters.

Thus have we come to the 1990s. The heroic period is over. Progress and reaction go hand in hand. Hybridity confronts essentialism. Divisions *within* racially defined groups compete for attention with the imperative of diversity in mainstream institutions. Tensions are everywhere, from Crown Heights to the university quad, from the Mexican border and the waters off Haiti to the suburban voting booth. There is no reason to think that race will preoccupy us any less in the next few years. Indeed, in just over a year we saw the Hill-Thomas hearings, the Los Angeles riot, and the election of Bill Clinton—the first racially moderate president in a dog's age.

Each of these rather momentous events, and many others we could name, calls into question the possibilities of racial politics in the contemporary United States. Thus it is not surprising that a number of progressive authors have produced books on race, seeking in general to intervene in what is correctly perceived as a shifting political climate. Most of these books were written well before the political winds shifted in the Democrats' direction, so few contemplated the serious ruptures that have now appeared in the Republican coalition that has held national power for so long. There is a sense in which some of the works discussed here are anachronisms; they were outdated at birth. Still, they provide a valuable starting point for any overview of current U.S. racial politics. Nor is it easy to go beyond them just yet. But that is precisely the task we face: to understand and overcome the theoretical and practical dilemmas posed by race after the heroic days of movement struggle, but well before any authentic equality, social justice, or radical pluralism has been achieved.

Compared to the long defensive action we have been fighting, the current situation is reasonably auspicious for the cause of racial justice. The Clinton administration's commitments have yet to be tested, but its accession to power will at least create some opportunities, if activists and movements know how to seize them. (As I write, Clinton's inauguration is about a month off.) Therefore, I address these remarks to those who, like myself, continue to believe that far greater racial justice is both possible and desirable, and that a far more nuanced and radical understanding of the meaning of race is within our reach.

In this essay, I propose first to consider a series of books whose subject is conflict between blacks and whites and the implications of this conflict for U.S. politics. I then examine efforts to expand this traditional bipolar framework, looking at books that address the experiences of other racialized groups—Asian Americans and Latinos—and that consider the interaction of race and gender in the contemporary United States. Next I look at two recent attempts to reconsider racial issues in global perspective. Not only have we North Americans got something to learn from the comparative analysis of race, but the salience of race also is increasing transnationally. In the conclusion, I attempt some theoretical notes that might begin to stitch together these disparate fragments of the racial mosaic.

Black and White and Blue All Over

Was the promise of the civil rights movement achieved? Twenty-five years after the legislative sea change, how much was dream, and how much was nightmare? Certainly, for some the dream was brought closer to reality, if not achieved. The destruction of formal segregation was itself a victory. Middle-class integration—the racial diversification of many formerly white enclaves from suburbs to professions, from universities to boardrooms and media—was another. And the spread of an ethos of racial pluralism, visible in current debates about multiculturalism, for example, was also a clear if not uncontested gain. But below the froth of these successes lay the stew of persistent poverty for many, and of continuing threat even for those whom Martin Kilson, specifically referring to the black community, has called the "coping-stratum" of the working class (Kilson 1989).

Over the past few years, several competent attempts have been made to assess the current dimensions of black-white inequality. Notable among these have been the survey project led by Gerald D. Jaynes and Robin M. Williams, Jr., which produced the volume *A Common Destiny: Blacks and American Society* (1989), and the recent book by Andrew Hacker, *Two Nations, Black and White, Separate, Hostile, Unequal* (1992). Both works amply illustrate the pattern of limited integration combined with persistent poverty that I have described. *A Common Destiny* was widely praised for its descriptive achievements, but criticized for its anemic efforts at interpreting the phenomena it documented. Hacker's statistical work too has received great accolades. His highly accessible book effectively describes disparities between blacks and whites in respect to employment and income, education, crime, and family structure, though it adds little to the information presented earlier by Jaynes and Williams.

Hacker at least attempts to *explain* why inequality has remained so pervasive, in contrast to the Jaynes and Williams volume. But his explanations seem almost unrelated to his data. A stickler for exactitude where numbers are concerned, Hacker is impressionistic and arbitrary where argument is required. In some places his impressions are convincing in a rather literary way, as for example in his sympathetic examination of the stresses and strains of contemporary black identity. Elsewhere he appears to resort to arbitrary and simplistic arguments, as for example in his heavy reliance on the familiar theory of "white privilege." This account focuses upon

> the weight Americans have chosen to give to race, in particular to the artifact of "whiteness," which sets a floor on how far people of that complexion can fall. No matter how degraded their lives, white people are still allowed to believe that they possess the blood, the genes, the patrimony of superiority. No matter what happens, they can never become "black." (217)

While there is obviously an important residual insight here into the operation of racism, as an *explanation* it leaves a lot to be desired. What distinguishes "white people" from one another where matters of race are concerned? Do they all benefit, or do some benefit and others lose, from racial discrimination? Some whites—women and gays, for example—have extensive experience as the victims of certain types of discrimination. Others who are considered white, such as Jews and Arabs, also know something about discrimination, and tend toward the liberal side of the political spectrum where race is concerned. Are all of them equally committed to their "privilege," or do they share some common interests with blacks? What is the role of ideology, of ethical and political conviction, of social policy in structuring this "privilege"? Who, particularly, "allows" whites to believe themselves superior? Hacker winds up blaming "white America" *tout court* for racial inequality, a position that is not only at odds with his spirit of empirical inquiry but also politically bleak to the point of cynicism. Indeed, when he argues that "our time is not one receptive to racial remedies" (xiii), he reveals a lack of the "optimism of the will" so necessary for politics.

Derrick Bell is equally unsatisfying on these points. His *Faces at the Bottom of the Well: The Permanence of Racism* (1992) is largely a cri de coeur about the limits of the civil rights vision. That vision depended in some respects on alliances with whites. But since whites cannot give up their dependence on racial discrimination, Bell suggests, racist social structures will persist. It was a mistake to accept Myrdal's reformist vision that "white America . . . *wanted* to abolish racism" (9, emphasis original). In contrast to this, the reality is that there remains an

> unstated understanding by the mass of whites that they will accept
> large disparities in economic opportunities in respect to other
> whites as long as they have a priority over blacks and other
> people of color for access to the few opportunities available.
> (ibid.)

This premise is not subjected to any serious scrutiny, but rather asserted as a given. It is the "nightmare" thesis as dogma.[1] As with Hacker, the idea that significant distinctions might be made among whites, or that social policy and political processes might be responsible for some portion of the racial injustice that persists in the United States, is not seriously investigated. The only concession Bell makes in this essentializing portrait of whites is occasionally to invent an antiracist white character, such as Erika Wechsler of the "White Citizens for Black Survival," an all-white armed underground poised to resist a potential black holocaust, or Dr. Sheila Bainbridge, who helps Jason Warfield, leader of the "African-American Activist Association," recover from an assassination attempt and then becomes his lover. (Sheila majored in black studies and has mostly black and Hispanic friends.)

Bell offers chapter-length parables on the proposition that "black people will never gain full equality in this country" (12, italics removed). Among other ideas, he contemplates the appearance of a new Atlantis ("Afrolantica") that only black people can enter; he considers taxing discrimination rather than legislating against it; he imagines "racial data storms" that would at last enlighten whites about the immensity and longevity of black suffering; and in his most controversial fantasy, he conjures up visiting "space traders" who offer to solve all the problems of the earth in return for just one thing: the entire U.S. black population, which they propose to remove to parts unknown. Perhaps upset at the message of hopelessness his approach conveys, he appends a coda to his book entitled "Beyond Despair," in which he argues that even if full equality cannot be achieved, black resistance to racism and injustice is still worthwhile in moral and spiritual terms. In the absence of a coherent vision of what "full equality" might look like, this gives small comfort.

In contrast to Hacker and Bell, Thomas Byrne Edsall and Mary Edsall consider the claim that *whites* have been the chief victims of the civil rights legacy in their book *Chain Reaction: The Impact of Race, Rights, and Taxes on American Politics* (1992). The main outlines of this argument are familiar from unceasing reiteration in neoconservative tracts. The Edsalls do not endorse the neoconservative view, but they don't treat it very critically, either, in the course of analyzing the political processes that have promoted it to near-hegemonic status.

Their main concern is the role of racial divisions in the rightward realignment of the Republican party—and with it the political spectrum in general—in the post-1960s period. The Edsalls' argument is that the successful attack on "racially preferential policies" (affirmative action in all its forms, busing, housing desegregation, etc.) not only brought the Republicans to power, but also led to the decline of cities, reduced social spending, and diminished support for the welfare state in general. Race played a central role in that shift, catalyzing the "chain reaction" of the book's title: white middle-class resistance to taxation, to the expansion of state-furnished rights of all sorts, and to integration.

This is not exactly news, but at least it is an argument. In contrast to Hacker and Bell, the Edsalls are able to show concretely how in the post-civil rights era political struggles over race were organized and orchestrated by the right:

> In spite of American success in eliminating legally protected racial
> subjugation, race remains a powerful wedge issue, and for as long

as that is the case, the incentive to capitalize on racial conflict will supersede pressures to address the economic bifurcation that increasingly plagues the country. (284)

Nor do they spare the Democratic party, and indeed the established civil rights leadership, for their often witless collaboration with the right's agenda. Although they place great stress on the link between class and race—note the reference to "economic bifurcation" in this passage—the Edsalls do not explore the issues involved in this connection. We are left with the familiar, and ever weaker, logic imposed by all class reductionisms of race: racial antagonisms are manipulated for economic or political gain.

In taking this position, the Edsalls agree with Hacker and Bell in an odd way: though they pay insufficient attention to continuing black inequality or to the solid evidence of discrimination that Hacker in particular presents, they accept the "white privilege" argument after a fashion. Their victims, however, are the *whites* who were sold out by liberal Democrats beholden to their black constituencies, and whose racial resentments were so effectively organized by the right. And their villains are not blacks but foolish liberal Democrats who thought racial equality could be achieved without substantial social struggle and economic dislocation. Indeed, they sympathize with the grievances of whites—fear of crime, dislike of welfare, resistance to tax increases, and above all resentment of "preferential treatment"—which Republicans seized upon and Democrats tried to ignore.

So the question comes down to values and victimology. The Edsalls at least have the merit of raising these issues, which Hacker and Bell seek to avoid by blaming whites in general for racial inequality. But the Edsalls fail to confront the question of racism, since they never really question the choice made by middle-class whites—the "Reagan Democrats"—to accept Republican blandishments, vote their own pocketbooks, and let their darker brothers and sisters be damned. What kind of "values" were those?

It was the misfortune of the Edsalls' book to appear just as the Republican party began its own self-destruction. (Politics moves too quickly for publishing schedules these days!) Although their long-range prediction of party realignment now seems off base, their analysis of the racial resentments underlying post-1960s politics should not be dismissed too quickly. The Clinton forces have clearly read them assiduously, as evidenced by the suburban tilt of the winning Democratic campaign. Clinton's victory was based to a significant extent on the need to allay white voters' resistance to the politics of "rights without responsibilities."

To take these authors seriously is to be caught in a dilemma. Which is correct: the position of Hacker and Bell that racism is fundamentally unchanged, that it is a basic component of U.S. society and culture, and that — at least in respect to the black experience — U.S. society harbors not a dream but a nightmare? Or the position of the Edsalls that civil rights and equal opportunity have reached their political limits in a society bifurcated by class divisions? The question is not "objective"; it is political. It cannot be resolved in an either-or fashion, because the two positions both partake of racial *"common sense."* However much these ideas conflict, they coexist in the minds of most North Americans. "Common sense" here is understood in Gramscian terms: it is a stew of attitudes and ideas — frequently inconsistent and sometimes anachronistic, but often accurate at least in part — through which people interpret their experiences, in this case their racial experiences.

In a series of books exploring North Americans' experiences of such matters as class, war, work, music, and national character, Studs Terkel has proved himself the greatest contemporary chronicler of "common sense" in the United States. Now, in *Race: How Blacks and Whites Think and Feel about the American Obsession* (1992), he addresses the issue of race with all his traditional emphases and sympathies. One turns to Terkel for an elucidation of the experiences and the conflicts that most deeply beset the mainstream psyche.

The interviews are deceptively simple. Terkel poses a question now and then, but more often lets the subjects speak for themselves. He is more of a systematizer than he lets on, though. The "common sense" he documents, though occasionally rough-hewn and contradictory, tends to acquire a consistency that only a certain selectiveness can bestow. His presence is, shall we say, directorial. As a result, nearly all of Terkel's many respondents express goodwill and a desire for unity on racial matters. Granted, a few admit to doubts about whether there is substantial discrimination in the present, and a very few give vent to sentiments of racial hostility, but the generalized sentiment of these pages is a longing for racial justice. There is a good deal of inspiration to be found here, but also, ultimately, the disappointment that comes from a refusal to engage difficult questions deeply.

Terkel sees race through a somewhat old-fashioned lens, which makes me wonder whether he and I inhabit parallel universes. Where are the equivalents to the many resentful and fearful white students I teach, who find themselves divided between guilt and anger toward the blacks, Latinos, and Asians with whom they share a classroom? Where is the anger at affirmative action in employment, the hostility to school integration and equalization of school budgets across district boundaries? Where is the resistance to residential desegregation, the neoconservatism of the suburban white voters discussed by the Edsalls? Where is the antiwhite hostility that many nonwhites feel? These sentiments appear only rarely in the book. Indeed, why is race conceived so largely in terms of black-white polarity? Yes, Terkel includes a small number of Latinos and Asians, not to mention a couple of South Africans, but as his subtitle indicates, he still thinks about "the American obsession" in dualistic as opposed to multipolar terms.

Finally, where is gender? Over and over, Terkel interviews exemplary black women, people whose political activities and characters display vast reserves of hope and courage in the face of poverty, racism, and cruelty that would have crushed the spirits of many. Yet almost nowhere does the book recognize the significance of gender issues, and of feminist perspectives, in interpreting race. The book assiduously ignores a whole host of difficult gender issues: the sexism inherent in welfare, the issue of violence, the hostility to women and gays displayed by the 1960s movements so venerated in the text, and the huge conflicts enveloping the black family. Since these themes are not addressed directly, they operate as subtexts that undermine the respondents' authority. To read the book takes a certain suspension of disbelief. As long as one can maintain that attitude, the book is inspiring; but as soon as critical thinking takes over, the book seems to beg many essential questions.

Other Others

So far, my discussion has focused on the mainstream political arena. It has adopted the bipolar racial typology of the books discussed. There's a lot wrong with that picture. Let's shake it up a bit by adding some new concerns: other racially identified groups, whose presence transforms the white-black bipolar model into a multipolar one; the interactions of race, gender, and class; and, finally, a word on the nature of racial identification itself.

There is now a wealth of theory and evidence about the social construction of race. It no longer seems necessary to argue that the racial politics and the racial identities that we know today are not fixed and eternal. They are flexible and contested, both at the large-scale or "macrosocial" level and as small-scale or "microsocial" relationships of family, friendship, and so forth (Omi and Winant 1986). In fact, even the racial identification of the individual is highly uncertain and conflictual. Our sense of ourselves and each other as racially identified persons and groups always involves not only external differentiation (I am different from another), but also internal differentiation (I contain differences within myself).

Over the past decade or so, these insights have generated promising research on a host of new racial themes, and in a wide variety of fields. Responding not only to new ideas, but more significantly to new and unexplained problems and social dynamics, younger scholars are busily overthrowing established orthodoxies in the study of race.

One such key problem is the generation and consolidation of new group racial identities. Such categories as "Hispanic" or "Latino," as well as that of "Asian American," are in fact very recent constructions in the United States. Their meaning is quite different from the designations that preceded them, terms that were often based in nationality: Chinese, Mexican, and so on. In an important recent book, *Asian American Panethnicity: Bridging Institutions and Identities* (1992), Yen Le Espiritu makes the first systematic attempt to document and analyze the processes that create new racialized identities in the United States. A recent collection from the journal *Latin American Perspectives*, subtitled "The Politics of Ethnic Construction: Hispanic, Chicano, Latino?," takes up some of the same themes (Gimenez et al. 1992).

For both Espiritu and the *LAP* authors, the process of constructing a new collective identity out of disparate—and sometimes antagonistic—ethnic and national ones inevitably takes on racial overtones.[2] Racialization or panethnicity develops over time as the result of a wide variety of pressures. In the Asian American and Hispanic cases, these pressures included demographic shifts as overtly racist immigration policies were eased after 1965. They involved various political factors as well. For example, different Asian and Latino groups had been subject to similar repressive state policies such as exclusionary immigration laws, restricted naturalization rights, and illegal internment and deportation. All had been forced together in substandard and segregated housing: Chinatowns, Manilatowns, and barrios. Other political factors that tended to unify disparate ethnic and national groups included the extensive influence that the black movement exerted (particularly on youth) during the heroic period of the civil rights struggle (Muñoz 1989); the threat posed by hostile forces such as the "English only" movement and the upsurge of hate crimes and racially motivated violence, which did not make fine distinctions between ethnic groups; and the strategic gains that were available from alliances. At the experiential level as well, the similar treatment afforded to those who "look alike," the wider society's inability to distinguish between Chinese and Korean, between Mexican and Ecuadoran, had the effect of "racial lumping," to use Espiritu's phrase.

Although these and other factors pushed disparate groups closer together, the creation of new racial categories with which people could identify also required the muting of profound historical, cultural, linguistic, and religious antagonisms and differences *within* the newly racialized groups. Distinct tensions and conflicts still exist over the use of the terms "Hispanic" and "Asian American," new immigrants particularly resist incorporation into such categories,[3] and intragroup rivalries, as well as class antagonisms, often flare up.

I find two points in the racialization/panethnicity process particularly fascinating. The first is the *ineluctable demand for categorization* posed in a highly race conscious society. However ambivalent or conflictual, the requirement of racial identification will always be terribly strong in the United States. This is true despite the schematic and often nearly arbitrary factors that work to create one category rather than another.[4]

Rather than lamenting this reality in the fashion of neoconservative nostalgia for a homogeneity that in fact never existed, we can learn an important political lesson from the inherent instability we discover whenever we seek the core components of racial identity. We are more than individuals, and indeed more than members of any single collectivity.[5] Both individual and group identities are multiply determined: individuals have class, gender, racial, and ethnic sources of identity, among others; groups may be constituted by narrow boundaries (e.g., mestizos from Jalisco—no *indios* or Oaxacans need apply), or by broad boundaries (e.g., Mexicans or, broader yet, Latinos). What constitutes identity is *political agency*, the construction of categories for strategic reasons and in response to perceived needs. Panethnicizing processes are thus harbingers of the multipolar and multicultural politics that progressive and egalitarian activity will require in the years to come. But such processes also contain the seeds of their own destabilization, for they tend to override interethnic group conflicts in the service of a greater whole.

A second notable feature of this particular pattern is the *competition and antagonism among racialized groups*. Spurred on by an economic system that encourages the creation of ethnic and racial niches, and by a political framework that tends to throw up leaders who can turn rivalries and fears into political capital, antagonisms *among* racially defined groups seem to be on the increase, even as newly racialized or panethnic categories mute older tensions. Thus, generalized anti-Asian violence arises from the middleman minority niche occupied by Korean shopkeepers, and from anti-Japanese hostility originating in economic competition.[6] The development of social policies designed to overcome such antagonisms will be an important progressive priority in the future.

Race and Gender

In October 1991 the nation was riveted, not to mention riven, by the Thomas-Hill hearings before the Senate Judiciary Committee. The hearings were reopened to examine charges of sexual harassment brought against Supreme Court nominee Clarence Thomas by a former subordinate, Anita

Hill. As Thomas's confirmation to the Court hung in the balance, a contest that was literally and obscenely *spectacular* took place: these two emblematic figures, both articulate lawyers, both conservative, and, of course, both black, became political gladiators. As if in ancient Rome, they fought before both immediate and removed audiences. The immediate audience—the imperial elite—consisted of the all-white and all-male Senate Judiciary Committee. But Thomas and Hill also struggled under the gaze of an enormous popular audience: a multiracial one, composed of women and men. This audience, this society, rediscovered in the spectacle its many deep divisions about the meaning and interrelationships of race, gender, and sexuality.

Novelist and critic Toni Morrison, angered and saddened by the Hill-Thomas spectacle, has edited *Race-ing Justice, En-gendering Power: Essays on Anita Hill, Clarence Thomas, and the Construction of Social Reality* (1992). The essays included here seek to interpret the hearings, which as Morrsion writes in her introduction, summoned up

> all the plateaus of power and powerlessness; white men, black
> men, black women, white women, interracial couples; those with a
> traditionally conservative agenda, and those representing
> neoconservative conversions; citizens with radical and progressive
> programs; the full specter [!] of the "pro" antagonists ("choice"
> and "life"); there were the publicly elected, the self-elected, the
> racial supremacists, the racial egalitarians, and nationalists of every
> stripe. (ix)

Indeed, if any recent racial event deserves the label "overdetermined," this was it. *Race-ing Justice* succeeds very well at exploring the pain, the contradictions, the ironies, and the lessons of the Hill-Thomas episode. Several essays are particularly on target in emphasizing our failure in the United States to exorcise the sexual stereotypes associated with black men and black women, respectively: what Nell Irvin Painter calls the "black-beast-rapist" and the "oversexed-black-Jezebel" (Painter 1992; Collins 1991: 163-80).

Another exceptionally valuable contribution made in many of these essays is the powerful critique of what Cornel West calls "the pitfalls of racial reasoning": the continued belief in "racial authenticity," in the political validity (or progressive character) of blackness *as such*, and in the necessity to "close ranks" in defense of any black person under attack. In the Hill-Thomas hearings these beliefs produced collusion with sexism, reactionary politics on a wide variety of fronts, and outright hypocrisy and dishonesty on the part of the nominee, in addition to his desperate resort to racism. For, as West and others point out, though Thomas had risen to prominence by denying the political significance of race, "when he saw his ship sinking, he played the racial card of black victimization and black solidarity at the expense of Anita Hill" (395). And Morrison's introduction—both fiery and ruminative—stands as a monument of integrity and resistance to all pretense, political sham, and manipulation.

Within all the analysis, most of it very useful, that *Race-ing Justice* provides, two themes stand out powerfully. One is the need to address not only conflicts of power, but also conflicts of *interpretation*, as manifested in the hearings. The other is the need to analyze racism and sexism *together*, in relation to one another. Some brief remarks on each of these points follow:

What these essays do very well, in general, is to look beyond the politics of conflicting interests and sources of power that constituted the "text" of the hearing to focus instead on the politics of conflicting interpretations and subjectivities that constituted the hearing's "subtext." It is not news that the subtext emerged so powerfully that it threatened to drown out the supposedly central issue of Thomas's confirmation. But what did the subtext demonstrate? Among other things: the continuities in black women's struggles for subject status and political rights from the nineteenth century to the present; the near-paralysis of the civil rights legacy as evidenced by the poor performance of many black organizations and leaders; and the failure to take seriously the linkage between mainstream (i.e., male) conceptions of sex and power, and thus to recognize the victimization of women through practices running from harassment to battering to rape.

One could go on with this list, and in fact the book's authors are fairly exhaustive about it. What is crucial here is to recognize not only the defeat that Thomas's eventual confirmation represented, but also the tremendous achievement of Anita Hill. Hill successfully exposed both what Paula Giddings calls the "silences and dissemblance in the name of a misguided solidarity" (463), which black women (and those who stood with them) could now begin to transcend, *and* the repressiveness and exclusion of the mainstream political system vis-à-vis racial minorities and women, which would now be challenged far more systematically as a result of her "defeat."

The authors of *Race-ing Justice* understand very well the significance of race for gender dynamics, and the importance of gender for race. But these insights, while important, are not enough. We have extensive literatures on both topics. What remains unresolved, not only in the book but more generally, is whether we can achieve a single theoretical account of oppression/subjection that is capable of explaining both racism and sexism—and, presumably, other forms of injustice as well.[7] The need for such a theory is great, for only through such a comprehensive understanding can we establish the political framework necessary to unify, or at least ally, the disparate but also overlapping subjectivities that events like the Hill-Thomas hearings put at odds. Intuitively, there are both significant grounds for such a single theory and important ruptures and breaches among any such theory's varied protagonists. Any acceptable account would unquestionably have to avoid the reductionism that would treat racism and sexism as manifestations of some single "fundamental" essence of social relations; it would also have to affirm both the correspondences and the uniquenesses of racism and sexism. On these large theoretical questions, *Race-ing Justice* is almost completely silent, although to be fair, we must recognize that its objectives were not primarily theoretical but polemical and denunciatory.

Globalized Race, Neo-Marxism, Poststructuralism

More than ever, the world is preoccupied with race. The Japanese struggle with their insularity and history of imperialism. Much of Europe has become thoroughly racialized—if it was not already—by its obsession with the immigration of former colonial subjects, the presence of former *gastarbeiter*, asylum seekers, Romani, and so forth. The formerly or soon-to-be-formerly communist world faces resurgent "ethnic" and "national" conflicts that quickly take on racial form once they are characterized as struggles for the "survival of peoples," the "resistance to alien cultures," and so on. The countries of the "South" confront the aftermath of colonialism, with its legacy of conquest, artificial borders, divide-and-rule approaches to subjugation, and Eurocentrism; such is the case, at least, in much of Africa and Asia. In Latin America, indigenous peoples and the inheritors of the African diaspora confront latter-day versions of the deadly inequalities they earlier faced in North America.

The heightened racial leitmotif of these global transformations caught many analysts by surprise. The mere persistence, not to mention the expansion, of racial antagonism ran counter to the predictions of most authorities, both academic and official. With rare exceptions, all had expected the gradual dissolution of race into some greater entity: free market or class struggle, cultural pluralism or nation-state.

The theoretical apparatus available to explain race has also been found wanting. Faced with the new worldwide dynamism of race, many mainstream thinkers—based in both the social sciences and the humanities—capitulated to neoconservative tendencies. Marxian currents were in general trapped by reductionisms of class, and poststructuralist approaches by an emphasis on subjectivity that verged too often on navel gazing. I shall have more to say about the possibilities for racial theory in the concluding section of this essay. Here I want to address two attempts to produce new analyses of the contemporary globalization of race, one undertaken from a neo-Marxian viewpoint, and the other from a poststructuralist vantage.

In *Race, Nation, Class: Ambiguous Identities* (1991), "structuralist" Marxist Etienne Balibar and world-systems theory founder Immanuel Wallerstein seek to go beyond established Marxian perspectives in order to explore resurgent racism and nationalism. Their book is not strictly a collaboration, since the two authors take separate responsibility for different chapters. At various points, however, they examine their agreements and disagreements and offer summaries of each other's positions. They tend to divide up their interests as well: as might be expected, Wallerstein is more concerned with "the economic," global processes of class formation, and the state; Balibar is more preoccupied with culture, social processes, and the nation. The book has a French density. Wallerstein is generally more intelligible but (to me) less innovative; Balibar is often recondite and, in translation at least, an uneven stylist, but his understanding of new racial phenomena is acute.

Wallerstein's chief contribution to the discussion on race is to reconceptualize the classic Marxian problem of the regulation of the labor force. Marx had argued that capitalism maintained a "reserve army of labor," a reservoir of unemployment from which additional workers could be drawn when needed, and that could also be used to hold down wage levels. Wallerstein suggests that this regulation has not only a "labor market" aspect but also an ideological aspect, which he finds in the dialectical tension between universalism and meritocracy on the one hand, and racism and sexism on the other. The capitalist system zigzags between the two, but unstably:

> The combination of universalism-meritocracy serving as a basis by which the cadres or middle strata can legitimate the system and racism-sexism serving to structure the majority of the workforce works very well. But only to a point, and that for a simple reason—the two ideological patterns of the capitalist world-economy stand in open contradiction to each other. This delicately poised combination threatens always to get out of hand, as various groups start to push the logic of universalism on the one hand, and of racism-sexism on the other too far. (Balibar and Wallerstein 1991: 35)

In some ways this is a useful analysis: it reemphasizes the interrelationships of race and class, and of gender and class. And it points to the social framework in which the conflicts and contradictions of contemporary capitalism are situated: inequality, the nation-state system (all these ideologies must be elaborated in the form of laws, organized and enforced by systems of schooling, qualification for posts, labor law, etc.), and uneven economic activity. In fact, Wallerstein associates the ups and downs of the "business cycle" (or capitalist economic crisis) with the "zigs and zags" of the contradiction between universalism and racism-sexism.

But in other respects this analysis is rather lame. It "explains" racism by its functionality for capitalism, a very old line of argument that by now—as Wallerstein should realize—has been widely criticized (Omi and Winant 1986: 25-37). Without reopening this matter too much here, let's just enter a few summary judgments about this position. It has its truth, for without question racism stratifies labor markets, comes into conflict with traditional individualistic notions of democracy and equality, and provides various grounds for political mobilization. But because it treats race as an epiphenomenon of supposedly more fundamental class conflicts, it notices very little about race: how racial categories are framed, how they change over time or vary comparatively, their centrality to key discourses of science, religion, and politics are all neglected. The reductionism of race to class, then, involves not only an overemphasis on class, but also a neglect of race.

Finally, Wallerstein's view lacks an argument, and thus fails to explain what it purports to explain. There is no effort to describe *how* racism acquires, much less maintains, its usefulness in dividing the workers; rather, we are informed that racism exists, that therefore the workers are divided, and that this division is functional for capitalism, provided of course that it is well-regulated. The latter notion is Wallerstein's only innovation in the matter; he points to the need for regulation, for the balancing of ideologically divisive racism and sexism with the ideologically unifying "universalism." But even here the functionalist limitations appear, because we have no sense of how, or by whom, this balancing act of ideological regulation is carried out. One cannot help but feel that Wallerstein has not consulted recent literature on race, but is more concerned with adding another piece to his world-systems jigsaw puzzle.

Balibar, though, is a different story. He is considerably less concerned with systematization, and therefore more open to complexity. His main project is to account for the present upsurge of racism in Europe. Looking at France in particular, he offers a powerful analysis of the phenomenon he calls "neoracism," which he suggests will be the main form racism takes in the near future. By this term he means a racism that is officially *anti*racist, in two senses. First, he says, neoracism has effectively rid itself of any overt adherence to racial prejudice or advocacy of discrimination. Second, and by far more important, neoracism has moved beyond biologism to an understanding of race rooted in supposed cultural differences, a position that permits a far more flexible range of racist political practices. Neoracism, according to Balibar,

> does not postulate the superiority of certain groups or peoples in relation to others but "only" the harmfulness of abolishing frontiers, . . . [and] the incompatibility of life-styles and traditions. (21)

As is often the case in racial politics, this position *rearticulates* arguments previously made by its opponents. The struggle against racism has for nearly half a century taken the principal form of the defense of difference, of the rights of minorities, of the irreducible variety and necessary plurality of human cultures. Balibar demonstrates how this position has become susceptible to a very conservative political reinterpretation, in the changed circumstances of a Europe "flooded" with racialized immigrants. Furthermore, neoracism's advocacy of the "naturalness" of racial difference also allows it to justify white resistance to the new immigrants, to antidiscrimination measures, and to any form of group recognition for racialized minorities. These reactions, it suggests, are only "natural" when the sudden appearance of new and foreign cultures threatens to disrupt the "traditional values and norms" of the majority. Indeed, from a neoracist perspective, it is the *abolition* of difference, the artificial effort to adjust social norms, to engage in "social engineering" or crudely seek to foster counterfeit forms of equality, that is racist. Neoracism, Balibar suggests,

> presents itself as having drawn the lessons from the conflict between racism and anti-racism, as a politically operational theory of the causes of social aggression. If you want to avoid racism, you have to avoid that "abstract" anti-racism which fails to grasp the psychological and sociological laws of human population movements; you have to respect the "tolerance thresholds," maintain "cultural distances" or, in other words, *in accordance with the postulate that individuals are the exclusive heirs and bearers of a single culture*, segregate collectivities (the best barrier in this regard still being national frontiers). (22-23, emphasis added)

Needless to say, this argument continues to operate as a cover for deep inequalities, for what Balibar calls the "theme of hierarchy," and as justification for racist practices of all kinds, up to and including widespread violence. Germany has recently been the most publicized case, but in fact throughout Europe, including in such countries as France,[8] Spain,[9] and even Sweden (Inter Press Service 1992), similar patterns of discourse and assault have become widespread. Balibar's analysis, though drawing principally on recent European experience, obviously also resonates with developments in the United States, where neoconservatism has worked out the main axes of "anti-racist racism," and where cultural difference arguments are daily becoming more central in racial discourse of all types.

An additional contribution offered by Balibar's analysis is its linkage between neoracism and anti-Semitism, whose rise in Europe has closely paralleled that of the new forms of racism. Balibar points out that anti-Semitism is the great prototype of cultural racism in that, despite various exercises in phenotypical stereotyping, anti-Semitism has never depended on biologism:

> The Jew is more "truly" a Jew the more indiscernible he is. His essence is that of a cultural tradition, a ferment of moral disintegration. Anti-Semitism is supremely "differentialist" and in many respects the whole of current differentialist racism may be considered, from the formal point of view, *as a generalized anti-Semitism*. (24, emphasis original)

Does this analysis mean that we should abandon notions of difference, that we must now revert to the crude assimilationism proposed in the first critiques of biologistic racism made in the early part of the century? Of course not. Rather, it highlights the crucial notion of *hybridity*. Today and in the next decade (at a minimum), the challenge will be to dismantle individualistic and essentialist conceptions of identity and culture. I shall have more to say about this concept in the concluding section of this essay.

Balibar's provocative account stands on its own terms, at its best when it is interrogating Marxism's inability as yet to explain new developments in racial politics. It can be rather sharply distinguished from Wallerstein's approach—more sharply than Balibar admits—because of its refusal of the kinds of totalizing theoretical gymnastics Wallerstein practices. In a sense the tension between the two authors of *Race, Nation, Class* mirrors the tensions within Marxism itself—or what is left of it. Certainly Marxism's failure to address the complexities of race has been one reason (among many) for its eclipse.

Taking this argument even further, Robert M. Young argues in *White Mythologies: Writing History and the West* (1990) that the major left philosophical currents of the postwar period have foundered precisely on the rocks of Eurocentrism and the universalizing historicism it seeks to make possible. In a general way, Young's book provides a useful overview of the misadventures of Western Marxism (a phrase that in Young's usage acquires new and more sinister connotations).

Young's primary territory is French poststructuralist thought, so he is especially at home in the recondite worlds of Michel Foucault, Gayatri

Spivak, and especially Jacques Derrida. His critical fire is directed chiefly toward Jean-Paul Sartre, the Frankfurt school, and Fredric Jameson. These latter writers, he argues, have in general sought to continue the totalizing traditions of left European thought. It is the effort to locate colonialism and racism (and to some extent sexism, though this is not Young's main theme) *within* the various Western Marxisms, to extend Europe's universalistic claims even to its victims and antagonists—in short, the attempt to constitute and then theorize "Europe's others" by Europe's own dialectical means—that Young most thoroughly damns. Those who have rejected the temptations of universalism (which to Young means a philosophical lineage from Hegel, not a Wallerstein-type world-system theory), and who have argued instead for the inherent discontinuities and partialities of history, are best suited to develop an account of "difference," whether it is racial, gender-based, or postcolonial.

The difficulty in Young's account does not lie in his poststructuralist critique of the variants of Marxism, but rather in the limited alternative he can provide. *White Mythologies* addresses many currents of poststructuralist thought, but it fails to answer the basic questions Young himself poses: How can we get beyond the corruption of social theory imposed by the epochal rise of Europe? How can we understand politics without at least implicitly accepting Europe's universalization of its own imperial history? How can we understand social relations of subordination without generalizing the appropriative and incorporative subjectivity associated with European notions of individual/state and self/other—not to mention male/female, white/nonwhite, settler/native?

Young takes his title from a well-known essay by Jacques Derrida (1982), and in general operates as a Derridean throughout the book. By that I mean that he criticizes other writers not primarily by opposing their accounts of postwar political phenomena, but by challenging the limits and biases of the categories they use. His deconstructionism seeks out instances in which concepts of history, for example, or of subjectivity, take on a false universality or occlude the subject position of the writer, or universalize the particular social context in which they were produced. Marxism in all its forms is particularly vulnerable to such charges, but much of Young's book shows how poststructuralist thought has tried, and failed, to escape the same problems. Foucault's substitution of genealogy for history, and of a "web" of power and multiple resistances for the agency of a revolutionary subject; Said's "dualism" of high European culture and its externalized Orient; Bhabha's quest for the "subversive" in postcolonial discourse; Spivak's "residual classical Marxism" juxtaposed with the immense heterogeneity of the subaltern—all these testify to the difficulties that any attempt to construct an alternative theoretical apparatus faces. Young himself notes that

> poststructuralism, which in its own way takes part in the history of Western Marxism, differs only insofar as it foregrounds the theoretical difficulties involved rather than repressing them in pursuit of the unrealized ideal. (24)

In the end, Young can conclude only that the legacy of colonialism lives on in "the West" in various ways: in the simple presence of millions of descendants of former colonial subjects in their "mother countries"; in the construction of the discursive forms in which people recognize their identities, their institutions, and their "nation"; and in the specific relations of power and authority that constitute contemporary racism. Historicism may be problematic, but the past continues to shape the present.

Conclusion: The Quest for Theory

Just as the meaning of race and the nature of racial identity change over time, so too do the meaning and nature of racism. Joel Kovel (1984) has argued, for example, that in the United States racism has taken three distinct forms: a dominative stage, an aversive stage, and a stage of *meta-racism*, which requires little active human agency to sustain itself. A further stage is suggested by Balibar's concept of neoracism, which—though it was formulated to address recent European developments—has substantial applications to the United States as well. It is a measure of the progress we have made that these insights, which only a few years ago were quite new and controversial, are now fairly commonplace. Such recognitions—embodied in the approach Omi and I developed in *Racial Formation in the United States* as well as in many other recent works—now constitute a new starting point.

But where do we go from here? The books reviewed in this essay are all state-of-the-art attempts to deal with aspects of current—and, needless to say, terribly complex—racial dynamics. They throw into sharp relief some of the main themes that any effort to achieve a comprehensive understanding of contemporary racial phenomena must address. At the risk of oversimplification I shall list these as follows: the endurance of racism even in the wake of substantial reform efforts; the persistence of racial mobilization in mainstream political arenas; confusion and conflict about the significance of race at the level of "everyday life" or "common sense"; the consolidation of a multipolar racial arena as a result of the panethnicity/racialization phenomenon; interaction between the race, gender, and class variables of oppression/subjection; and the globalization of racism as a key dimension of politics in the postcolonial era.

The difficulties of linking these themes in a general theory of race and racism are certainly enormous; yet the mere fact that we can enumerate key issues such a theory would have to address is a big step forward. In this brief conclusion I can only point to some of the elements a more adequate *racial formation theory* can potentially bring to bear. Here I shall present four such elements or, more precisely, four commitments that any such theory should incorporate and uphold:

Anti-Individualism. Individuality is a "social fact," in the Durkheimian sense, an experiential reality that is not going away and that, for many reasons both theoretical and practical, one would wish to defend. Yet the foundation of the large-scale, even transcendent, structural and cultural features of contemporary society on the basis of *individualism,* on the belief in a unitary bearer of identity, rights, and duties, is highly problematic. It is an artifact of a now wholly defunct period in societal development and political thought (Polanyi 1957 [1944]). We do not need to abandon our commitments to individual rights to recognize the constructed and unstable character of individual identity and the significance of "standpoint" — that is, politics — in establishing conceptions of the self (S. Harding 1987). Nonexclusive notions of identity explain hybridity better, and more effectively delineate the overlaps between different forms of oppression and resistance.

As Balibar demonstrates, it is only through the reassertion of undifferentiated individualism that neoracism can be consolidated. Where more nuanced conceptions of identity can be elaborated — as in the case of the group SOS-Racisme in France or various antiracist and "rainbow" approaches elsewhere — a radicalized pluralism becomes an effective counterweight to efforts to exhume a reactionary individualism.

The Centrality of the Body. The body serves as the preeminent racial signifier. This is a reality that — among other things — should alert us to the permanence of race, to its presence as a fundamental axis of power/ knowledge, in Foucauldian language. That much is obvious, but there is a further point: bodies are "scaled," as Iris M. Young (1990) notes; they are placed in a hierarchy such that all forms of oppression/subjection are necessarily interrelated. The psychological dimensions of Young's account of the process of "scaling" — which draw heavily on a particular neo-Freudian version of object relations developed by Kristeva — seem to me overly schematic. But recognition of "scaling" does not require acceptance of a single source of this process, much less an ontogenetic one. In fact, "scaling" has many alternate readings and sources — philosophical, political, and cultural as well as psychological. As Young points out, again employing Foucault, the pattern of "scaling" is very generalized, very imbedded:

> The gaze of modern scientific reason . . . is a normalizing gaze. It is a gaze that assesses its object according to some hierarchical standard. . . . In accordance with the logic of identity the scientific subject measures objects according to scales that reduce the plurality of attributes to unity. Forced to line up on calibrations that measure degree of some general attribute, some of the particulars are devalued, defined as deviant in relation to the norm. (125-26)

Once we recognize the permanent presence of the body in political processes of all types, including both oppression/subjection and the various forms of resistance, the continuities and discontinuities among these different forms of politics appear less circumstantial, less "accidental." The deep conflicts among various types of subordination may persist, or they may be superable, but theoretical work along the lines suggested here ought to be able to tell us more, in either case, about why.

Dual Consciousness, Authenticity, and Politics. Almost a century ago, W. E. B. Du Bois wrote of "this peculiar sensation, this double-consciousness, this sense of always looking at one's self through the eyes of another" (1989 [1903]: 5). The recognition that inequality and injustice involve a doubling and splitting of awareness, of subjectivity itself, continues to inform all politics, but it is particularly important for racial politics. Today we can see that dual consciousness is an immensely significant phenomenon. It can be theorized as resistance and subversion, as ambivalence, as standpoint and critique. Furthermore, it has collective as well as individual traits: it structures not only "personality," but also "culture." When we speak of the "dominant culture," for example, we recognize that inequality *always* involves the imputation of undifferentiated, integrated subjectivity to a hegemonic group. The "normal" or relatively transparent subject position is white, male, heterosexual. Thus it is only the subaltern who have color, day care and parental leave are "women's issues," and so on.

Elsewhere I have pointed out how resistance to inequality tends to fissure the hegemonic subject position, leading to the beginnings of dual consciousness even among whites and men, as well as to furious attempts to ward off this new and radicalized pluralism. These are the kinds of right-wing rearticulations of race and racism highlighted by Balibar in *Race, Nation, Class*.

Here I wish to stress not only the theoretical but also the political value of such a split or fragmented awareness. Such ruptures serve as the foundation for oppositional politics, since having more than one sense of one's subjectivity potentially allows for comparisons and empathetic judgments, as well as critique, parody, and subversion of the dominant forms of (un)consciousness. Further, an awareness of the pervasiveness of dual consciousness serves to check assertions of unmediated authenticity, whether hegemonic or subaltern. Appeals to "traditional values," to the national culture, to canonized texts that exemplify hegemonic claims must therefore be treated with the extreme suspicion that awareness of standpoint demands. Subaltern claims, as expressed for example through invocation of supposedly direct experiences of oppression—of the form "As a black person, I know X," or "As a woman, I know X" (where X is an undifferentiated generalization about blacks' or women's experience)—are also suspect. Our experiences are *never* authentic, but always mediated, fissured, refracted.

The Ethical Dimension and the Contribution of Pragmatism. The effort to frame a new racial politics, and indeed to grasp the unlimited potential of a politics based in the varieties of subjectivity, is inherently an attempt to reintroduce ethics into the core of the political. Here we can find inspiration in Levinas's work, in which the effort to *understand* the other replaces the effort to *incorporate* and thereby transcend the other. In this framework (which is obviously beyond the present essay's scope), otherness is not antagonism, and is located *within* as well as *outside* the subject.[10]

The prospects for racial theory, and more generally for any reconceptualization of left politics, not only in the United States but also more globally, are dependent on the reformulation of such categories as justice, equality, domination, and oppression. This is so because, although the struggles of racially defined minorities, women, gays, and the exploited and impoverished remain in general separate struggles, they also confront a variegated but ultimately unified hegemonic order. If they fail in their quest for the common ground among the different axes of oppression/subjection, if they abandon the effort to link their distinct but related aspects of resistance, they fail generally and as political projects. Such dangers are anything but abstract.

The prospects for theory therefore depend on the pragmatic possibilities of linking, of connecting, different but potentially related concrete experiences of oppression/subjection. These connections have as their starting point ethical commitments: to the reduction of injustice and its consequent pain and suffering; and to the enabling of difference or alterity, and its consequently differentiated subject positions. In other words, we should recognize a *radicalized pluralism* as a desirable political goal. We can do this in a pragmatic fashion, drawing upon long-standing ethical traditions in the United States.[11] As Martha Minow has argued (also employing central themes in the pragmatic tradition):

> What we need to do is work, in specific contexts, on problems of difference. There is no ultimate resting place but instead an opportunity for dialogue, conversation, continuing processes of mutual boundary setting, and efforts to manage colliding perspectives on reality. It is not even enough to imagine the perspective of the other; we must also try to share deliberations with the other person. History should remind us that none of us can resolve dilemmas of difference alone. None of us should rest confident that we have found the correct version of reality once and for all, or that we may fully trust the exercise of power. (1990: 383)

PART III

The Comparative Sociology of Race

Chapter 8

Racial Formation and Hegemony: Global and Local Developments

Race in all its forms continues to preoccupy us, to surprise us, to shape our world. In North America, the political clamor and deep cultural divisions over race stubbornly refuse to subside. Throughout the Americas the quincentennial anniversary of European conquest was more deeply resisted than celebrated, for the arrival of Europe in the "new world" was a foundational racial event that echoes down the centuries to us today. In Africa we observe the crumbling of apartheid and its likely replacement by something more "American"; will the African National Congress's goal of a "non-racialist" South Africa prove chimerical? In Europe the permanent installation of African, Turkish, and Asian immigrants is reshaping national identities as much as the inexorable drive toward integration; to what extent, and in what form, will the venerable currents of exclusivism and neo-fascism reappear as the cold war and the Soviet presence fade into the past? On the Pacific rim of Asia, the Chinese and Japanese struggle anew with heterogeneity and pluralism, often imbued with racial themes. While perhaps more properly defined as "ethnic," ferocious conflicts taking place at the fringes of the "developed" world, from South and Southeast Asia to the Middle East, from Burundi to Burma, from Azerbaijan to Bosnia, exhibit at least "protoracial" features. Arguably, the world today is a vast racial battlefield.

But what is this quality we call race? At once evanescent and formidable, ephemeral yet intense, simultaneously conspicuous and unspecifiable, race is a fascinating and recondite theme precisely because of its slippery and contradictory character. There is a recognizably "interior" side to race—for anyone raised in a racialized social order—in which one's identity is indelibly marked, indeed formed, by the phenomenon. The "exterior" side of race, though, is equally familiar: it is there, for example, in systems of stratification, of segregation and coercion, of racial oppression, however various and flexible their particular forms. We see the exterior side of race in the very ubiquity of racial order, in social policy and political organization, where it takes such forms as exclusion/inclusion, pluralism/assimilation, or even genocide; in collective action, both institutionalized and spontaneous; and in the political economies of localities, nations, and, indeed, much of the globe.

This chapter is an effort to specify some of the racial dimensions of *hegemony* in the contemporary world. It is necessarily a preliminary effort and chiefly a theoretical one. The argument is organized as follows: first I present a view of hegemony that dispenses with any notion of core agency (i.e., Gramsci's "fundamental class") and focuses instead on the interrelated structural and signifying dimensions of hegemony.[1] Such a view, necessarily schematic and open to all sorts of theoretical objections, retains from Gramsci a deep concern with hegemony as politics; it adopts from numerous poststructuralist currents an abiding interest in meaning and interpretation (R. Young 1990).

Next I argue for a particular theoretical approach, *racial formation theory*, as the most useful framework with which to analyze contemporary racial phenomena within this view of hegemony (Omi and Winant 1986). This approach understands race as pervasive throughout social life; it recognizes the expansion and intensification of racial phenomena in the contemporary world; and it adopts a much-needed historicism in the effort to connect contemporary and past racial orders in a single, unified framework.

From this perspective, the link between race and hegemony can be more deeply explored. The epochal process that has constructed and reconstructed the meaning of race, and that has over and over again engraved racial signifiers on social and political institutions, collectivities, and individuals, continues to do so in the present. The study of racial phenomena is particularly relevant in a global political economy where class-based politics are weakening, and where flows of people, capital, and ideas are ever more rapid. Racial identities are transnational and some form of racial difference nearly universal; they are also highly personal and experiential, an instantly recognizable part of who one is. Thus, I maintain, race is simultaneously a global and a local phenomenon, politically contested from the largest to the smallest of social terrains.

Having established this framework for thinking about race in terms of hegemony, I next consider the global and local dimensions of contemporary racial formation processes. After general discussions of each, I present two "case studies," each focused on the *relationship between race and class*, which I am convinced is central to hegemony in many different societies today. In respect to the global aspect of racial formation, I examine the internationalization of this relationship. I am particularly interested here in the reemergence of fascism, and in the capacity of radical democratic movements to defeat it. As a local instance of racial formation processes, I analyze the so-called underclass debate in the contemporary United States.

Theorizing Hegemony

For present purposes, hegemony may be defined as a form of rule that operates by constructing its subjects and incorporating contestation. In this interpretation, hegemony can be clearly distinguished from domination because under hegemonic conditions opposition and difference are not repressed, excluded, or silenced (at least not primarily). Rather they are inserted, often after suitable modification, within a "modern" (or perhaps "postmodern") social order. Hegemony therefore involves a splitting or doubling of opposition, which simultaneously wins and loses, gains entrance into the halls of power and is co-opted, "crosses over" into mainstream culture and is deprived of its critical content.

Hegemony organizes various themes, axes, and cleavages, which can be characterized, but not fully captured analytically, by using the familiar terms: race, gender, class, and neocolonialism might be the top categories on the present epoch's list. Such concepts are essentially metaphors for institutionalized social relationships that combine processes of exploitation and domination, on the one hand, with processes of subjection and representation, that is, with struggles over meaning and identity, on the other.

For simplicity's sake, and leaving many important questions out for the moment, let us call the former set of questions, in which we can include both mainstream and radical views of politics and economics, the *structural* dimensions of hegemony. These include organized political processes of various kinds (elections, workplace struggles, policy-making), as well as distributional conflicts and the institutionalized aspects of social movements of all types, ranging from national liberation to civil rights and feminism.

Struggles over meaning and identity I shall awkwardly call the *signifi-cation* dimensions of hegemony. By this I mean the "cultural" and "social psychological" processes of identity formation and socialization through which, and however unstably, individuals and collectivities are constructed and assigned their structural locations in society: as rulers, subordinates, nurturers, natives, "political classes," and so on.

Of course, the frameworks of "culture" and "social psychology" do not adequately capture the complex struggles over political meanings and con-cepts, over the representations of power and identity that have been cen-tral to both Gramscian and poststructuralist political theory. Nor does this division between structure and signification adequately address all cases of identity formation and collective action. For example, the volatility with which collectivity can emerge or disintegrate in everyday experience, and the complex interplay of political themes and personal identifications such quotidian events imply, cannot be theorized adequately by the crude di-chotomy proposed here. One thinks of Sartre's discussion of the interplay of "fused" and "serial" identities in the *Critique of Dialectical Reason* (1976) or of Bhabha's (1993) analysis of the parodic and subversive themes in the discursive practices of the colonized. Nor do I wish to suggest an undue benignity in the operations of hegemony: no hegemonic system in-corporates *all* its opposition. If we look at racial issues, there is certainly plenty of room in societies across the globe for exclusion, segregation, dis-crimination, malevolence, ignorance, and outright violence. Therefore, to suggest that we may detect a general trend from domination to hegemony, away from outright coercion and toward "consent" (in the Gramscian sense) as a more effective form of rule, is not to argue that violence and repression are on the wane, either in racial matters or in other spheres of conflict. Would that this were so.

But I do not wish to be detained here. The point is clear enough: hege-mony is a form of rule in which the subjective dimensions of politics ex-pand significantly. An effective hegemony constructs its own subjects. An effective counterhegemony subverts those subjectivities; it disrupts and re-interprets the seemingly unified conceptions, memories, symbols, and identities of the "establishment" against which it contends.

Finally, it bears repeating that hegemony both structures *and* signifies. In concrete experience there is no break between, say, "economic" and "cultural" life. Inequality, for example, is a complex sociopolitical phe-nomenon that "socializes" individuals and groups, that stigmatizes the many and exalts the few, deeply identifying us, distinguishing us, and allowing us to interpret our world. Inequality has to be "policed," not only in the literal sense, that of controlling the opposition that injustice tends to stimulate, but also in the cultural sense. Inequality requires constant interpretation. Why is there poverty amid plenty? How can the "North" justify its excesses before the impoverished and increasingly desperate "South"? How much responsibility do the poor bear—how much do "I" bear—for my own poverty?

Thus any theory of hegemony begins by recognizing that institution and interpretation, structure and culture, society and self are concretely linked, that they are in fact congruent at the level of experience, of material life. Their distinction can only be a conceptual one, useful for purposes of analysis and, hopefully, to inform opposition.

Racial Formation

Racial formation theory was developed as a response to postwar understandings of race, both mainstream and radical, that practiced "reductionism": by this I mean the explanation of racial phenomena as a manifestation of some other, supposedly more significant, social relationship. Examples of racial reductionism include treatment of racial dynamics as epiphenomena of class relationships, or as the result of "national oppression," or as variations on the ethnicity paradigm established in the United States in the early twentieth century after successive waves of European immigration.

In contrast to these approaches, racial formation theory suggests that race has become a fundamental organizing principle of contemporary social life. At its most basic level, race can be defined as *a concept that signifies and symbolizes sociopolitical conflicts and interests in reference to different types of human bodies*. Although the concept of race appeals to biologically based human characteristics (so-called phenotypes), selection of these particular human features for purposes of racial signification is always and necessarily a social and historical process. There is no biological basis for distinguishing human groups along the lines of "race," and the sociohistorical categories employed to differentiate among these groups reveal themselves, upon serious examination, to be imprecise if not completely arbitrary. Indeed, we can speak of racial formation as a *process* precisely because the inherently capricious and erratic nature of racial categories forces their constant rearticulation and reformulation—their social construction—in respect to the changing historical contexts in which they are invoked.

The implications of this view are manifold. First, race is understood as *a phenomenon whose meaning pervades social life*. Race operates both micro- and macrosocially; not only the individual psyche and relationships among individuals, but also collective identities and social structures are racially constituted. Because race is not a "natural" attribute, but a socially and historically constructed one, the racial dimensions of social structures, identities, and signification systems must be understood as flexible and contested. They are often explicitly, but always at least implicitly, political terrain.

Second, racial formation theory addresses the surprising *expansion and intensification of racial phenomena* occurring in the contemporary world, the new global context of race mentioned earlier. This is discussed more extensively later, but can be crudely formulated here in terms of the cross-cutting nature of racial identities. Race is a transnational, interclass phenomenon, not simply in the abstract, but concretely. The legacies of enslavement and colonization have established powerful (though not unproblematic) linkages between dispersed communities—often geographically distant from one another, often resident within distinct nation-states—who share some experience of racially organized subjection. The same shared experiences can create cross-class solidarities that defy the supposed "rational expectations" of both mainstream and Marxist economic analyses.

Third, racial formation theory suggests *a new conception of racial history and racial time*. In respect to race, at least two dimensions of historical time can be distinguished, one genealogical, one contingent. In *genealogical* terms, the social construction of race is a millennial phenomenon whose origins lie in an immense historical rupture encompassing the rise of Europe, the onset of African enslavement, the *conquista* and colonization of the Western Hemisphere, and the subjugation of much of Asia. Across the centuries, there has been never-ending dispute over the meaning of race, controversy that was integral to the struggles of the oppressed and enslaved with their rulers. By now we have substantial scholarship on these matters that quite effectively explains the framing of supposedly unified collective identities (e.g., Europe) in terms of externalized "others" (Connolly 1991; Todorov 1985; Anderson 1991 [1983]). The temporal dimensions of this account are in my view extremely significant.

"Western" or colonial time completed its synchronization of the globe during the nineteenth century, demarcating human "difference" in terms of the traditional or primitive versus the modern (Wolf 1982). Complicit in the racialization of time were not only the propagandists of colonialism, but also the great social theorists of modernity. Weber's "spirit of capitalism," Durkheim's account of the division of labor and the wellsprings of sociocultural solidarity, and Marx's analysis of the brutal but also ultimately progressive extension of the capitalist mode of production to the "ends of the earth" (consider the subtext of this term: where does the earth begin?) all privileged European time. This millennial process through which vast expanses of the earth were slowly brought under European control was among other things a thoroughly racial affair, an enormous explanatory and self-justificatory act in which, as Spivak (1988) has argued, the only "speakers" were the rulers. Genealogical racial time, then, is an archetypal *longue durée*: a slow agony of inscription upon the human body, a murder mystery, if you will, but on a genocidal scale. The phenotypical signification of the world's body took place in and through conquest and enslavement, to be sure, but also as an enormous act of expression, of narration.

Another type of historical time accessible to racial formation theory is that of *contingency*. Particular racial meanings and social structures are always context-driven. The presence of a racial order consolidated by coercion (e.g., the antebellum South, classical colonial rule in Africa) grants little political terrain to racial conflict. In such an absolutist context, I suggest, the racial order is "naturalized" and publicly unproblematic. Racial time can appear nearly frozen — until the repressive social order is shattered by violence, the only meaningful form of resistance. In such situations, the dominant groups seek to monopolize not only the means of violence, but also those of knowledge;[2] opposition is marginalized and may be rendered nearly invisible, until, like the dream deferred, it explodes.

On the other hand, once they abandon the *herrenvolk* mode, democratic politics are forced to develop more hegemonic forms of racial rule. That is, they must incorporate their racial oppositions, make concessions to their demands, and engage in ever-widening debate about the meaning of race in society. In such a context, the racial order is necessarily and publicly problematic, resistance to racial oppression becomes increasingly multiform, and racial time appears to move swiftly indeed. We North Americans have only to consider the rapidly moving events of the last quarter century to ratify this perception. Contemporary African and European racial time is also accelerating.

To summarize, racial formation theory as presented here is compatible with the decentered conception of hegemony outlined above: it resists the temptation to dismiss race as an "illusion," mere "ideology," while at the same time rejecting any objectivist or essentialist interpretation of the concept.[3]

The Global Dimensions of Racial Formation

I have already suggested that on a global comparative scale the continuing and indeed expanding significance of race has defied the predictions of most high officials, as well as most social critics and movement leaders. Until quite recently, mainstream economists and Marxists, liberals and conservatives, ethnicity theorists and nationalists all expected the dissolution of race in some greater entity: free market or class struggle, cultural pluralism or nation-state. Although the full implications of the endurance of racialized societies and identities have yet to be plumbed, it is clear enough that the heyday of liberalism, modernism, and Marxism is finished. Far from appearing as an aberrant phenomenon, a survival of more benighted times, the facticity of racial phenomena now seems rather overwhelming. Their perseverance seems rather less mysterious than belief in their imminent superannuation, which today seems almost willfully naive.

Yet the elementary forms of racial life vary tremendously from one culture, one society, to another. To what extent can a theory of racial formation address the bewildering variety of racialized experiences, identities, and social structures on a global scale?

Once more easily seen in terms of imperial reach, in terms of colonization, conquest, and migration, the geography of race is becoming *globalized* and thus accessible to a new kind of comparative analysis. Today the movement of capital and labor has internationalized all nations, all regions. Thus former (neo)colonial subjects, now redefined as "immigrants," challenge the majoritarian status of the European groups (the whites, the Europeans, the Americans or French, etc.) that once ruled over them. While ex-colonial subjects immigrate to the metropoles, the formerly well-paying and supposedly secure jobs of metropolitan workers emigrate toward the former colonies, there to exploit a more vulnerable labor force congregated on export platforms, herded into industrial enclaves designed to produce cheaply for the "developed" countries.

Culturally too the internationalization of race proceeds apace. Such phenomena as the rise of "diasporic" models of blackness, the creation of "panethnic" communities of Latinos and Asians (in such countries as the United Kingdom and the United States), and the breakdown of borders in both Europe and North America all seem to be hybridizing and racializing previously national polities, cultures, and identities. Because of these transformations, the comparison of local social/political orders based on race becomes more necessary. Likewise, for the first time we can begin to think of variations in racial identity not as deviations from some supposedly modal (and actually quasi-imperial) norm, but as a flexible set of context-specific repertoires. As a final note, the dissolution of the transparent racial identity of the formerly dominant group, that is to say, the increasing racialization of whites in Europe and the United States, must also be recognized as proceeding from the increasingly globalized dimensions of race.

A Global Case: The Internationalization of the Race-Class Relationship

Race and class are interwoven all around the world. These two figures describe basic axes of inequality, of power, of separation. At times they compete for significance in framing a social order or nation-state; at times one is eclipsed by the other; at times they fuse. Colonialism and empire, for example, were organized from the compounding of these two materials. Race is no mere by-product of capitalism, as reductionist theories would have it; rather, capitalism is a racial entity. Without its ability to racialize those whom it exploited, capitalism could not have accumulated the wealth needed to subdue the world. In this matter Marx's well-known denunciation is fully justified:

> The discovery of gold and silver in America, the extirpation, enslavement, and entombment in mines of the aboriginal population, the beginning of the conquest and looting of the East Indies, the turning of Africa into a warren for the commercial hunting of blackskins, signalized the rosy dawn of the era of capitalist production. These idyllic proceedings are the chief momenta of primitive accumulation. (1967: 751)[4]

Can anyone seriously argue today that these "idyllic proceedings," these multiple enslavements, this series of fatal plagues, these orgies of cultural deracination, would even have been attempted, let alone successfully accomplished, if their intended victims had been other Europeans?[5] Only the Jews, the "other within," could be placed on the receiving end of such barbarity, and when they were, the Jews were appropriately racialized as well. In my view, the mere origin of capitalism in racially rationalized conquest definitively refutes all class reductionisms of race.

Yet of course the genealogy of race, replete with variations on this theme of "racial capitalism," proceeds unbroken up to the present (West 1987). Every secondary labor market, every ghetto, casbah, and native reserve, every segregated neighborhood testifies, in this account, to the interdependence of class and race. So what's new? On what basis can I claim that today we are witnessing the internationalization of the relationship between race and class?

I have already suggested that today hegemony takes a decentered form, one that is not organized around a fundamental class antagonism. This is not merely a theoretical revision of Gramsci, but also reflects a new historical moment in which class antagonisms are definitively displaced from the central political significance they have occupied since, say, 1848, since the end of "the age of revolution" (Mouffe and Laclau 1985; Hobsbawm 1962). There are many signs of this: the incoherence and consequent popular rejection of "actually existing" (or should we say "recently existed"?) socialism, the reversal of capitalist development in the "South," the internal rot affecting all the so-called developed countries.

This decentering of hegemony means that other antagonisms, differences other than class, which were always present but lacked visibility and politicization due to the apparent centrality of class struggle, can now come to the fore. The continuing significance of race (and gender as well) is no doubt related to the partial political eclipse of class.

To be sure, the predominance of class on the political stage was always uneven: in the United States, the inability of a true class-based politics to develop cast some early suspicions on the supposed universality of this "motor of history" (Sombart 1976 [1896]). The sustained ferocity of racial antagonisms, their presence from the beginning of the colonial period (in respect to native peoples), their early unification of color and enslavement (in respect to African peoples) made the phrase "American exceptionalism" something of a cliché in Marxist analysis. The early emergence of feminism as an offspring of abolitionism rather than as a key factor in socialism also signified the relative weakness of class politics in the United States. In the colonial and neocolonial world, the nationalist forms in which politics were arranged always clashed with Marxist logic, even when their practitioners were avowed Marxist-Leninists. Class as the "fundamental contradiction" of the modern world was, then, something of a European framework.

Today this situation has been complicated even further, as the legacies of "northern" dominance begin to erode. The luxury of corporatist pacts between capital, labor, and the state, trading off wage gains for productivity increases, is effectively at an end. The ability of established unions and their political representatives to speak for their national working classes is at best stretched to its limit, and frequently is ruptured. The capacity of political democracy to discipline capital, to restrict capital flight, for example, to levy effective taxes on capital, or to enact environmental or social legislation perceived by capital as disadvantageous, has declined dramatically.

Political battle lines are being redrawn in many countries as the new dimensions of the relationship between race and class, the racial dimensions of capitalism, are recognized. Mobilization of white racial antagonisms has proved indispensable for the "respectable" right, and even for some sectors of the left, in many "northern" countries. In the United States it has been an indispensable feature of Republican presidential politics since 1964.

Conversely, there now arises the difficult task of mobilizing (in some cases, newly) heterogeneous racial minorities in order to counter this trend. This task falls to social movements, for all too often established social democratic and trade union groups seek principally to defend the interests of their traditional, white constituencies. Such defensiveness is going to accelerate the dissolution of class politics, if only because the presence of large numbers of immigrant workers portends radical demographic shifts in the "developed" world. In a quarter century, whites may be a minority in the United States. In a quarter century, substantial racially defined minorities will exist in integrated Europe; though nowhere near approaching the numbers that exist in the United States, these Asian and African immigrants and their descendants will have to be reckoned with.

The political logic this situation presages, I think, goes well beyond the mere interpenetration and increasing complexity of the relationship between race and class. What it foreshadows is nothing less than a global struggle between fascism and democracy.

Unquestionably, a clear potential exists for the *resurgence of fascism.* Organized fascist movements already exist in most countries, as does a fascist international of sorts. Contemporary fascism lacks ideological depth and consistency, but what internal coherence it does have derives directly from its appeals to racial fear. Such positions are all too familiar: the racial enemy, often in league with the Jew, is a parasite upon the national body, a despoiler of sacred national and cultural traditions; the country is in danger of being "swamped" by immigrants; the key institutions of society have already been subverted; only through a massive appeal to the true, hardworking folk "who built this country" (white, French, American, English, Christian, etc.), only by return to the "traditional" values, can we restore the grandeur . . . In its aspirations to hegemony, fascism too must construct its subjects: they are the producers, the patriots, the "true" Americans, Frenchmen, and so on. The nation has been betrayed by its "others," people who are different, who don't really belong in the fatherland, who don't believe in hard work, who don't share "our" values.

Fascism's potential constituencies are the displaced workers, the downwardly mobile members of the middle classes, those whose vulnerabilities are most clearly articulated by what Ronald Walters (1987) has called (in the U.S. context) "white racial nationalism." The ideological narrative addressed to them can take various forms; it can be "coded" as a subtext for elections and propaganda, or it can be grunted or shouted while carrying out beatings or lynchings, defacing synagogues, or attacking immigrant workers' hostels or neighborhoods. What is crucial is its reliance on the politics of resentment, fear, and exclusion, its ability to link race and class (and often gender as well), and its hunger for an authoritarian solution to uncertainty and vulnerability.

Confronting the resurgence of fascism is the potential for *radical democracy.* Radical democracy must compete with authoritarianism of all sorts to articulate an open and plural vision of politics. I have argued that as the relative significance of class declines, other forms of social organization, in particular racial and gender differences, come to the fore. These differences constitute the very opposite of the authoritarian order that racial reaction seeks to create through its politics of exclusion and repression. They counterpose the possibility of inclusion to that of exclusion; they oppose repression with self-expression. Radical democracy potentially represents a subversive, as well as celebratory, counterhegemonic tendency: for those who were never effectively addressed by mainstream politics, for the millions whom class politics either excluded outright or included only indirectly, radical democracy and the "politics of difference" offer a precious glimmer of recognition.

Yet if it is effectively to counter reactionary and authoritarian initiatives based on race—initiatives that have had considerable success in France, Britain, Germany, and the United States, among other countries—radical democratic politics will have to acknowledge the fears to which the right appeals. That is, radical democratic politics must link race (and gender) with class more energetically through inclusion than reactionary politics can do through exclusion. There are, I suggest, two keys to this process, one social structural and the other a matter of signification, of interpretation of identities and cultural meanings.

On the social structural side, radical democratic politics must articulate concepts of *social and economic justice, fairness, and equality*. There are substantial historical precedents, as well as powerful political arguments, for this connection. In many countries deep democratic traditions can be mobilized in favor of social justice and fairness, especially when combined with long-standing class-based demands for greater economic equality and redistribution. Recent decades have been marked by the diminution of living standards in most countries of the so-called West; popular antagonism to this trend is high. Additionally, a radical democratic articulation of race and class must acknowledge that racial minority status still serves as a negative marker, a stigma, in the class formation process. All across the globe, dark skin still correlates with poverty.[6] Thus class position is in many respects racially assigned. It follows from this that radical democratic challengers should reopen the question of discrimination as a racial process with class consequences.

On the side of signification, radical democratic politics must *acknowledge and accept the uncertainty and fragility of social and cultural identities*, and the fears that threats to these identities can produce (Przeworski 1986). This can be done without the flirtation with neoconservatism evident even on the left (Sleeper 1990); a more effective approach evokes the ethical dimensions of the racial crisis and asks to what extent we permit ourselves to know the racialized other (West 1991; Lechner 1988). Such a politics invites us to examine the contingency and multiplicity of our own identities. No individual belongs to "just" one socially constructed category: each has her/his racial, gender, class-based, and national identities, and that is just a start of the list. Nor are these categories uniform or stable; we are Whitmanesque, we contain multitudes. To recognize our many selves is to understand the vast social construction that is not only the individual, but history itself, the present as history. A radical democratic politics must invite us to comprehend this.

But merely issuing the invitation is not enough; indeed, I suggest that the earlier postwar social movements organized around race, gender, and peace in fact did this and no more, thus setting themselves up for the reaction that subsequently engulfed them. Why? Because to understand the fragility of our identities can be profoundly disconcerting, especially in the absence of a political and moral vision in which the individual and the group can see themselves included, supported, and contributing to the construction of a better society. To counter the authoritarian interpretation of fear and uncertainty, to resist the imposition of exclusive and repressive models of order, a radical democratic politics must acknowledge fear and uncertainty while at the same time offering a way to accept and interpret these emotions publicly and collectively. Not through repression but through knowledge of the differences within ourselves can we achieve the solidarity with others that, though necessarily partial, is essential for the creation of a more just and free world.

The Local Dimensions of Racial Formation

My argument so far has focused largely on the contemporary amplification of racial conflict across the globe. It would be a mistake, however, to assume any overarching uniformity in this upsurge of tension over, and heightened awareness of, racial matters. Applying the model of hegemony I have advanced here, which focuses on the interaction of social structure and signification, it is logical to expect a great deal of variation among local racial orders. Of course, each nation-state, each political system, each cultural complex necessarily constructs a uniquely racialized social structure, a particular complex of racial meanings and identities. Thus the global similarities, the increasing internationalization of race, can only be understood in terms of prevalent patterns, general tendencies; in no sense can such generalizations substitute for detailed analyses of local racial formations.

With what questions should we approach the examination of particular racial formation processes? Many variables, particularly structural ones, are already familiar: In what way are the social dynamics of race affected by such demographic patterns as immigration and fertility rates? What is the extent of racial inequality, of stratification by race, and what trends are evident in its development? To what extent are racial equality and social justice concerns incorporated into the national policy agenda? How do social and political institutions mediate racial divisions and conflicts? In what way has the mutation or even outright decay of previously effective political forms — such as various versions of socialism, nationalism, and developmentalism — refocused racial politics and policies? Answers to these and many other similar questions can give a good empirical view of the local social structure of race.

None of these questions, of course, addresses such questions as the meaning of race, the boundaries of racial identity, or the means by which these meanings and boundaries are defined and changed. To examine such issues we must turn to the process of signification, that is, to the way in which hegemonic sociopolitical orders construct their subjects. Here our empirical focus is necessarily imprecise: What is the degree of variability in racial identities, both collective and individual? To what extent is race "essentialized," "biologized" in a given society? How much autonomy is available to the individual in the construction and selection of racial identities? In what ways are traditional forms of racial representation — for example, in religion, art, or science — undergoing modification?

Here we are asking questions about signification that also have crucial structural implications. When we inquire, for example, as to how much flexibility a national-popular culture allows in the constitution of racial groups, we are in practice examining the state, various ideological apparatuses, institutions of socialization, and so forth. Are there rigid, castelike color lines à la apartheid? This is as much a political economic question as a cultural one. Is mobility possible among racially defined subordinate groups? The answer to this question depends not only on their degree of organization and political capabilities, but also on their access to the means of representation and rearticulation, their capacities, indeed, for parody and subversion (Bhabha 1993).

Furthermore, the dynamics of racial signification are necessarily *relational*. How much autonomy does the individual have to choose her/his racial location? To what extent is national identity bound up with racial identity? The construction of racial meanings is about the position of groups (and individuals) vis-à-vis one another: identity is constituted through differentiation, difference through identification (Connolly 1991). Thus the increasing empowerment of a racial minority formerly subject to intense exclusion and discrimination will engender an "identity crisis" for the group formerly more absolutely superordinate. Here the interdependence of the structural and signification dimensions of hegemony is clearly demonstrated. Some examples of these kinds of shifts might include minority enfranchisement, upward economic mobility, and increased access to cultural forums such as media and curriculum. The United States, South Africa, the United Kingdom, and many other countries furnish ready contemporary cases. In the following section, I discuss some of these processes with particular reference to present-day developments in U.S. racial formation processes.

A Local Case: Racial Hegemony and the "Underclass"

I have already suggested that throughout much of the world, race and class serve as interrelated figures of inequality and difference. How these frameworks are constructed, as institutions and ideologies, and as systems of social organization and of cultural representation, varies greatly. In the United States, where significant social inequality coexisted for many years with well-developed racial ideology, a caste-based social structure developed to guarantee white workers their racial identity as a signifier of their "freedom" (Roediger 1991). From slavery through the Jim Crow era this framework underwent many adaptations, without fundamentally altering its character as a *herrenvolk* —that is, a white and male—democracy.[7]

But by the end of World War II the *herrenvolk* formula had been seriously undermined. Emigration from the South of the previously rural black population, and its subsequent transformation into an urbanized working class, reinforced long-standing efforts to build a movement for racial justice. Emerging affinities between that movement and various anticolonial struggles around the world combined with the legacy of antifascism and the competition of the cold war to frame a national interest in racial reform. When the civil rights movement overthrew de jure segregation in the mid-1960s, then, it also deeply wounded the racial caste system.

The old system did not die, though; it mutated instead. The destruction of rigid rules of racial exclusion, the recognition that the principle of equal justice under law must extend to all, did not overcome de facto white supremacy any more than had the Thirteenth, Fourteenth, and Fifteenth amendments to the Constitution a century before. The enactment of civil rights laws meant that the state officially rejected the norms and values of white supremacy. But it did not mean that long-standing racist practices, often informal or even unconscious, would cease. It did not mean that racist attitudes had disappeared. In fact, by eliminating the most egregious forms of racial injustice, by distancing the state from the overtly antidemocratic ideology of white supremacy, the civil rights reforms perversely facilitated the maintenance of racial inequality in some respects. For in the post-civil rights era, the sources of racial inequality would be far more dispersed. Difficult as it was to achieve the various civil rights laws that outlawed discrimination, guaranteed voting rights, and so on, it would prove far more difficult to change racial attitudes and informal practices.

The overt racial *domination* of the Jim Crow era thus gave way to the racial *hegemony* of the post-civil rights period, as the state both adopted and demonstrated the limits of the movement's principal demands. In this transformed atmosphere of racial hegemony, the chief problem of rule was no longer to subdue the masses of disenfranchised minorities who sought racial equality and social justice. That single project of subjugation now turned into a twofold strategy of accommodation: first, it was essential to incorporate those black, brown, etc., individuals who were able to make use of the new, more open racial climate and policies to achieve greater mobility for themselves. For these largely middle-class folks it was crucial that the old, caste-based logic of race be consigned to the dustbin; their race must not continue to mark them out for inferior status, lest they reconstitute themselves as the leadership of the mass movements only recently contained by reform (Williams 1991).

Second, the vast majority of racially defined minority group members—those who for various reasons could not avail themselves of the 1960s racial reforms—were to be left to their own devices. Indeed, it was now argued that their fate was totally in their own hands. Egalitarian policies now reigned; all could advance based solely on their merits. What could be fairer than that?

Once this logic was in place—roughly by the mid-1970s—the new outlines of racial stratification *by class* could be discerned.[8] Beneath the black middle classes lay the residual working classes, those who had been able to avoid the deindustrialization and deunionization, the capital flight and urban decay that marked the U.S. urban landscape, particularly after 1980. And beneath this stratum lay the "underclass."

The debate on the constitution of this latter group, and on the best policies for dealing with it, has run continuously since the late 1970s, though the term was in use as early as 1969.[9] Although it has produced a number of valuable insights, the striking thing about discussion of the "under*class*," from the standpoint of the shifting dynamics of racial hegemony, is the way this term masks continuing *racial* stratification. Here I have neither the desire nor the space to sort through the voluminous literature this debate has produced. But I do wish to point out the clear association between the emergence of accounts focused on this black "underclass" in the 1970s and beyond and the simultaneous abandonment of the movement-based agenda of racial equality and social justice. The deep significance of the underclass thesis was the revival of the old "culture of poverty" analysis, which attributed failure to achieve upward mobility to the shortcomings and indeed deviant behaviors of the poor themselves.

That the very concept of an American underclass was very imprecise, and that it was subject to tremendous ideological tugging and hauling, cannot be disputed. Indeed, how many people did the category include? "Drastically different estimates of the size of the underclass reflected its imprecise definition," says Katz, who cites studies putting its dimensions at anywhere from 500,000 to 8 million people (1989: 204-5). But this vagueness did not prevent the steady invocation of the term by politicians, journalists, and academics during the 1980s (Auletta 1982; Moynihan 1986; Wilson 1987; Lemann 1991; Jencks 1992). For present purposes, the most notable feature of the emerging focus on the "underclass" was its implicit racial selectivity: "Two groups—black teenage mothers and black jobless youths—dominated the images of the underclass." Furthermore, discussion of poverty

> virtually ignored both the majority of the poor, who were not black and did not live in female-headed families, and the explosive growth of poverty among white adult males. (Katz 1989: 195)

In other words, the designation "underclass" was the product of an emergent effort to explain and control racially assigned poverty in the post-civil rights era. Despite its surface-level racelessness, the term was never applied to the poor *tout court*. Whatever their other differences, all participants in the underclass debate sought to explain not the continuity of poverty itself, not the existence of extreme income or class inequality, but the persistence of specifically *black* poverty, inequality, and marginality after the enactment of civil rights and equal opportunity legislation.

Enter William Julius Wilson, who produced the best of the underclass studies—because his work integrated more information and set up a large number of research hypotheses for further testing. As defined by Wilson, the underclass was "a heterogeneous grouping of inner-city families and individuals whose behavior contrasts sharply with mainstream America (Wilson 1987: 8). By using the phrase "inner-city" he signaled that his focus would be on blacks alone. And although at times his book offered data on white poverty (172) and recognized the existence of urban (Latino) barrios and "Chinatowns" (180), where race and class factors jointly shaped poverty, this was done strictly for comparative purposes. Wilson reserved the term "underclass" exclusively for ghettoized African-Americans. Indeed, he castigated "liberals" for "emphasizing racism as the explanation" of black impoverishment (10).

Wilson accepted many of the "culture of poverty" arguments made by the right, though he recast "pathological" underclass behavior as a product of structural problems, notably endemic unemployment, rather than any inherent defect in the black poor themselves. He thus sought to rearticulate the new hegemonic discourse of race in a more progressive, "social democratic" direction (viii).

Wilson argued for a new antipoverty strategy that would not be "race-specific," and would thus have a greater likelihood of being adopted by legislators and voters. He recognized the transformed racial climate of the post-civil rights era, in which new right and neoconservative politicians had ridden to power by covert race baiting combined with proclamations of having achieved a "color-blind" social policy. His intervention had much to recommend it as a political strategy, but it also involved a great limitation: Wilson's denial—already apparent in his previous work (1980)—that race remained as constitutive of the U.S. social structure as ever.

Even though he denies it, Wilson's own analysis goes a long way toward demonstrating not the existence of an underclass in a society where the significance of race is decreasing, but rather the continuing significance of institutional racism, or what Joel Kovel (1984) called "metaracism." This is the form of racism appropriate to the present historical moment, in which the state no longer organizes and enforces white supremacy, but retreats behind an official policy—or facade—of race neutrality. The sociopolitical and legal justification offered for supposedly "color-blind" policies is a conservative, individualistic reinterpretation of the civil rights measures of the 1960s, and of the meaning of equality itself. This metaracist state in practice cultivates the stratification of racially defined minority communities, going beyond mere tokenism to foster large-scale organization of pliable—and suitably rewarded—minority allies on the one hand,[10] while draining resources from low-income minority communities on the other. The predictable results are the trends Wilson documents: concentrated unemployment and misery in ghetto (and barrio, and reservation) communities. Such has been the trajectory of the new racial hegemony in the United States.

As a practical matter, the shift recommended by Wilson may well be a necessity, but in my view it is still a mistake to accept the hegemonic view that the racial dimension of inequality is a thing of the past. Racism, whether it takes the form of overt white supremacy or metaracism, has class consequences. Up to a certain point it protects whites from the violence of economic dislocation, a pattern that has been discerned in the 1980s (Edsall and Edsall 1992). But beyond that point, when the state's refusal to maintain public investment and an adequate level of social provision (Amenta and Skocpol 1988; Skocpol 1988) begins to affect whites and suburbanites adversely as well, the political terrain available for race bait-ing and manipulation of white racial fears shrinks.

If this point has indeed been reached, we may expect polemics about the threat posed by the "underclass" to recede. What remains to be seen is how far the pendulum of social policy will swing back. Will new measures take only a minimal step toward the center, content simply to address the fears and uncertainties of the white suburban constituents, the "Reagan Democrats" (Greenberg 1985), who responded to the resolutely middle-class rhetoric of Bill Clinton's presidential campaign? Or will a new social policy be forged, an initiative committed to eliminating—or at least signif-icantly reducing—the post-civil rights racial stratification that only wors-ened in the 1980s? On this the jury is still out. Clinton has played it both ways, recasting neoconservative rhetoric about the "responsibilities and obligations" of the black poor on the one hand, and inveighing against ra-cial injustice on the other. Much will depend on whether a new movement for social justice—one that can expose the limitations of post-civil rights racial hegemony and demand a truly egalitarian social policy—can be built.

This analysis has focused on the vicissitudes of racial identity—globally as well as locally—as a continuing, and often neglected, dimension of he-gemony. I have sought to demonstrate the continuing crisis that besets our notions of who we are and of what our all-too-easy racial categorization signifies. Today more than ever, effective political opposition demands a concerted critique not just of inequality, not only of the lack of political representation, not simply of social policies of benign neglect (or in some cases malign neglect), but also of the system of racial signification itself. "Commonsense" notions of the meaning of race and of the permanence of racial identities in any given society need to be exposed—along with ra-cialized structures of inequality—as supports of the local hegemonic or-der, in whatever country they appear.

Chapter 9

Rethinking Race in Brazil

Introduction: The Repudiation of the *Centenário*

May 13, 1988, was the 100th anniversary of the abolition of slavery in Brazil. In honor of that date, various official celebrations and commemorations of the *centenário*, organized by the Brazilian government, church groups, and cultural organizations, took place throughout the country, even including a speech by President José Sarney.

But this celebration of the emancipation was not universal. Many Afro-Brazilian groups staged actions and marches, issued denunciations, and organized cultural events repudiating the "farce of abolition." These were unprecedented efforts to draw national and international attention to the extensive racial inequality and discrimination that Brazilian blacks—by far the largest concentration of people of African descent in any country in the Western Hemisphere—continue to confront. Particular interventions had such titles as "100 Years of Lies," "One Hundred Years without Abolition," "March for the Real Liberation of the Race," "Symbolic Burial of the 13th of May," "March in Protest of the Farce of Abolition," and "Discommemoration *(Descomemoração)* of the Centenary of Abolition" (Maggie 1989).

The repudiation of the *centenário* suggests that Brazilian racial dynamics, traditionally quiescent, are emerging with the rest of society from the long twilight of military dictatorship. Racial conflict and mobilization, long almost entirely absent from the Brazilian scene, are reappearing. New racial patterns and processes—political, cultural, economic, social psychological—are emerging, while racial inequalities of course continue as well. How much do we know about race in contemporary Brazil? How effectively does the extensive literature explain the present situation?

In this chapter I review and critique the main theories of race in Brazil in light of contemporary racial politics there. I focus largely on postwar Brazilian racial theory, beginning with the pioneering studies sponsored by the United Nations Educational, Scientific, and Cultural Organization (UNESCO) in the 1950s. This body of theory has exhibited considerable strengths in the past; it has been particularly effective in dismantling the myth of a nonracist national culture in which "racial democracy" flourished, and in challenging the role of various elites in maintaining these myths. These virtues, largely understandable in light of the analytical horizon imposed on critical social science by an antidemocratic (and indeed often dictatorial and brutal) regime, now exhibit some serious inadequacies when they are employed to explain current developments.

I intend this essay to be a critical reappropriation of this literature that both accepts much of its insights and rejects its limitations. Such a reinterpretation, I argue, sets the stage for a new approach, based in *racial formation theory*. In the concluding section of the essay I set forth this perspective and suggest that it offers a more accurate view of the changing racial order in contemporary Brazil. Racial formation theory can respond both to the ongoing racial inequalities and persisting salience of racial difference and to the new possibilities opened up by the transition to democracy; it can do this in ways that the established approaches, despite their considerable merits, cannot.

Theoretical Perspectives: The Debate Thus Far

Until quite recently Brazil was seen as a country with a comparatively benign pattern of race relations.[1] Only in the 1950s, when UNESCO sponsored a series of studies—looking particularly at Bahia and São Paulo—did the traditional theoretical approaches, which focused on the concept of "racial democracy," come under sustained attack.[2] The work of such UNESCO researchers as Thales de Azevedo (1966), Roger Bastide (1973, 1978), Florestan Fernandes (1969, 1978; Bastide and Fernandes 1959), and Marvin Harris (1964) documented as never before the prevalence of racial discrimination and the persistence of the ideology of "whitening." This set of overtly racist attitudes and beliefs had supposedly been discredited in the 1930s and 1940s after the interventions of Gilberto Freyre (Freyre

1940; Skidmore 1974) and the advent of the more modern "racial democracy" view. In a word, the UNESCO-sponsored research set new terms for debate, constituting (not without some disagreements) a new racial "revisionism."

The Revisionist Approach   — reductionist too

Racial revisionism was full of insights into Brazilian racial dynamics, but it also had significant limitations. Chief among these was a tendency to reduce race to class, depriving racial dynamics of their own, autonomous significance. In the space available here, I offer only a summary criticism of this perspective, concentrating on the leading members of the revisionist school.

In Florestan Fernandes's view, Brazil's "racial dilemma" is a result of survivals from the days of slavery, which came into conflict with capitalist development and would be liquidated by a transition to modernity. "The Brazilian racial dilemma," Fernandes writes,

> constitutes a pathological social phenomenon, which can only be corrected by processes which would remove the obstruction of racial inequality from the competitive social order. (1978, vol. 2: 460)

Fernandes's work probably remains the most comprehensive sociology of race relations in Brazil. The greatness of his work lies in his recognition of the centrality of race in Brazil's development, not only in the past or even the present, but also in the future. However, race remains a "dilemma" whose "resolution" will signify sociopolitical maturity. In other words, Fernandes still understands race as a problem whose solution is integration. Implicitly there is a new stage to be achieved in Brazilian development, in which racial conflict will no longer present an obstacle or diversion from class conflict.

Fernandes at least recognized the continuing presence and significance of race; other revisionists tended to dismiss or minimize it. While Fernandes's basic optimism was tempered by the question of whether the full modernization of class society could be achieved, Thales de Azevedo saw evidence that this process was already far advanced: according to him, class conflict was *replacing* racial conflict in Bahia (Azevedo 1966: 30-43).[3] Marvin Harris, who worked closely with Azevedo, suggested that the Brazilian system of racial identification *necessarily* subordinated race to class.[4] Comparing Brazilian and U.S. racial dynamics, Harris argued that the absence of a "descent rule" by which racial identity could be inherited, and the flexibility of racial meanings, led to a situation in which "racial identity is a mild and wavering thing in Brazil, while in the United States it is for millions of people a passport to hell" (Harris 1964: 64).

Actually, there are various theoretical accounts of the process by which race is supposedly subordinated to class. For the original revisionists, the question was whether this process was a social fact, already in progress and perhaps even well advanced, or a mere possibility. For Azevedo, it was already well under way; for Fernandes, it was a tendency that might—tragically—never come to pass unless the Brazilian people exhibited enough political will to transcend the racial dilemma and modernize their social order.

Later work, such as that of Carl Degler and Amaury de Souza, suggested various ways in which racial dynamics could persist while still remaining subordinated to class conflicts. Degler, in a rich comparative analysis of Brazil and the United States, concluded that because Brazil distinguished mulattoes from blacks, and afforded them greater social mobility—the so-called mulatto escape hatch—racial polarization had been avoided there. Pointing to the same flexibility of racial categories that Harris had documented, Degler found ample evidence and logic for the "escape hatch" in Brazilian racial history. If there was an escape hatch, then the United States pattern of growing racial solidarity would not occur; thus at least for some blacks (that is, mulattoes) questions of class would automatically take precedence over those of race. Other blacks, recognizing that mobility was available to the lighter skinned, would seek this possibility, if not for themselves then for their children.

Besides tending to confirm the traditional wisdom about "whitening" as the preferred solution to Brazil's racial problems, this analysis also saw economic mobility (and thus, integration in class society) as the key question in Brazilian racial dynamics. Because the escape hatch already provided this opportunity for the lighter skinned blacks, the task was to extend it to blacks in general.

Amaury de Souza made a similar argument that had less recourse to historical data and instead focused on whitening as a sort of rational choice model in which blacks had to weigh the costs of individual mobility against those of racial solidarity; consequently a type of "prisoner's dilemma" confronted any effort to organize black political opposition (de Souza 1971; see also Bastide 1965).

While the UNESCO studies offered an unprecedented wealth of empirical detail about Brazilian racial dynamics, the racial theory they employed was less innovative. They consistently practiced reductionism; that is, they understood race epiphenomenally, as a manifestation of some other, supposedly more fundamental, social process or relationship. In the vast majority of studies, race was interpreted in terms of class. Racial dynamics were seen simply as supports for (or outcomes of) the process of capitalist development in Brazil.

While it is certainly not illegitimate to examine the linkage between race and class, reductionism occurs when the independence and depth of racial phenomena go unrecognized.

The counterargument to class reductionism is that, as a consequence of centuries of inscription in the social order, racial dynamics acquire their own autonomous logic, penetrating the fabric of social life and the cultural system at every level. Thus they cannot be fully understood, in the manner of Fernandes, as "survivals" of a plantation slavocracy in which capitalist social relationships had not yet developed. Such a perspective ultimately denies the linkages between racial phenomena and postslavery society. There can be little doubt that since abolition the meaning of race has transformed tremendously; it has been extensively "modernized" and reinterpreted. To grasp the depth of these changes, one has but to examine the intellectual or political history of the race concept itself. Late nineteenth century racial vocabularies and assumptions about white supremacy are as repugnant in contemporary Brazilian discourse as they would be in the present-day United States (C. M. de Azevedo 1987; Skidmore 1974).

Nor is it tenable to suggest that in Brazil racial distinctions are ephemeral, mere adjuncts to class categories, as do Harris and Azevedo. Substantial racial inequality may be observed in levels of income, employment, and returns to schooling, in access to education and literacy rates, in health care, in housing, and, importantly, by region (Costa 1983; Silva 1985; Hasenbalg 1979, 1983).[5] In order to substantiate the thesis of transition from race to class, it would be necessary to demonstrate that inequality levels were tending to equalize *across* racial lines; the fact that 100 years after the end of slavery blacks are still overwhelmingly concentrated in the bottom strata certainly suggests that race is still a salient determinant of "life chances."

Degler's and de Souza's emphasis on the distinction between blacks and mulattoes — and the consequences of mobility for mulattoes — is more difficult to evaluate. On the one hand Nelson do Valle Silva's detailed study of racial stratification reveals no significant difference between black and mulatto mobility. Looking at a variety of indicators (income, returns to schooling, etc.), and using 1960 and 1976 census data that distinguish between blacks and mulattoes, Silva finds that "Blacks and mulattoes seem to display unexpectedly familiar profiles." Further,

> these results lead us to reject the two hypotheses advanced by the
> Brazilian sociological literature. Mulattoes do not behave
> differently from Blacks, nor does race play a negligible role in the

process of income attainment. In fact it was found that Blacks and mulattoes are almost equally discriminated against. . . . This clearly contradicts the idea of a "mulatto escape-hatch" being the essence of Brazilian race relations. (Silva 1985: 54-55; see also Silva 1980)

On the other hand, the significance of this finding may be overstated, vitiated by Afro-Brazilian practices of racial classification. For example, a recent black movement campaign, Campanha Censo 91, sought to counteract the tendency toward "auto-embranqecimento" (self-whitening) in responding to the national census's questions on race.[6] Thus Silva's claim that the traditional notion of mobility no longer holds may be correct statistically but false in terms of Afro-Brazilian perceptions. The mulatto escape hatch, an absolutely central theme in Brazilian racial ideology, might thus retain an ambiguous, if weakened, relevance.

Perhaps the most striking limitation of the revisionist literature is its nearly exclusive focus on racial inequality. This is not to deny the importance of the economic dimensions of race. However, the preoccupation with inequality to the near total exclusion of any other aspect of race is a logical feature of approaches that treat racial dynamics as manifestations of more fundamental class relationships. These approaches tend to take the meaning of race for granted and to see racial identities as relatively rigid and unchanging.

To summarize: despite their success at exposing racial inequalities in Brazil and thus destroying the racial democracy myth, the revisionist approaches encountered difficulties when they had to explain transformations in racial dynamics after slavery, and particularly the persistence of racial inequality in a developing capitalist society. Their tendency to see the persistence of racial inequality as a manifestation of supposedly more fundamental class antagonisms (reductionism) resulted in an inability to see race as a theoretically flexible, as opposed to an a priori, category. In writing about racial dynamics the revisionists tended to ignore the changing sociohistorical *meaning* of race in Brazil.

The Structuralist Approach

Beginning in the 1970s, and with greater frequency in later years, a "postrevisionist" or *structuralist* approach to race in Brazil began to emerge. This perspective saw race as a central feature of Brazilian society. "Structuralist" authors sharply refocused the agenda of racial theory. They did not seek to explain how racism had survived in a supposed racial democracy, nor how true integration might be achieved. Rather, they looked at the way the Brazilian social order had maintained racial inequalities without encountering significant opposition and conflict.

In a brief essay originally published in 1971, Anani Dzidzienyo combined a critique of racial inequality with a discussion of both the macro- and microlevel cultural dynamics of race in Brazil. He challenged the

> bias which has been a hallmark of the much-vaunted Brazilian "racial democracy"—the bias that white is best and black is worst and therefore the nearer one is to white, the better.

Further, he noted that

> the hold which this view has on Brazilian society is all-pervasive and embraces a whole range of stereotypes, role-playing, job opportunities, life-styles, and, what is even more important, it serves as the cornerstone of the closely-observed "etiquette" of race relations in Brazil. (1971: 5)

Here in embryo was a far more comprehensive critique of Brazilian racial dynamics. Dzidzienyo argued that racial inequalities were both structural and linked to a formidable racial ideology. This "official Brazilian ideology achieves *without tension* the same results as do overtly racist societies" (14, emphasis original). Structural inequality and the system of racial meanings were linked in a single racial order; each served to support the other. In this connection between structure and culture the structuralists saw a pattern of *racial hegemony*. But how was this hegemony attained and maintained, "without tension"?

In a contribution of great importance, Carlos Hasenbalg developed a new synthesis of race and class, building on but also departing from the work of Fernandes (Hasenbalg 1979: 72-75). Post-*abolição* racial dynamics, Hasenbalg argued, have been steadily transformed as Brazilian capitalism has evolved; thus, far from being outmoded, racial inequality remains necessary and functional for Brazilian capitalism.[7] The essential question, then, is not to account for the persistence of racism, but rather to explain the absence of serious racial opposition, what Hasenbalg calls "the smooth maintenance of racial inequalities."

Both Dzidzienyo and Hasenbalg recognized that neither the powerful cultural complex of "whitening" and "racial democracy" nor the brutal structural inequalities between black and white would have been sustainable on their own. Both writers analyzed the racial order in Brazil in terms of the linkage between culture and structure, between ideology and inequality. In this sense, these writers adopted early versions of a racial formation perspective.

Yet their analyses still bore some of the marks of class reductionism. To be sure, Dzidzienyo and Hasenbalg granted Brazilian racial dynamics a significant degree of autonomy vis-à-vis class dynamics. But their structural approach was still limited by the one-dimensionality of a view that explained the shape of the Brazilian racial order almost entirely in terms of its "management" by white elites. Few constraints are recognized as limiting white management, either in the form of social structures inherited from the past, or in the form of resistance on the part of the racially subordinated group. Inequality is "smoothly" maintained by a combination of ideological manipulation and coercion, all with the objective of maximizing elite (i.e., capitalist) control of the developing Brazilian economy.

In Hasenbalg's view, for example, the crucial action that permitted the system of "smooth maintenance" to evolve occurred when the elites decided to encourage massive European immigration, thus displacing black labor after *abolição* (1979: 223-60). Plentiful supplies of white labor prevented the emergence of a racially split labor market, such as developed in the United States, and effectively defused racial antagonisms. The infusion of white labor insured that class divisions among whites, rather than competition between whites and blacks, would shape the pattern of Brazilian capitalist development. It also fueled the cultural/ideological complex of whitening, and later the ideology of racial democracy. Thus the system of racial categorization, as well as the ideological and political dynamics of race in general, were shaped by capitalist development in the post-*abolição* years.

This approach does not deviate very far from that of Fernandes. It simply assumes the primacy of capitalist development and the secondary character of race. It does not take into account the fact that racial ideology was entirely present at the supposed foundations of Brazilian capitalist development. Indeed, it was in part because of their fear of blacks that the Brazilian elite turned to European immigration in the first place (Skidmore 1974: 130-31, 136-44). Hasenbalg recognizes this empirical fact, but cannot incorporate it in his theory.

In fact, Hasenbalg's argument would operate equally well in reverse: in place of his suggestion that capitalist development demanded the smooth maintenance of Brazilian racial inequality, it would be equally logical to suggest that the course of development followed by Brazilian capitalism was shaped in significant measure by preexisting racial patterns.[8] However significant the absence of a split labor market was to the development of Brazilian racial dynamics, it was clearly not determining; at most it was one factor among others. Indeed, the political authoritarianism—the *coronelismo*, paternalism, clientelism, and so forth that characterized elite-mass relationships in the first republic and beyond—was a carryover from slavery into the post-*abolição* framework in which capitalist development began in earnest. Thus not only the framework of Brazilian class relations but also in large measure the traditional political structure may be said to have their origins in racial dynamics.

Without derogating the importance of the structuralist contributions, it may be worthwhile to note that they were written during the most repressive phase of the Brazilian military dictatorship (1968-1974), when all opposition, including black movement activity, was at its nadir. The mobilization that did exist largely took the form of cultural and "identity" politics, typified most centrally by the "black soul" movement (which I will discuss later). It is not unreasonable to suggest that the structuralist problematic—of a frozen racial inequality, "smoothly maintained" by an all-powerful elite—stemmed from the conjuncture in which it emerged.

Furthermore, despite their recognition of important cultural dimensions in Brazilian racial politics, the structuralists still theorized these elements as strictly subordinate to those of inequality and discrimination. Their view was that Brazilian racial discourse largely served to mask inequality; they did not see the cultural dynamics—the racial "politics of identity"—as conflictual, contested terrain. Perhaps this residue of class reductionism also limited their ability to recognize potential flexibility and changing patterns in Brazilian racial dynamics.

Summarizing once more, we can say that despite its considerable strengths, the literature on race in Brazil suffers from a series of debilitating problems, including a neglect of the discursive and cultural dimensions of race, an exaggerated belief in the omnipotence of elites where racial management is concerned, and a tendency to downplay the tensions and conflicts involved in Brazilian racial dynamics. These limitations largely derive from a deep-seated tradition of class reductionism, which is manifest in the classic studies of the early postwar period (the revisionists), but latent even in more recent work (the structuralists).

Such criticisms point to the need for a new approach, one that would avoid treating race as a manifestation of some other, supposedly more basic, social relationship. In the concluding section of this essay I propose an alternative in the form of *racial formation* theory. This perspective, I think, offers a more accurate view of the changing racial order in contemporary Brazil. It can respond both to ongoing racial inequalities and to persistent racial difference in Brazil. It can address the new possibilities opened up by the transition to democracy. Finally, it can do this in ways that the established approaches, despite their considerable merits, cannot.

The Racial Formation Perspective

Racial formation theory seems particularly well suited to deal with the complexities of Brazilian racial dynamics. Developed as a response to reductionism, this perspective understands race as a phenomenon whose meaning is contested throughout social life (Omi and Winant 1986).

From such a perspective race is both a microlevel matter of the individual psyche and of relationships among individuals, and a macrolevel component of collective identities and social structures. Once it is recognized that race is not a "natural" attribute, but a socially and historically constructed one, it becomes possible to analyze the processes by which racial meanings are decided, and racial identities are assigned, in a given society. These processes—those of "racial signification"—are inherently discursive. They are variable, conflictual, and contested at every level of society, from the intrapsychic to the supranational. Inevitably, many interpretations of race, many racial discourses, exist at any given time. The political character of racial formation stems from this: elites, popular movements, state agencies, religions, and intellectuals of all types develop *racial projects*, which interpret and reinterpret the meaning of race.

The theoretical concept of racial projects is a key element of racial formation theory. *A project is simultaneously an explanation of racial dynamics and an effort to reorganize the social structure along particular racial lines.* Every project is necessarily both a discursive or cultural initiative, an attempt at racial signification and identity formation, on the one hand, and, on the other, a political initiative, an attempt at organization and redistribution (Omi and Winant 1986; Winant 1990).

The articulation and rearticulation of racial meanings is thus a multidimensional process in which competing "projects" intersect and clash. These projects are often explicitly, but always at least implicitly, political. "Subjective" phenomena—racial identities, popular culture, "common sense"—and social structural phenomena such as political movements and parties, state institutions and policies, market processes, and so on are all potential sources of racial projects.

Racial formation theory suggests that the logic of race is multiply determined and decentered at any given historical moment. The pattern of racial meanings and identifiable racial identities, the racial dimensions of social inequality, and the degree of political mobilization based upon race all exhibit instability and flexibility. Thus, at a particular moment or in a certain society, race may appear to be a nearly "natural" phenomenon, unquestioned and apolitical, simply a matter of "common sense"; at another moment or in another social context, race may be highly politicized, the site of significant social mobilization. In the former situation, we would expect to find little racial contestation, and at the most only a small number of marginalized racial projects. In the latter situation, we would encounter a large-scale national debate, a great deal of popular uncertainty about the significance of race in everyday life, and numerous antagonistic racial projects.

From this perspective, too, we can develop important cross-national and historical comparisons about race. Comparing the United States and Brazil, for example, we would find that race has in general been a far more politicized category in the United States, that racial divisions have been more absolute and explicit, and that consequently racial conflict has been more fundamental and antagonistic than in Brazil. This comparison would also begin to account for the far greater social mobility and political power of racial minorities—especially in recent decades—in the United States.

Looking historically at Brazilian racial formation processes, we see a few significant periods of racial awareness and mobilization, on the part of both Brazilian elites and Afro-Brazilians. The periods of agitation for *abolição* and of the 1920s and 1930s, as documented for example by Celia Marinho de Azevedo and Florestan Fernandes, were such moments. At many other points, of course, racial formation processes have been largely uncontested. From this perspective, then, we can agree with accounts emphasizing the general lack of antagonism and persistent inequality characteristic of everyday Brazilian racial dynamics, without ignoring occasional periods of conflict and mobilization, both of blacks seeking change and of whites fearful of it.

Racial Formation in Contemporary Brazil: The Impact of Democratization

When we ask why the Brazilian black movement is newly stirring after a relative absence of half a century, an important part of the answer must be the impact of democratization. It was the *abertura*, the painfully slow re-emergence of civil society, that created the conditions under which black political opposition could reappear. At first tentative and meliorist, and still marginalized relative to black movements in the United States and Europe, the black movement in Brazil has now taken a permanent place on the political stage. Of course the process of democratization is still far from consolidated, and the room for maneuver available to an explicitly race-conscious movement is still quite limited. But as the various protests against the *centenário* showed, not since the days of the Frente Negra Brasileira in the 1920s and 1930s has so explicit a racial politics been possible.[9]

The reappearance of the black movement also demonstrates the limits of the various analyses of Brazilian racial dynamics that I have reviewed. Nothing about the current upsurge squares with either the revisionist or the structuralist accounts. From the revisionist perspective, one would have expected a diminution of racial conflict as Brazil became a more fully capitalist society, less characterized by the residues of its slaveholding past. The experience of rapid industrial growth under the military dictatorship, the "miracle" that made Brazil the eighth-largest national economy in the world (in terms of gross national product) by 1985, should also have made race a less salient marker of political identity. In fact, the reverse occurred.

From the structuralist perspective, one would have expected the elite's "smooth maintenance" of racial inequality to be nowhere more efficiently carried out than under the military dictatorship. This was a system of elite rule par excellence, and one that managed quite "smoothly" the excruciatingly slow return of democracy during the 1970s and 1980s (Stepan 1988); furthermore, the military had been at pains to deny, in quintessentially Brazilian style, the existence of racism in the country (Skidmore 1985). Yet, not long after the *abertura* began in earnest (in 1974), the first attempts at national black movement building were initiated by the Movimento Negro Unificado (MNU),[10] and throughout the later transition period a slow but steady drumbeat of black oppositional voices, actions, and organizational initiatives was under way.

From a racial formation perspective, by contrast, these developments do make sense. The black upsurge was a combination of two factors: the *reemergence of civil society*, which necessarily opened up political terrain for social movement activities, and the *politicization of racial identities* upon that terrain.

The Reemergence of Civil Society

The *abertura* took place as a conflictual dialogue between democratic oppositional forces and the military dictatorship. It was a gradual relaxation of repression both prompted by and fueling opposition forces. The Brazilian democratic opposition in general, traditionally compromised and co-opted by elite control, *coronelismo*, and corporatism, faced enormous difficulties in the atmosphere of military dictatorship. The decades-long process of military rule rendered ineffective many of the traditional sources of political opposition in Brazil; others it eliminated outright. Thus the popular strata had to adopt new forms of struggle and contestation. Here the new social movements—human rights groups, women's groups, residential associations, and, very important in the Brazilian context, ecclesiastical base committees (CEBs)—became important political actors.

The new social movements *recreated civil society* by expanding the terrain of politics. They addressed issues that had formerly been seen as personal or private—that is, not legitimate themes for collective action—as public, social, and legitimate areas for mobilization. In these groups a range of radical democratic themes—religious, feminist, localist, but chiefly "humanistic"—were encountered in new ways (or for the first time). For many people, particularly those of humble origin whom the traditional political processes had always been able to ignore, the new social movements provided the first political experiences of their lives.[11] For those of the middle classes—priests, journalists, lawyers, health workers, educators, and others who shared explicit democratic and egalitarian aspirations—the new social movements offered a political alternative to leftist and populist traditions that the military dictatorship had effectively stalemated (Scherer-Warren and Krischke 1987; T. dos Santos 1985: 47-48; Boschi 1987; Schmink 1981; Cardoso 1983; Mainwaring n.d.).

Brazilian blacks were intimately involved in the quest for democracy (J. R. dos Santos 1985; Mitchell 1985; Moura 1983; Sodre 1983; Gonzalez 1985). They were among the *favela* dwellers, the landless *boias frias*, the metalworkers. In the early phases of the *abertura* they did not organize *qua* blacks, but the interrogation of social and political reality, the quest for *citizenship* emphasized in many movement activities, placed a new focus on racial themes. By the later 1970s, with the consolidation of democratic oppositional politics, a new generation of black movement organizations began to emerge.

It would be impossible to list all the political influences that blacks encountered in this process, nor can the variety of positions and currents within the nascent black movement be elaborated here. Certainly by participating in the panoply of oppositional social movements that confronted the dictatorship, many blacks acquired fresh political skills and awareness. Among those mobilized were black activists in *favela* associations, in CEBs, and in rural struggles for land (especially in the northeast); blacks who participated in strike activity (especially in the heavily industrialized, so-called ABC region of São Paulo); blacks involved in cultural activities and organizations;[12] black students (Turner 1985); blacks concerned with issues of African liberation; black researchers and intellectuals involved in studying Afro-Brazilian history and culture; and black women involved in feminist activities.[13]

Thus, as the *abertura* advanced and democratic opposition consolidated and expanded, blacks began to mobilize and organize as blacks. With the creation of the MNU in 1978 a national black political movement was brought into being.[14] More recently still other black organizations have appeared, notably the Grupo União e Consciência Negra, which claims organizations in fourteen Brazilian states, the Centro de Articulação de Populações Marginalizadas (CEAP), the Centro de Referencia Negro-mestiça (CERNE), the Instituto Palmares de Direitos Humanos (IPDH), and the publication *Jornal da Maioria Falante*. These are the means by which blacks are participating in the struggle to create democracy and social justice in Brazil.

A variety of political projects can be identified in the black movement upsurge that accompanied the *abertura*. "Entrism" (the effort by marginalized groups to operate in the political mainstream), socialist positions, and "nationalist" currents are all clearly in evidence. Strong debates and dissension characterized the development of the MNU. For example, major sectors of the organization rejected Abdias do Nascimento's project of *quilombismo* (Abdias do Nascimento 1985), his effort to develop an "Afrocentric" ideology for the black movement (Gonzalez 1985: 130). There have also been major debates about the role of feminism within the movement, and about the relationship of race, sex, and class in general.

Alongside such "nationalist" currents as that of *quilombismo*, "entrists" in the movement, oriented to both mainstream and left parties, have urged greater organized black participation in trade unions and political parties. Many radical blacks have joined the PT (Workers Party); within that organization they have created a Commissão de Negros that operates at both the national and regional levels. One of the few national black leaders, Benedita Souza da Silva, is a PT federal deputy.[15] There are also blacks in the PMDB (Brazilian Democratic Movement Party), the PSDB (Brazilian Social Democratic Party, a center-left split-off from the PMDB), and even rightist political parties such as the PDS (Social Democratic Party). Many blacks, however, even among those most committed to entrism, continue to criticize political parties, as well as unions and other popular organizations, as insufficiently committed to racial equality.

Additionally, there is a pronounced tendency toward co-optation of movement activity, for which Brazilian politics is notorious. Entrist groups are particularly susceptible to this. Whether they are effective or largely symbolic, various government entities have established mechanisms of liaison with the black community.[16] At the national level, there is now an Assessoria para Assuntos Afro-Brasileiros in the Ministry of Culture. Several state governments, particularly those of São Paulo and Rio de Janeiro, also have established agencies to foster cultural events and to investigate complaints of discrimination.

The Politicization of Racial Identity

Today the meaning of race and the complexities of racial identity are contested far more intensely than ever before in Brazil. We have only to look at the mobilization against the *centenário* to see this debate in progress. To understand this point it is useful to contrast expressions of black identity articulated at the repressive peak of the military dictatorship and in the

black soul

afoxes

present climate of relatively free expression. The "black soul" upsurge of the 1960s is used here to exemplify the first period, and the development of the *afoxés* in the 1980s to illustrate the second. Although many examples of public discourse on the subject of black identity could be cited, these two are not arbitrarily chosen: they are the most important manifestations of black cultural politics in their respective epochs (Fontaine 1985; Mitchell 1985).

During the most repressive periods of military rule, when overt political mobilization against racism was almost impossible, cultural movements sustained black awareness and challenged racial stereotypes, making use of "identity politics." Probably the most effective (or controversial) of these currents was "black soul," which flourished in the later 1960s, drawing inspiration from the black cultural and political upsurges then engulfing the United States (Rodrigues da Silva 1980). Black soul was a youth-oriented current; it had little appeal beyond the big cities (most notably Rio). To describe it as a movement probably overstates its political resonance.

Yet because it identified the interests of blacks in Brazil with those of blacks elsewhere, because it addressed issues of racial identity, black soul drew considerable attention from the military and from other official custodians of Brazilian racial ideology. For example, its obvious inspiration by cultural developments in the United States—where the black movement was entering its radical phase—prompted considerable unease. It was denounced as "un-Brazilian," implicitly antinationalist. In terms of racial formation theory, this reaction can be understood as a conflict over the meaning of race prompted by the black soul phenomenon. The fact that its rather superficial aspects (Afro hairstyles, dashikis, a taste for Motown and Stax/Volt records) became cause for official harassment indicates that, at least in the eyes of its opponents, black soul represented a challenge to Afro-Brazilian isolation from the global assertion of black identity. By drawing attention to blacks *qua* blacks, this current echoed the sporadic efforts of previous generations to highlight and discuss the nature of race in Brazil. Thus black soul raised the same hackles that the Frente Negra Brasileira had raised decades before, and that the Movimento Negro Unificado was to raise a decade later. In this way it contributed to debate over the nature of black identity in Brazil, at a moment (the mid-1960s to early 1970s) when repression was increasing. Black soul was important, then, in ways that transcended mere style and musical tastes. It was a transitional moment, a bridge between the limited but important black mobilization taking place in the predictatorship periods (I am thinking of such organizations as the Comité Democrático Afro-Brasileiro and the Congresso Brasileiro do Negro), and the activities of the MNU in the 1970s.

More recently, black identity has been stressed in the work of the *afoxes*. These are groups whose origins lie in African cultural traditions that have survived in Brazil, for example, the religion of *Candomblé*, and the West African language (Nagó) that slaves of Yoruban origin spoke. Originally the *afoxes* acted largely through *Carnaval*, consciously seeking to accentuate and focus black awareness through the powerful (and frequently subversive) discursive framework offered by this annual popular festival. Largely because of their subversiveness, the *afoxes* were outlawed, and were legalized only under the impact of *abertura* in the late 1970s.

In the northeast, and particularly in Salvador, Bahia, the "black capital" of Brazil, *afoxes* are not only active in *Carnaval*, but also serve as political organizations, performing educational tasks (racial *conscientização*), organizing *favela* dwellers and *moradores* (neighborhood) groups, and so forth. Salvador is also the home base of the group Olodum, which began as an *afoxe* but has become an important "nationalist" influence through its recordings. Olodum's music is consciously and complexly Afrocentric, drawing on the *afoxe* tradition, addressing Afro-Brazilians about their history, their links to Africa and to blacks in the diaspora, and their collective racial identity. Not only in their lyrics, but also in their incorporation of musical forms such as reggae, Olodum presents a view of black identity that radically challenges traditional concepts of race in Brazil. Its deliberate evocation of the African diaspora explicitly refuses the official Brazilian racial ideology in all its forms, from Freyre's "Lusotropicalism" to "racial democracy." Acting through popular music, Olodum attempts to reinterpret the question of race, and to valorize black identity, in a manner that addresses millions of Brazilians. Certainly this rearticulation of black identity is not unprecedented. It bears important resemblances to the message of Abdias do Nascimento, for example; in its treatment of Zumbi, the hero of black resistance to slavery, it resonates with many other efforts at mobilization and analysis. But what distinguishes the project of Olodum from those of many other Afro-Brazilian militants past and present is its immense appeal to the masses of blacks. Because it is a popular musical group, indeed *the* black band in Brazil, Olodum has become a sort of national *afoxe*.

Conclusion: Rethinking Race in Brazil

The issue of race is making its belated but inexorable entrance on the Brazilian political stage. Because today there is—at long last and with all its warts—political democracy in Brazil, there is an upsurge of overt racial conflict. There are two major themes to this conflict: the first is about racial inequality, mobility and redistribution along lines of race, and racially based political action. The second is about the meaning of race, the nature of racial identity, the logic of racial categories, the centrality of the African currents in Brazilian culture and history, and the links between blacks in Brazil and elsewhere in the African diaspora.

Certainly none of these themes is absolutely new—how could it be? Nor do I mean to suggest that a radical transformation of Brazilian racial dynamics is in the cards. There are many reasons to think that a far more incremental process than that which occurred elsewhere in the Americas—in the United States, say, or in the Caribbean—is in the works. Many factors in Brazil's history point to a more gradual politicization of race, for example in comparison to the United States. In Brazil there has been no apocalyptic national conflict over racial slavery, such as the U.S. Civil War; there has been far less state-enforced racial segregation, so that race is inherently less politicized than elsewhere. Further, there are far fewer established and independent black institutions, such as universities or media. The fact that Brazil lacks a viable democratic tradition, capable of incremental extension to previously excluded groups, is also of great importance. This list could be extended, and of course the comparison has been made far more systematically in other literature. I simply offer it here to suggest that no explosive racial upheaval is to be expected in Brazil.

Still, while traditional patterns of race and racism have by no means been invalidated, a qualitative change is evident in the sociopolitical dynamics of race in Brazil. The many examples I have cited in this essay demonstrate, I think, that this shift is under way: the protests against the *centenário*, the proliferation of black organizations, the attempts of established institutions—political parties, state agencies, unions—to address racial issues, and the arrival on the national cultural scene of black consciousness-raising efforts.

If indeed these changes are taking place at the sociopolitical level, they must be accompanied by changes in the theoretical and analytical tools with which we view race in Brazil. Just as we can no longer accept the premodern biologistic racism of the nineteenth century or the idyllic panorama of tropical racial harmonies imagined by Freyre in the 1930s, so we can no longer agree with the class reductionism that the UNESCO studies, for all their merits, generated in the 1950s and 1960s. Brazilian racial dynamics cannot be understood as reflections of an underdeveloped political economy that failed to attain full capitalist status. No transition from race to class, however elaborate, is under way.

Nor can we accept the argument of the structuralists that racial politics are, in essence, permanently marginalized. While there can be no question that the diffusion and denial of racial conflict has operated as effectively in Brazil as anywhere in the world, the *abertura* and its aftermath are providing extensive evidence as to the proliferation and deepening of racial conflict and racial consciousness. The argument that effective elite management of racial conflict could continue was refuted by the events of the *abertura* itself, an elite management scheme of unprecedented sophistication, which nevertheless resulted in the upsurge of racial opposition we have seen since the late 1970s.

Rethinking race in Brazil, then, means thinking about *racial formation*, about a process of permanently contested social institutions and permanently conflictual identities. Racial formation theory tells us that in Brazil the full range of racially salient sociopolitical and cultural dynamics hasn't even been identified yet. Language, geography, science, dress, farming, style, food, education, sports, media, literature, medicine, religion, the military . . . all these topics contain a wealth of hitherto unidentified racial dimensions, even those that have attracted significant research. Can anyone imagine that Bastide, as estimable a writer as he was, has exhausted the field of Afro-Brazilian religion? Or that Stephens's excellent English dictionary of Afro-Brazilian Portuguese has completed etymological and sociolinguistic investigation (Stephens 1989)? Academic research is driven by popular activity, cultural demands, political mobilization. If democracy can truly take hold, the racial dimensions of many spheres of Brazilian life will be interrogated and examined by those who must live them out. This is the heart of the racial formation process.

Chapter 10

"The Fact of Blackness" in Brazil

My title, evoking Fanon's famous discussion of race and colonialism (1967 [1952]), signals the principal objective of this chapter: to use Fanon's work to discuss some dilemmas in the analysis of race in Brazil. There has been relatively little application of Fanon's analyses of race to the Brazilian context. I offer some remarks about the particular relevance of his insights to Brazil, but because my chief interest here is to address Brazilian racial dynamics, I do not attempt an overall interpretation of Fanon. I am well aware that his work is almost as hotly debated as that of Marx, Gramsci, or Freud (Bhabha 1990b; Gates 1989), but I claim the right to use some of his core perceptions in an applied, rather than exegetical, mode.

But before taking on that task, I shall first discuss race in Brazil, framing what I see as the dilemmas posed by the available analyses. Then I shall reintroduce the Fanonian framework and employ it to reinterpret Brazilian racial politics.

Explaining the Relative Absence of Racial Politics in Brazil

The analytical and theoretical dilemmas posed by the question of race in Brazil, and particularly "the fact of blackness," are really daunting. Racial dynamics simply refuse to behave as social scientists, both Brazilian and otherwise, might expect. The chief dilemma is this: vast inequalities that we can identify by various types of social scientific research stubbornly resist political articulation. The immediate corollary of this assertion is that the question of "difference" is intensely contested in Brazil.

Of course there is *some* mobilization along racial lines, and however continuous as opposed to dichotomous, racial identities are framed along lines of color and hierarchized from light to dark. Thus all the basic dimensions of a racialized society can be specified in the Brazilian case. Indeed, most blacks, if not most whites, will acknowledge the racism that exists in Brazilian society.

This, incidentally, is one area where, as far as I know, data is limited and out of date: Brazilian racial attitudes have not been studied in depth since the late 1950s and early 1960s (Bastide and van den Berghe 1957; Fernandes 1978). As far as I know there has never been a comprehensive, methodologically sophisticated survey of racial attitudes, something on the order of Schuman, Steeh, and Bobo's *Racial Attitudes in America* (1985). Of course survey research on racial attitudes is notoriously difficult, as Schuman et al. recognize. The veracity of respondents is always a crucial problem, as is the reliability of research instruments. But if nobody even attempts such work, then all of us qualitative and theoretical types are really left in the dark.

So in the absence of good information on attitudes, and with plenty of social change going on in every area one would want to name—from demographic shifts to democratization, from the intense political climate surrounding the impeachment of the president (taking place as I write in late 1992) to the endless economic crisis, from struggles over land, the environment, and the role of women in Brazilian society to conflict within the Catholic Church—the near absence, or let us say the relative weakness, of a black movement is rather striking.

Many people have professed to see that movement on the horizon many times. Indeed, I freely admit that I am among that number; I have also argued, and am still prepared to argue, that in some respects U.S. and Brazilian racial politics are converging. The Afro-Brazilian movement's failure to present itself has thus come to constitute a rather glaring challenge to those of us who have so eagerly awaited it.

Meanwhile, many important analysts have devoted their energies to explaining why such a movement has *not* come into existence. These explanations are also unsatisfying, since they tend to demonize or grant inordinate powers to the Brazilian powers that be. To consider just a few of these approaches, let us look at the work of Abdias do Nascimento (1978a, 1978b) and Carlos Hasenbalg (1979).

Nascimento has claimed that Brazil has the most effective system of apartheid in the world: in his view this system is based in the well-known myth of racial democracy. Nascimento's analysis makes some telling points about how a superficially "tolerant" ideology of race can mask and indeed foment racial injustice and inequality. But a dilemma arises at the heart of this approach. Is the myth effective among blacks as well? If so, then Nascimento must portray his constituency as duped, an inherently limited political position. If, on the contrary, it is improbable that many blacks believe in this myth, if (as appears more likely) the effectiveness of the myth tends to be greater among whites and racial apologists, whether right or left, if—in short—blacks don't think they have democracy, why do they not act collectively with greater effectiveness to obtain it?

Another important analyst, Carlos Hasenbalg, has pointed to effective management of racial tensions by Brazilian elites—over long historical periods up to the present—as the chief reason for the lack of black political mobilization. Hasenbalg argues that through various means, including the manipulation of immigration policy, the adroit deployment of populist politics, and the incorporation of nationalist and culturalist ideologies provided by figures such as Gilberto Freyre and Sergio Buarque de Holanda, the dominant sociopolitical apparatus was able to defuse racial tensions and to insure the "smooth maintenance" of racial inequalities.

This is obviously a powerful argument as well, but it still has significant problems. It views elite power as highly effective when it comes to racial management, but this is the same elite power that, in every other area of Brazilian political, economic, and cultural life, has proved itself incompetent, craven, and corrupt. Hasenbalg conceives of elite power as relatively undifferentiated, undivided by controversy or competition. But what and who constitutes this elite? Without going very far back into the tortured history of race in Brazil, indeed looking only at recent decades, can we see in Vargas, Kubitschek, Goulart, the various military factions, Sarney, and Collor a consistent elite-based racial policy? Or indeed any evidence of "smooth maintenance"? To my North American eyes the racial policies of these leaders, and of the various interests they expressed and represented, seem rather more like variations on the theme of benign neglect.

One other explanation for the lack of heavily contested racial politics in Brazil is more culturalist: here I am thinking of analyses that focus on racial identity, such as Degler's analysis in *Neither Black nor White* of the so-called mulatto escape hatch (Degler 1986 [1971]). Other writers with similar perspectives include Amaury de Souza (1970) and Bolivar Lamounier (1968).

Situated in a comparative context (i.e., compared with the United States), the "escape hatch" idea might make some sense. It evokes Harry

Hoetink's "two variants in Caribbean race relations": one variant is northern, Protestant, and relatively absolutist about racial categories; the other is southern, Catholic, and more capable of eliding the categories (Hoetink 1967, 1985). Yet looked at in Brazilian terms, it is less satisfactory.

Analyses of racial stratification indicate that the difference in socioeconomic status (SES) between those classified as *preto* or *negro* (in other words, black) and those seen as *mulato* (or mixed race) is minimal. Blacks of various shades recognize the prevalence of racism, as I have already mentioned, and the distinction between *negro* and *mulato* itself is a function as much of SES as the reverse, because "o dinheiro embranquece."[1] So how far does it get us in explaining political demobilization?

To summarize, the relative absence of racial politics in Brazil remains problematic. Although there has been some racial mobilization, and awareness of racial inequalities has increased somewhat, the situation has not fundamentally altered since the period when "the myth of racial democracy" flourished. Indeed, in some respects the even earlier ideology of "whitening" remains in effect.

Social scientific analyses have also made some progress in identifying patterns of racial inequality and injustice. We have come a long way since the UNESCO studies first broke the news that Brazil was not the racial paradise its apologists claimed it to be. Yet in important ways social science is no more able than "common sense" to account for the relative lack of racial politics in Brazil. Although they make powerful contributions, the best studies available are still marked by serious shortcomings.

Fanon and Brazil

Frantz Fanon's theoretical insights on racial dynamics may contribute to our understanding of the Brazilian situation. No intensive effort has been made to apply Fanon's insights in depth to Brazilian racial dynamics. There are only passing references in the major recent authors—Fernandes, Bastide, Ianni, Sodre, Moura, and Hasenbalg, for example. Indeed, Fanon has been seen primarily as an anticolonial theorist, a polemicist for national liberation movements, and particularly of the Algerian revolution. It may be that these prevalent interpretations unduly confined interest in his work and limited appreciation of his general usefulness to racial theory in Brazil. Brazil's colonial status terminated relatively peacefully in 1822, and the country has experienced no serious revolutionary upheavals. Its few "uprisings"—the *tenentes* movement, the Prestes column, the urban guerrilla activity of the 1960s—can hardly be counted as national liberation movements, and certainly did not have major racial dimensions.

The only relatively deep reflection on Fanonian themes in the Brazilian context is a little book by Neusa Santos Souza, *Tornar-Se Negro* (1983). This volume focuses on psychological dimensions of racial dualism, and makes a significant contribution, but it does not address the theoretical implications of Fanon's perspective.

Fanon's importance extends far beyond his thought on anticolonial revolution. For one thing, as an Antillean, a Caribbean, Fanon can be seen as a representative of Hoetink's "southern," Catholic, flexible variant of race relations (not that I want to endorse all of Hoetink's perspective). And as a "Frenchman"—Martinique being, let it be recalled, a *departement* of France, and Fanon having long since extended his horizon beyond strictly Caribbean concerns—Fanon had to wrestle with the question of "otherness" on a world-historical, anticolonial stage. It is in this global arena (albeit French-inflected) that the imperial "civilizing mission" so crucial to French colonialism confronts the implacable resistance of "native others" determined to regain or redefine their own collective identities. Thus, Fanon is also a racial "dualist," though of a uniquely sophisticated sort.[2] To recognize Fanon's dualism it is enough simply to repeat any of the famous formulations in the essay from which I take my own title, for example:

Mama, see the Negro! I'm frightened! (Fanon 1967 [1952]: 112)

I came into the world imbued with the will to find a meaning in things, my spirit filled with the desire to attain to the source of the world, and then I found that I was an object in the midst of other objects." (Fanon 1967 [1952]: 109)

So Fanon's racial theorizing occupies a very wide space. His view of race is both continuous and split; it transcends the "two variants"; it recognizes but refuses to be bound by "otherness"; it embraces the uncertainty and flexibility of racial identities but insists on a fierce antiracism. Fanon, then, is among the few theorists who can overcome the opposition of the two variants of race relations. His analysis *maintains a certain tension*, viewing racial identity and racial politics as both fungible and contested on the one hand, and as a comprehensive framework of dominance and subordination, power and opposition on the other.

The Fact of Blackness in Brazil

This Fanon, Antillean and Frenchman, racial dualist and racial relativist, cosmopolitan and native, therapist and theorist, can tell us quite a lot about race in Brazil. Applying his insights would require us, to begin with, to recognize race as a *social fact*, in the Durkheimian sense; it would require acknowledgment of the deep presence of black identity, and of a racial gulf between rulers and ruled. Therefore, the contorted apologetics of Brazilian theorists of *mestizagem*, of *luso-tropicalismo*—notably those of Gilberto Freyre (1940, 1959)—cannot be sustained in a Fanonian perspective, simply because they reject the fact of difference, however much that difference itself partakes of its particular historical context, however much flexibility that difference retains. Nor can there be any room for victim blaming in a Fanonian view. To analyze racial dynamics this way is to reject the common Brazilian charge that race thinking is itself a problem, that to denounce racial injustice is somehow to indulge in racism.[3] Furthermore, because Fanon was a movement theorist who sought above all to assist racism's victims in confronting their objectification at the hands of their rulers and exploiters, any analysis drawing on his insights would have to recognize the need to politicize race, to develop racially based movements.

The difficulties of politicizing race in Brazil, from this Fanonian approach, arise from the many ways in which race is rendered politically "invisible." They spring from the ways in which "ambivalent" racial identity—both black and white—is created and fostered. Such an analysis, of course, would not deny the existence of widespread prejudice and discrimination in Brazil, but would insist that these phenomena are the results, not the causes, of the thoroughgoing racialization of Brazilian society.

Although there are many excellent analyses of racial stratification and inequality in Brazil (Silva 1980, 1987; Andrews 1991; Lovell 1991; Wood and Carvalho 1988), these studies generally stop short of examining the dimensions of race that interest Fanon, most notably the complex interrelationships between ambivalent racial identities and the political process.[4] This is what I propose to do—in a very preliminary way—in the conclusion of this essay.

Conclusion: Racial Identity and Democratic Politics

We can easily compare Fanon's accounts of many of his cases to statements made by patients of Neusa Santos Souza, author of *Tornar-Se Negro*:

—"Ser negro é ter que ser o mais."

—"Ele e' mais primitivo, talvez. Primitivo no sentido do primário, primeiro: a emoção é primaria a razão. Talvez o discurso racista tenha razão quando diz que o negro é mais emocional."

—"Minha avo . . . dizia que crioulo, sobretudo o negro, não prestava. Se voce vir confusão, saiba que é o negro que esta fazendo; se vir um negro correr, é ladrão. Têm que casar com um branco pra limpar o útero."

—"Ser negro é ter que mostrar algo—é ter uma serie de espaços vedados e mostrar que pôde atingir um nivel mais alto, uma cultura diferente." (Santos 1983: 61-62)[5]

And on and on. Neusa Santos Souza offers pages of these testimonies. Without relying unduly on her account—which will be immediately recognizable to anyone with knowledge of Brazilian racial dynamics—it seems fair to say that racial identity in Brazil places its bearers—black and white—in a state of deep uncertainty. The variations on this theme are familiar: perhaps one is struggling to accept one's black identity, to move toward the pride and self-assertion that is the thrust of Santos's title; perhaps one seeks to reinforce a white identity by repudiating all that is associated with the black;[6] perhaps one is intermittently aware of the extent to which race shapes one's interactions with the police, educational opportunities, or "life chances" in a general sense.

Perhaps nowhere else in the world is it more difficult to achieve a clear understanding of who one is according to the prevailing system of social categorization. Perhaps in no other country is it as arduous to assess the significance of race in everyday life, to take race into account in one's negotiation of survival, not to mention in one's quest for happiness or prosperity. In no other country is the *salience* of race so uncertain, so disguised in its quotidian manifestations, so explicitly denied and implicitly upheld. This ambivalence about race has not been measured—I am not sure how it could be—but it is widely recognized. What are its political implications?

What if the political demobilization of blacks (or the very slow and difficult process of mobilizing blacks), were the result of an inability to develop a meaningful black agenda? What if the ambivalences of racial identity in Brazil made that agenda particularly hard to develop? In that case we who have been analyzing race in Brazil may have been asking the wrong question, or asking the right question in the wrong way. This is something we can derive from looking at Fanon.

Our questions have been the traditional ones: about equality and citizenship, about "getting beyond" race, about democratizing race. We have been concerned with racial democracy, not merely the mythical racial democracy of Freyre, but the more modern notion—the rationalized and disenchanted version of what we mean by democracy—the vision of discrimination overcome, of prejudices discarded, of participation equalized.

If these are the questions, then the answer can only be a determinist one: first let us establish and fortify democracy, and then we will address the problems that remain. I too certainly hope Brazilian democracy is consolidated. But I doubt whether this kind of stage theory of racial progress can be anything more than a delaying device, a way of limiting black demands by placing race in a liberal-humanist framework. Such a political orientation, though admirable in many respects, fails to take into account the complexities, the ambivalences, of race.

It is a vision of *admission into civil society*, what we might label a civil rights vision. It assumes that Brazil can somehow get "beyond race," beyond the question of "the other." In place of this, we must recognize that in Brazil too identity is ambivalent and contradictory. The racialized other is within everyone. Indeed, having a racial order at all involves the doubling and splitting of identities, and the politics of ambivalence that goes with it. This is a key Fanonian insight.

Perhaps even more than in the "northern" societies such as the United States, where the state attempted to enforce the white-black distinction (however ineffectually), perhaps even more than in the colonial societies that Fanon most centrally addresses, where the white-black distinction was articulated in national terms (however unsuccessfully), in Brazil there was and is the most extensive development of *racial ambivalence*. This ambivalence lurks as a subversive racial presence within the body politic and within everybody. Its presence, its partial and often denied awareness of race, can be repressed and negated, incorporated and celebrated, or—as is most often the case—simultaneously romanticized and detested. But at the level of politics the articulation of this universalized and half-hidden racial awareness—it is feared—would unleash widespread disorder and imperil progress, thus challenging the two basic ideological pillars of the nation.

Contrast this analysis—imported from "without," from the globalized and historicized racial conflict that provides Fanon's logic—to the analysis of Freyre, who works from "within" and seeks almost desperately to preserve the particularities of Brazilian racial logic. Seen in this light Freyre seems a "loyal" twin brother to the "rebellious" Fanon. For Freyre too recognized the omnipresence of an ambivalent racial otherness, but rationalized and thereby repressed it as the "new man of the tropics," a new racial synthesis, what Michael Hanchard (1992) would call a new racial exceptionalism. But where Freyre's approach demanded the repression of racial difference in the service of *ordem e progresso*, Fanon is willing to confront the ambivalence of otherness, and to disrupt the society in order to achieve justice.

To go beyond the present understandings both academic and practical, to advance in a deeper way toward racial justice in Brazil, would involve calling into question not only the ambivalences of black identity, but also those of white identity. Drawing on Fanon's work, we can see in the struggles of Afro-Brazilians not only an effort to gain admission, not only an effort to be recognized as individuals with equal rights, but also an effort to partake in the general social movement to create democracy from below, to achieve not only formal representation but also participation.

From this perspective, and with this objective, black mobilization could take a very different shape. Rather than emerging at long last from the quiescent black masses and thus fulfilling what more and more seems an elusive, almost utopian hope, mobilization might appear as a series of options for identification, in which blacks could recognize themselves—at least partially—in various organizational and ideological forms. The public articulation and exploration of *racial dualism* would itself be a major advance. To be sure, it is inevitably painful to acknowledge the incompleteness, the fissuring, involved in racial identity, to own up to the existence of what Du Bois famously called "two souls, two thoughts, two unreconciled strivings; two warring ideals in one dark body" (1989 [1903]: 5). But for Afro-Brazilians to be able to mobilize *both* in respect to the singularities of racially framed experiences *and* simultaneously around the commonalities of inequality and deprivation experienced as citizens of Brazil, a deeper recognition of the depth of racial ambivalence and the conflicted nature of Brazilian racial identities would be essential.

To be sure, such a mobilization could not occur without a serious war of position, to use the Gramscian phrase, without the mounting of a significant cultural and political challenge aimed at the current terms of debate and organization. Such a challenge would have to be directed at transcending previous forms of racial struggle, such as pan-Africanism or *quilombismo* and orthodox Marxism. Whatever historical merits those political and ideological currents may have had in the past, today they beg the key questions of ambivalence and instability in racial identity.

As an end result of such a struggle we might imagine a Brazilian racial politics that recognized the racial ambivalence imposed—perhaps permanently—not only upon Afro-Brazilians but upon all Brazilians. Such a politics, such an awareness, would constitute a singular contribution to the effort to understand and transcend racism throughout the world. It would constitute a uniquely Brazilian interpretation of "the fact of blackness."

Chapter 11

Democracy Reenvisioned, Difference Transformed: Comparing Contemporary Racial Politics in the United States and Brazil

For a long time, the touchstone of all comparative studies of race in the United States and Brazil was the *contrast* between the two countries. In the United States, so the argument went, a rigid color line divided white and black, and "hypodescent" or the "one-drop rule" made all gradations of racial difference insignificant. In Brazil, by contrast, the gradations were of immense importance, since they were organized along a "racial continuum" (Harris 1964; see also F. J. Davis 1991). In the United States, race was a matter of state policy, of politics. The state established and policed the color line, through slave codes and slave patrols under slavery, segregation in the pre-civil rights period, and equal opportunity and affirmative action policies in the post-civil rights era. In Brazil, by contrast, the state and political system have been extremely reluctant—at least in the century since abolition—either to enforce or to suppress racial boundaries; far more prevalent has been the blanket denial that racism exists in Brazil, and the assertion that it is in fact racist to denounce racism.[1]

As a consequence of these contrasts (so the argument has traditionally run), racial antagonisms have been polarized and politicized in the United States, and diffused and depoliticized in Brazil. At a certain point, before the emergence and consolidation of the U.S. black movement in the late 1950s and early 1960s, the contrast-based comparison seemed to extol the virtues of the Brazilian model. In contrast to what was essentially a *herren-volk* democracy in the United States, and in sharp distinction to the U.S. hyperconsciousness of racial difference in every dimension of sociopolitical and cultural life, Brazil seemed a lot more relaxed and accepting of race. Miscegenation was not a big deal there, it seemed, and overt racial conflict hardly existed.

Later, however, after serious confrontations had taken place in the United States over racial issues, and after extensive though essentially moderate reforms had been initiated, the contrast-based argument began to turn against Brazil (Skidmore 1985). Suddenly, Brazilian racial dynamics seemed ossified and anachronistic, plagued by something like a false consciousness and subject to manipulation by elites. Helped along by the publication of the UNESCO studies, which demonstrated what such writers as Azevedo and Fernandes labeled "the myth of racial democracy" in Brazil, the question of the absence of a robust black movement was raised with ever greater intensity (T. Azevedo 1966; Fernandes 1978; Bastide and Fernandes 1959). The contrast between the United States and Brazil now appeared as one of progress (however uneven and conflictual) versus stasis (however smooth and cordial). And although this synoptic account does not address the many subtle dimensions through which race is organized in the two countries, in general terms it describes where matters rest even today.

But matters *don't* rest, especially racial matters. Race is constantly being transformed and recast as political, cultural, and indeed global developments affect our sense of who we are and shape the demands we place upon social institutions. Today race takes new forms in both countries as a result of new conflicts and new perceptions—about racial identity, about racial politics, and about the very meaning of race in everyday life. As a result, a new comparative examination may be in order.

Sociological and historical comparison of the two countries' racial dynamics has long been recognized as useful because of their similar development as settler states and slavocracies in the Americas, their subsequent abolition of slavery, and their acceptance of large waves of European (and Asian) immigration. While these parallels obviously have their limits, they have been sufficient to inspire a host of scholarly investigations. New developments in both countries, I want to suggest, invite a renewed comparative analysis of U.S. and Brazilian racial politics.

What could we learn from such a reexamination? Simply as an effort to describe developing racial trends and to communicate these views between the countries involved, I believe, such work is useful. But beyond that, the comparative analysis of race responds to a growing awareness of race as a global phenomenon whose importance, far from diminishing in the postindustrial, post-cold war, post-Marxist, and incipient postapartheid world, is in fact increasing. Finally, at the most concrete level, as conditions change, they must be reexamined and theory must be developed or revised as appropriate. And racial conditions are changing dramatically in both the United States and Brazil.

In this essay I examine these shifts from two related but distinct perspectives. I begin with transformations in the political systems of the two countries that relate to race. This discussion focuses on a term that is highly charged (especially in Brazil): *racial democracy*.

Brazilian democracy overall remains fragile, and Brazil's "racial democracy" was, of course, a myth that played the authoritarian role of denying racial difference and suppressing racial mobilization. Yet, beginning in the *abertura* and continuing in the renewed democratic Brazil of today, blacks have been able to experiment with modes of racial organization and protest that surpass anything achieved since the 1930s. I do not think it is possible yet to speak of a general politicization of race in Brazil. But today the increasing level of political awareness—itself a function of democratization, as well as of economic crisis and the impeachment of Collor—also has a stronger racial component than before. In such a context there is a tendency, gradual to be sure but hopefully permanent, to turn the myth of racial democracy into a reality of racial politics and opposition

The United States, by contrast, has been for most of its history a *herrenvolk* democracy in which basic political rights extended only to white men, and in some respects it remains so today. Yet U.S. society has been significantly transformed as a result of the civil rights reforms achieved a quarter century ago. Here I analyze the multiple consequences of these reforms in terms of racial mobility and stratification, fragmentation of racially defined communities, and, finally, problematization of racial identities themselves.

The second focal point of this essay is the complexity and permanence of *racial difference* in each country. In the United States, race is becoming more complicated and nuanced, largely as a result of the struggles of the recent past, so that the color line and the traditionally bipolar, black-white foundation of racial politics and identity is eroding. In Brazil, race is becoming more politicized, so that the color continuum and the techniques available to elites to deny and diffuse racial difference, and to disrupt and suppress racially based politics, are breaking down. Yet because this politicization has thus far been expressed through collective action only to a limited extent, its chief consequence has been to increase the sense of dualism experienced by Brazilian blacks. These developments have crucial consequences for the politics of racial identity in each country. In the United States the "double consciousness" once posited by Du Bois is becoming much more variable in response to shifting demographic, political,

and class-based factors. In Brazil, something like a black double consciousness is developing now, as the realities of racism are increasingly exposed
but not yet challenged in a fundamental and organized way. The result is a
situation that in some respects resembles the pre-civil rights movement
United States in which the ideological work required to process and survive racism is done to a large extent intrapsychically by blacks.

In a concluding note I offer some speculative remarks on the comparison of racial politics in the United States and Brazil and on the general relationship between democracy and racial difference.

Racial Democracy Reenvisioned

Comparative analysis of recent racial politics in the United States and Brazil
suggests the centrality of a "transition to democracy" in both cases. This is
perhaps a controversial assertion. There were certainly substantial differences between the *herrenvolk* democracy of the United States, which was
based on a formalized and legally constituted racial caste system with a
nearly rigid color line, and the "racial democracy" of Brazil, which was
based on a combination of factors:

> (a) the assumption, mainly by white elites, that . . . racism does not
> exist in Brazil or at least not on the level of countries such as
> South Africa and the United States; b) the continuing reproduction
> and dissemination of stereotypes denigrating blacks and valorizing
> whites which results in low, distorted self-images and an aversion
> to collective action among the former; and c) coercive sanctions
> and the pre-emption of dissent imposed by whites upon blacks
> who question or threaten the fundamentally asymmetrical patterns
> of racial interaction. (Hanchard, forthcoming; see also T. Azevedo
> 1975)

But there were significant similarities as well. Both systems—to begin
with the obvious—were considered to be democracies, a fact that can only
inspire either irony or dread. In both systems it was whites who advocated
the merits of the particular brand of "racial democracy" that operated in
each country. The effect of each system was to suppress (or even better,
avert) any demand for the extension of full rights to blacks. Thus, for a long
period after abolition, inequalities and even the fundamental absence of
citizenship rights, rights to equality before the law and in access to state
institutions, and rights to participate equally with whites, all went unrecognized in both countries.[2] Finally, the particular racist practices employed
in both systems bore more than a casual resemblance to one another, for
example, in terms of the content of stereotypes.

The similarities between the two systems should not be exaggerated. Their chief difference — the presence of explicit and legally sanctioned racial difference in the postabolition United States, and its relative absence in postabolition Brazil — was of course extremely important. This disparity had a centuries-long gestation in the singular racial formation process that each country underwent. The contrast was further heightened by distinctive paths to abolition, which came in the United States as an aftermath (and afterthought) of a disruptive and bloody civil war, and in Brazil as a much-belated recognition by the state that as many as 95 percent of Afro-Brazilians had already obtained their own emancipation. Nor should persistent racial violence in the United States — and its relative absence (until recently)[3] in Brazil — be ignored.

Overall, the comparison of U.S. *herrenvolk* democracy and Brazilian "racial democracy" is justified not because the two countries experienced overarching similarities in their developing racial politics, but rather because in both countries the claim that the system was democratic served to deny racially defined groups their democratic rights. The low status ascribed to these groups, their availability for exploitation and abuse, and their sociocultural marginalization were thus assured. It is the deeply ideological — or more properly, hegemonic — character of these two racial regimes that ultimately justifies comparing them.

There can be little question that the Brazilian myth of racial democracy retained a greater grip on its black subjects (though by no means as great a grip as it did on white Brazilians) than white supremacist ideology did on U.S. blacks. The informality alone of the Brazilian system — in contrast with segregation in the United States — went a long way to mask its character. Indeed, it was precisely the formality of the U.S. racial order, its politicization and enforcement by the state, that provided the black movement with a suitable target for mobilization. But it should also be noted that even this contrast is not an absolute one. The Brazilian state *did* intervene in racial politics, though rarely — witness Vargas's suppression of the Frente Negra Brasileira in the 1930s.[4] And the U.S. civil rights movement was to discover to its chagrin that the informal elements of white supremacy are a good deal more difficult to dismantle than the laws that enforce it.

The Brazilian transition to democracy was shaped by the prolonged *abertura* of 1974-85 (Mitchell 1985). During the preceding six-year period, the dictatorship's most brutal and repressive years, the military adopted the racial democracy myth *tout court*, denouncing any antiracism activity as a species of leftist subversion. But from the mid-1970s onward, a general upsurge of democratic aspirations took place, nurtured in various sectors such as the church, the unions, feminism, and the neighborhood movement. Blacks participated in all these activities, but *qua* blacks launched the most significant racial organization of the period, the Movimento Negro Unificado (MNU), in 1978. The appearance of the MNU signaled the greatest upsurge in black political activity since the 1930s (Hanchard, forthcoming: 221-40; M. E. Nascimento 1989; Gonzalez 1985). Not only did the MNU explicitly attempt to fight racial discrimination, but alongside it and in its wake there appeared a wide variety of black political organizations, caucuses, study groups, and journals. Black cultural groups proliferated, including the *afoxes* and *blocos afros* (especially in the northeast).[5] Many of these had a specific political orientation to community organization and racial consciousness raising. Important black feminist tendencies also gestated within the MNU, giving rise to black women's organizing projects and strategies that continue in the present (Carneiro and Santos 1985; Mills 1992: 15).

As the *abertura* gave way to greater civilian rule and finally to a full-fledged democracy (though not one without warts), black movement organizations and activities proliferated. The 1982 elections saw the participation of numerous black candidates, though their performance was generally poor (Valente 1986). By 1992 the leading Afro-Brazilian elected official, PT (Workers Party) federal deputy Benedita da Silva, was able to mount (and nearly win) a campaign for the mayoralty of Rio de Janeiro. Mainstream cultural and political institutions began to address racial issues more directly: for example, racial themes appeared in party platforms, religious services (Andrews 1991: 202-4), and, with increasing frequency, in the mass media. Government agencies began to address issues of racism with greater openness, and the Constituent Assembly of 1987 debated the merits of a new constitutional prohibition on racial discrimination, though it ultimately adopted only a minimal provision. Perhaps most revealing, the centenary of the *Lei Aurea*, the final decree of abolition, was celebrated in 1988 with a significant debate on the continuities of racism in Brazil. Mainstream media demonstrated in numerous articles the persistence of racial discrimination; there were numerous obituaries for the myth of racial democracy. Black organizations—by now plentiful—denounced the celebration as a farce and stated their intention to commemorate not May 13, the date of the 1888 decree of Princess Isabel, but November 20, the date of the fall of the *quilombo* of Palmares in 1695 (Maggie 1989). The year saw numerous actions of opposition and protest, including the suppression by the military of a black march in Rio (Hanchard, forthcoming: 265-85). In the last few years, black campaigns have continued, for example in respect to the census, the murders of street children, and abusive sterilization practices.[6]

Something has definitely changed in Brazil—the Afro-Brazilian movement is now an established presence. The movement still has significant limitations: it is small and lacks a substantial base among the millions of Afro-Brazilians for whom daily survival is the only issue. There is no established national black organization; the MNU, though it continues to exist, has not been able to overcome various problems, chiefly a range of factionalisms. But the movement overall exhibits a certain robustness that argues against any claim of transience and places even its faults in a new light.

Brazilian racial politics — by the mere fact of their existence — now resemble their counterparts in the United States more than ever before. The appearance of the black movement in the 1970s could not have the same ruptural impact on the Brazilian political scene that the U.S. civil rights movement had; it was marked by its birth in an atmosphere of dictatorship and repression, and also by the greater effectivity of the racial democracy myth. Still, today it is possible to say that a transition to racial politics is under way. It will be lengthy and undoubtedly not as confrontational as in the United States, but it will take place.

In the United States, the logjam of white supremacist racial politics — which had been eroding steadily under legal pressure since the 1930s and political pressure since the 1950s — finally broke in the mid-1960s. In the United States in the 1960s, a massive movement succeeded in overthrowing the system of *herrenvolk* democracy and instituting moderate but nevertheless far-reaching racial reforms. Among the consequences were significant social mobility for some, though by no means all, members of racially defined minority groups; reorganization of the political system to accommodate minority voters, interests, and officials; increased politicization of race throughout U.S. society; emergence of a range of related social movements, such as "second wave" feminism, that drew inspiration from the black freedom struggle; and the eventual resurgence, in suitably modified form, of racial reaction. This upheaval had the overall effect of seriously damaging but by no means destroying white supremacy, and of extending the possibility of democracy to racial minority (and other formerly disenfranchised) constituencies, without fully consolidating those gains (Omi and Winant 1986).

As a consequence, the United States today is experiencing a totally unprecedented racial situation in which there is large-scale uncertainty about the meaning of race and the proper orientation of state racial policies. On the one hand, race continues to structure everyday life, social practices of all types, and the personal — indeed even the unconscious — dimensions of everyone's identity. On the other hand, the susceptibility of race to further state intervention or political action — beyond that deriving from the moderate egalitarianism of the civil rights movement — is denied, not only on the racial right, but also among many on the left and in various nationalist currents. Prominent among such arguments is an assertion that would be familiar in Brazil: that today, the issue confronting racially defined minorities is less centrally one of racism per se, and more crucially one of class.[7] And prominent too is the idea, also quasi-Brazilian, that racial identity is becoming more flexible (Omi and Winant 1991). It is to the issue of the politics of racial identity that I now turn.

Racial Difference Transformed

In both Brazil and the United States, contemporary racial politics have changed dramatically over the past few decades. The current racial situations in these two countries themselves may be understood in terms of "transition to democracy": in both countries, as a result of substantial movement activity, far more political freedom exists for racially defined minorities than in the past. Yet in neither country has the racial dimension of stratification and social inequality been seriously transformed. Rather, the more overt manifestations of racism have receded, as white supremacy in the United States and the blanket denial of racism in Brazil have been weakened, *without any fundamental reorganization of the racialized social structures of the two societies.*[8]

As reform has undermined the more overtly racist features of state institutions and discredited the formerly established ideologies of white supremacy and racial democracy, the political significance of the issue of racial *identity* has increased in importance. In the United States and Brazil, however, the new racial politics of identity are taking very different forms. In the United States, racial identity is being transformed from dualistic to multipolar in the case of minorities, and is becoming more visible and uncertain (or dualistic, if you prefer) in the case of whites. In Brazil, black identities are becoming more dualistic (as opposed to continuous), while white identities remain largely unitary and unreflexive.

In the United States, the characteristic that formerly defined racial identity most centrally, the color line, has been deeply eroded. Yet this process has not taken place evenly or openly; rather, a conservative racial ideology whose focus is on the equality of individuals, the invidiousness of racial distinctions, and the equivalence of race and ethnicity has become hegemonic. The official denial of the significance of race combines with constant, daily, practical reminders that race is as crucial a factor as ever in shaping life chances and experiences. As a result, both individuals and groups suffer from confusion and anxiety about the impact and significance of race in their lives. This situation bears some resemblance to that of Brazil.

In *The Souls of Black Folk* (1989 [1903]), W. E. B. Du Bois argued that a "veil" divided the black psyche into "two warring souls." The veil had many manifestations, but at its core it was a line drawn within black people. It was a survival mechanism that permitted a person to see her/himself not only from within, as a black person with a particular identity, but also allowed for an externalized self-recognition: a person could learn, out of necessity, to see her/himself as the white does. The veil thus served, social psychologically, for protection against racism, but also operated dialectically to limit and stifle the very identity, the very black self, that it preserved.[9]

This "double consciousness," I suggest, was a logical analysis of the dynamics of racial identity when it was written, and for a good while thereafter. But today it requires, if not rejection, at least updating. At the turn of the century, and indeed in important ways until the mid-twentieth century, the rule of the color line was all but absolute in the United States. Segregation was the norm in the residential, educational, social, cultural, military, and political mainstreams. Only in very limited social, economic, and political circles was a modicum of race mixing practiced.[10] If this remained largely true on the eve of World War II, it was just about absolutely true when Du Bois first set it down in 1903.

But the postwar political transformations wrought by the civil rights movement dramatically altered racial identity, in ways that we are still discovering a quarter century later. The civil rights movement wrenched from the state a recognition of the realities of discrimination and forced the development of limited but real policies, such as affirmative action and minority set-asides, that were designed to counter it. It also succeeded in overcoming discriminatory immigration law and in democratizing voting rights. Such changes created incentives for the consolidation of racial identities among "other" groups, that is, groups that were neither black nor white, groups that had substantial experience of racial discrimination, but that had previously been divided by ethnic, regional, or political differences and antagonisms. Vastly aided not only by the transformation of the U.S. racial landscape wrought by the civil rights reforms, but also by the realities of "racial lumping"—since many North Americans cannot distinguish between a Korean American and a Chinese American, or between Chicanos and Ecuadorans, for that matter—this *panethnicizing* or racializing experience generated the racial categories "Latino" (or "Hispanic") and "Asian American" (Espiritu 1992; Oboler, forthcoming). It also consolidated the category "Native American" (Cornell 1988). The long-term result of this process was the transformation of the U.S. racial order from its earlier black-white bipolarity to a more multipolar system.

The shift to racial multipolarity also spelled changes in racial identity. For black people, it meant a new series of antagonisms with burgeoning Latino and Asian American groups. These "other" minorities competed for the resources of a welfare state that was under severe attack from the right. They also occupied "middleman" economic niches in the black community, thus giving rise to a host of familiar antagonisms and conflicts.

Furthermore, stratification *within* the black community was also stimulated in the aftermath of the 1960s, as the black middle class discovered new opportunities and achieved greater mobility, abandoning the ghettos for the suburbs, entering the professional and corporate worlds, and so on. Meanwhile, the black working class was severely pressured by deindustrialization, and the poor were abandoned by the welfare state. The result was increasing division among blacks, and a greater tendency in the society at large to correlate race with class. Although the color line was not superseded, its salience diminished for blacks; the result was a situation that in limited but real respects resembled the Brazilian one in which "o dinheiro embranquece."[11]

Finally, the shifts brought on by the civil rights movement and the reforms it engendered also had an impact on white racial identity, which was rendered much more problematic than in the days of segregation. Whites had to change their attitudes toward minorities, which meant (since all identity implies difference) that they had to change their attitudes toward themselves. A desirable feature of this shift was the beginning—and this was obviously just a beginning—of racial dualism in whites: in other words, whites had to begin looking at themselves from the standpoint of *how they were being perceived by nonwhites*. On the negative side, whites were threatened by minority gains. They sensed a loss (actual or potential, real or imagined) of their majority status, their dominant position. They suddenly noted an *identity deficit*: formerly their whiteness, since it constituted the norm, was invisible, transparent, but now, in a more highly racially conscious atmosphere, they felt more visible, and indeed threatened (Alba 1990; Waters 1990). The result was a rearticulation of the egalitarianism embodied in the civil rights agenda in a far more conservative and individualistic direction, a kind of antiracist racism. This view, which denies the significance of race (espousing a "color-blind" approach), also claims that affirmative action and similar programs employ racism "in reverse." Such a perspective would certainly be recognizable in Brazil, where many whites claim that to focus attention on race or racism is itself racist.

In Brazil, the development of a black movement since the 1970s, while achieving tremendous successes in challenging the myth of racial democracy, has not resulted in more than very limited reforms in the institutional structure of Brazilian racism. These should not be dismissed; the creation of various state entities specifically charged with addressing discrimination and other Afro-Brazilian issues (Andrews 1991: 205-6), the restoration to the 1990-91 census of questions regarding race, the clear-cut (though brief) recognition of racism in the new constitution, and the various acknowledgments made by high state officials in recent years (and particularly during the 1988 centennial of abolition) of the existence and severity of racism in Brazil were all important departures from the traditional denial of racism that has characterized the Brazilian state in the past.

Yet all these actions and measures do not add up to much more than a symbolic shift. The major change in Brazilian racial dynamics has been the emergence of a viable movement, one that recognizes the political dimensions of race and the necessity of naming and defending Afro-Brazilian interests as such. This movement has focused its attention on campaigns against discrimination, against the murder of street children, and on community organization in poor areas. Undoubtedly the majority of the many black organizations founded since the 1970s are primarily cultural groups, which stress such issues as consciousness raising, linkages with Africa, the role of Afro-Brazilians in Brazilian history, and the commemoration of the Palmares *quilombo*. And there remain significant debates, well analyzed by Hanchard, between the primarily "Africanist" orientation of culturally based Afro-Brazilian groups and the primarily "Americanist" orientation of more explicitly political groups (Hanchard, forthcoming). In my view, given the early stage of the modern black movement, the ideological conflicts that have occurred between "culturalists" and "politicals," and between "Africanists" and "Americanists," have been understandable but premature. There is as yet no necessary incompatibility between such tendencies.

The combination of limited reforms with rising black consciousness and organization spurred by democratization suggests that blacks in Brazil will experience an increasingly contradictory situation. Indeed, as the number of racially conscious Afro-Brazilians increases, the Brazilian scene may in some respects come to resemble racial politics in the United States before the upsurge of the modern civil rights movement. In such circumstances individuals and personal relationships must undertake much of the ideological work needed to manage the stresses and contradictions of a pervasive "practical" racism that social institutions by and large refuse to address. Meanwhile, viable black organizations will have to act as what Aldon Morris (1984) calls "movement halfway houses," preserving and slowly building the movement.

Such are the conditions, mutatis mutandis, that Du Bois sought to address in his discussion of double consciousness or racial dualism. As race becomes more politicized in Brazil, as the state recognizes officially that

Brazil is not and never has been a racial democracy but neglects any effort to overcome the inequalities that exist, as a black movement builds slowly and painfully to challenge this situation under conditions of extreme poverty, Afro-Brazilians can be expected to experience greater stress than ever before. Their awareness of themselves as both black *and* Brazilian, both discriminated against and expected to deny the significance of race, can only increase.

As a final note: there is little evidence that white racial attitudes are changing significantly in Brazil. I am not aware of any recent survey research on racial attitudes, black or white, but anecdotally it is possible to affirm that, far more than blacks, whites continue to uphold the familiar positions: "No Brasil não da racismo. O negro conhece o seu lugar."[12] This suggests that a crucial indicator of the next turning point in Brazilian racial politics—one that appears quite distant, unfortunately, today—will have been reached when white Brazilians begin to experience an "identity deficit," a sense of threat, that a powerful movement for racial justice tends to invoke, especially when it has gained some foothold within the state. Of course, before such a moment is reached, one would expect substantial numbers of whites to join the movement for racial equality in Brazil.

Conclusion

The battle for racial justice is fought not only in the open political arena of the state and social movements, not only in the struggle for adequate cultural representations, significations, and consciousness of difference; it is also fought on the interior terrain of the individual—her/his intrapsychic world and immediate relationships. As Norbert Lechner (1988) has argued, democracy has not only an outside but also an inside, whose principal terrain is the construction of subjectivity. To be sure, these two "spaces" of democracy are deeply intertwined, so that developments in one area necessarily create changes in the other.

In both the United States and Brazil, the relationship between racial subjectivity—what I have called here the politics of racial identity—and the state has undergone enormous changes in the past few decades. These shifts have been more far reaching in the United States, but this is no more than the whole comparative literature on racial politics in the two countries would have led us to predict.

The surprising feature of this comparison, I think, is how much has changed in Brazil. I make this assertion in the full awareness that in terms of general racial inequality, as well as in terms of the stratification of education, employment, health and mortality, and so forth, little has improved. In fact, the general economic crisis of the country, as always enacted most intensively in the lives of its poorest citizens, has almost certainly increased levels of inequality by almost any measure. What, then, has changed?

The existence of a modern Afro-Brazilian movement, in my view, is the big change. This movement appears permanent, although such an assertion is inevitably speculative; it also appears to be comprehensively linked to the consolidation and expansion of democracy.

In both the United States and Brazil, the extension of democracy to address racial issues has generated a vast increase in racialized subjectivity. This ran counter to what most observers—both activists and pundits, politicians and academics—expected to happen. Most saw racism, whether it was white supremacy in the United States or the myth of racial democracy in Brazil, as anachronistic, something that would disappear when basic rights were extended and fundamental inequalities addressed. Of course, that has not happened, and not only because reform programs have been limited (as in the United States) or negligible (as in Brazil). It has not happened because racial difference, racialized subjectivity, is a permanent feature of both societies, and of much of the world.

The liberation of racial identity is as much a part of the struggle against racism as the elimination of racial discrimination and inequality. That liberation will involve a reenvisioning of racial politics and a transformation of racial difference. It will render democracy itself much more radically pluralistic, and will make identity much more a matter of choice than of ascription. As the struggles to achieve these objectives unfold, we shall gradually recognize that the racialization of democracy is as important as the democratization of race.

Notes

1. Introduction

1. Depending, of course, on whom one considers to be black, an issue that unsurprisingly transcends demography and involves cultural reference points (see Wood and Carvalho 1988). To North American eyes, Brazil looks roughly half black, but of course Brazilian eyes see differently.

2. The Theoretical Status of the Concept of Race

1. Page references will be given in the text.

2. Minor objections would have to do with Fields's functionalist view of ideology, and her claim that the race concept only "came into existence" (101) when it was needed by whites in North American colonies beginning in the late seventeenth century. The concept of race, of course, has a longer history than that.

3. Fields's admirer David Roediger also criticizes her on this point: "At times she nicely balances the ideological creation of racial attitudes with their manifest and ongoing importance and their (albeit ideological) *reality*. . . . But elsewhere, race disappears into the 'reality' of class" (Roediger 1991, 7-8; emphasis original).

4. Another important thinker who has at least flirted with the idea of race as illusion is Kwame Anthony Appiah. See Appiah 1986, 1990.

5. This concept is developed in Harris 1964.

6. "The question of identification is never the affirmation of a pregiven identity, never a self-fulfilling prophecy—it is always the production of an image of identity and the transformation of the subject in assuming that image" (Homi K. Bhabha, "Interrogating Identity," p. 188).

7. The work of Paul Gilroy (1991) on the significance of black music in Afro-diasporic communities is particularly revealing on this point.

8. There is a vast literature by now on these matters. The founding statement is undoubtedly Edward Said's *Orientalism* (1978); also useful is Bhabha 1990a.

9. I borrow this phrase not from George Lucas but from the book of that title edited at the Centre for Contemporary Cultural Studies, 1982.

171

10. David Lopez and Yen Espiritu define panethnicity as "the development of bridging organizations and solidarities among subgroups of ethnic collectivities that are often seen as homogeneous by outsiders." Such a development, they claim, is a crucial feature of ethnic change—"supplanting both assimilation and ethnic particularism as the direction of change for racial/ethnic minorities." While panethnic formation is facilitated by an ensemble of cultural factors (e.g., common language and religion) and structural factors (e.g., class, generation, and geographical concentration), Lopez and Espiritu conclude that a specific concept of race is fundamental to the construction of panethnicity (Lopez and Espiritu 1990: 198).

11. Similar points are made in Mudimbe 1988, Rabinow 1986, and Harding 1987.

12. For example, the magisterial work of Fernand Braudel 1981.

3. Where Culture Meets Structure: Race in the 1990s

1. For reports on some recent developments in rock, rap, and race, see Dave Marsh et al. 1990; on rap, see the magazine the *Source*.

2. Studies on the general subject of postcoloniality are replete with examples and analyses of this complex. For some representative analyses see Gates, ed., *"Race," Writing, and Difference*, 1986.

3. This approach obviously involves an interpretation of Gramsci that cannot be spelled out within the limits of the present essay. The Gramsci literature is vast and rewarding for students of race. I rely here upon Gramsci 1971, Hall 1986, and Mouffe and Laclau 1985. I have also found useful material in Guha and Spivak 1988.

4. Nor for nonwhites. As I have argued, even cultural forms deriving from the experiences of particular racially defined minorities (such as rap, hip-hop, or, for that matter, *norteña*) have "crossed over." A related issue is whether any group may legitimately retain its exclusive racial character. Various minority organizations on university campuses—the African-American student unions, the Asian and Pacific Islanders associations, the MECHA (Movimiento Estudiantíl Chicano de Aztlán, or Chicano Student Movement of Aztlán) groups—have been attacked as exclusionary. Here I think the resemblance is more superficial than real between past segregation and white exclusivism on the one hand and present racial minority efforts to construct associations solely for members of their own group on the other. Exclusivism acquires force when it is directed by a dominant majority against a subordinated minority. Hence neoconservative criticisms leveled at such groups (or at events scheduled "for women only," or gay dances, for that matter), seem either misconceived or disingenuous.

5. In 1986, blacks were three times as likely to be poor as whites; 44 percent of black children lived in poverty in 1985, as compared to 16 percent of white children. Latinos were roughly twice as likely to be poor as whites, though this group is far more stratified than are blacks. Similar variations exist for Asians. Among Native Americans, poverty rates approach or exceed those of blacks.

4. Dictatorship, Democracy, and Difference: The Historical Construction of Racial Identity

1. "*Herrenvolk* democracy" is a phrase coined, as far as I know, by Pierre van den Berghe (1967), in regard to apartheid. Roediger prefers the term "*herrenvolk* republicanism," since this brings in the notion of small (white) producers and artisans fighting for their rights—in this case against encroaching blacks.

2. I rely throughout this section on Roediger 1991 and Saxton 1990.

3. Racial slavery of course existed in Texas, but did not have the extensive roots it had established elsewhere in the South.

4. This paragraph draws heavily on Montejano 1987: 30-41.

5. Saxton 1971 remains the best single study of anti-Asian politics in the United States; Asian exclusion is treated in depth in Takaki 1990.

6. In respect to locale, the case of Hawaii, where Asian immigrants came to constitute a substantial majority of inhabitants, is revealing. Hawaii was distinct from the West Coast, where Asians were a significant presence but still a minority, and from other regions of the country, where their numbers were relatively small. The regional dynamics of racialization until relatively recently affected not only Asians but also blacks in the South and Mexicans in the Southwest.

7. Omi and Winant 1986: 74. A certain adaptation of Gramsci's conception of "war of maneuver," and of the related "war of position," is required before these terms can be applied to U.S. conditions. Gramsci's frame of reference is mainly that of the bourgeois revolution in Europe, and occasionally that of the Russian revolution. See, for example, Gramsci 1971: 238-39.

8. I provide this litany in lieu of a real history, for which there is no room here. The historical literature on the early civil rights movement is voluminous. A few good accounts are V. Harding 1981, Meier and Rudwick 1973, and Franklin 1969.

9. For example, the idea that the personal is political, though properly associated with the women's movement, has its origins in the black movement. As Carson (1981) shows, women civil rights workers had to fight to participate in decision making and leadership. Furthermore, the movement's efforts to challenge personal racism led to an overall increased level of awareness about oppressive attitudes and behaviors. This then translated into women's liberation and planted the seeds for the feminist reawakening of the late 1960s. See also Evans 1980.

10. I am thinking here of the upsurge, beginning in the early 1970s, of neoconservatism among racially defined minorities. This fascinating subject is beyond the present essay's scope. For a good treatment, see Boston 1988.

11. "When we were in Africa we were called Africans or blacks; when we were in Africa we were free. When we were captured and stolen and brought to the United States, we became Negroes" (Carmichael 1971: 149-50).

12. Black psychiatrist Alvin Poussaint has pointed out that "there's a lot of pressure on the black middle class to stay black. . . . It's kind of a contradiction. Your kids are living in an integrated community, and you want them to feel part of the community, participating equally in it. Then you feel very ambivalent about it psychologically, when they do" (quoted in Garreau 1987; see also Feagin 1991, Landry 1987, and Dent 1992).

13. Martin Kilson notes the increasing division of the black working class into "coping" and "noncoping" strata. See Kilson 1989; Kilson and Cottingham 1991.

14. On the "demise of Jim Crow" in Texas, see Montejano (1987: 262-87). Muñoz (1989: 86) argues that it was the cultural nationalist currents of black power that most attracted young Chicanos.

15. The Vincent Chin case was crucial in galvanizing Asian-Americans around the issue of anti-Asian violence. Chin, a twenty-seven-year-old Chinese American, was murdered in Detroit by several auto workers after getting into an altercation at a bar. The attackers apparently mistook him for Japanese (Espiritu 1992: 141-55). Also crucial in this regard is black antagonism to "middleman minorities," often Korean Americans, who operate small stores in ghetto neighborhoods. The spring 1992 riot in Los Angeles was the most extreme example of this, but cases of black-Korean tensions have flared from coast to coast.

16. This account draws heavily on Alba 1990 and Waters 1990.

17. This Weberian term puts a positive spin on the matter; a recent negative reading that invokes the "white privilege" argument is Hacker 1992.

18. Waters 1990: 147-55. "Symbolic ethnicity" is a phrase coined by Herbert J. Gans (1979).

5. Contesting the Meaning of Race in the Post-Civil Rights Period

1. Indeed, the very meaning of political labels such as conservative, liberal, and radical has been transformed by ongoing debates about race, including those on affirmative action, social welfare policy, and immigration reform.

2. In a similar vein, Stephen Small (1991: 4) has elaborated what he calls the *racialization problematic* as "a paradigm within which different theories can be advanced for the description and explanation of the creation and maintenance of 'racialised' group boundaries in different socio-historical contexts."

3. Interestingly enough, one of the earliest applications of the "panethnic" framework applied the term to whites. See Erickson 1975.

4. Mounting evidence in the field of medicine, for example, suggests that race and ethnicity can and should be factors in the diagnosis and treatment of specific illnesses. Some medical researchers and practitioners, however, fear that such "race consciousness" could result in a return to racist, eugenic notions. See Leary 1990.

6. The Los Angeles "Race Riot" and Contemporary U.S. Politics

1. Bush did not hesitate to use racial "code words" in this and other comments on the riot. See Rosenbaum 1992: A14.

2. In other writings, Michael Omi and I have charted in some detail the vicissitudes of the racial formation process in the postwar and post-civil rights periods. See Omi and Winant forthcoming and 1986.

3. The voluminous neoconservative literature is firm on this point. Thomas Sowell, for example, has argued that one's "human capital" is to a large extent culturally determined. Therefore, the state cannot create a false equality that runs counter to the magnitude and persistence of cultural differences. Such attempts at social engineering are likely to produce negative and unintended results: "If social processes are transmitting real differences—in productivity, reliability, cleanliness, sobriety, peacefulness [!]—then attempts to impose politically a very different set of beliefs will necessarily backfire, for the truth remains the same, regardless of what is transmitted through social processes" (Sowell 1983: 252).

4. It should be noted that one of Clinton's chief advisers, Stanley B. Greenberg, is an important racial theorist. He is the author of an influential intraparty analysis that pointed to Democratic party racial politics as the key factor in the defection of suburban and white voters—the "Reagan Democrats"—in the 1980s (Greenberg 1985). He is also the author of a major comparative study of racial politics and global development (Greenberg 1980).

5. "My proposal for dealing with the racial issue in social welfare is to repeal every bit of legislation and reverse every court decision that in any way requires, recommends, or awards differential treatment according to race, and thereby put us back onto the track that we left in 1965. We may argue about the appropriate limits of government intervention in trying to enforce the ideal, but at least it should be possible to identify the ideal: Race is not a morally admissible reason for treating one person differently from another. Period." So says Charles Murray in his book *Losing Ground* (1984: 223).

6. These debates are too voluminous and complex to be treated adequately, or even referenced, here. Some worthwhile beginning points might be, for Native Americans, Cornell 1988; for Latinos/Hispanics, Rodriguez 1989; for Asian-Americans, Lopez and Espiritu 1990.

7. Light and Bonacich 1988 remains the best account of the development of Koreatown.

8. These comments rely on published accounts, whose inaccuracy (to judge by 1960s reference points) is likely to be high. Advance apologies for errors may thus be in order.

9. Based on material provided by the Central American Refugee Center (CARECEN), which has worked to defend this community for many years. They can be reached at 668 S. Bonnie Brae, Los Angeles, CA 90057.

10. Davis's generally marvelous book is conspicuously lacking when it comes to the Asian communities of Los Angeles.

11. "[L.A. District Attorney Ira] Reiner, whose tenure in office has been marked by a series of failures, had himself selected Terry L. White, a black prosecutor with an undistinguished record, to try the King case. . . . Reiner faces stiff competition in the June primary from two of his deputies. When he chose White, he seemed to have his eye on potential black voters; in any case, he had chosen him before a change of venue was granted, not anticipating that a black prosecutor would face a jury without any blacks" (Rutten 1992: 52).

12. Paul de Pasquale, one of the defense attorneys, put it this way during his closing argument: "This unpleasant incident [the beating] is what we have police for. The circumstances here were consistent with the job the man was hired to do. He was part of the line between society and chaos. . . . This is not some orgy of violence. This is careful police work" (quoted in Mydans 1992: A1).

13. In the wake of the riot and the attention directed toward the LAPD, many reports of systematic racism and brutality came to the surface. A recent lurid exposé is Rothmiller and Goldman 1992. Here an insider describes being trained in racial bigotry, misprision and subornation, harassment, and torture. An excellent analysis of the regime of the LAPD, and its links to state power at all levels of U.S. society, is provided by Mike Davis (1990: 216-317). Note too that Davis's book appeared before the Rodney King incident.

14. For this reason Ronald Reagan's attacks on "welfare queens" seemed especially vicious. Who else did Reagan (and Bush after him) think was going to care for low-income children? To assault the one group that — against all odds — was still attempting to nurture and protect the most vulnerable members of society, and to do this while rendering that job more difficult by slashing and burning what meager resources were yet available to these low-income and disproportionately minority women, seems an act so obscene and cruel that it makes ordinary child abuse look benign by comparison.

7. Hard Lessons: Recent Writing on Racial Politics

1. "What is looked upon as an American dream for white people has long been an American nightmare for black people" (Cone 1991: 89).

2. Elsewhere, I have argued that "racialization" is the most appropriate term for this pattern. See Omi and Winant 1986: 64 and forthcoming.

3. A point that is forcefully made in Oboler 1992.

4. Jack D. Forbes (1992) points out the many peculiarities of American (in the hemispheric sense) racial classification. The high degree of *mestizaje* among Latinos means that many millions of those who now think of themselves in this category could equally well be classified as Native Americans, if sociohistorical circumstances had made this an option. In earlier work (1988), Forbes documented the significant intermingling of Native Americans and African-Americans throughout the hemisphere. Espiritu (1992: 172) notes that Filipino Americans have at least some claim on the "Hispanic" designation, despite their stronger identification with the "Asian American" panethnic category. These are merely examples of what could be a truly endless and fascinating enumeration of the complexities of racial classification.

5. A good statement of this notion of identity, grounded in a critique of the political

project of the Enlightenment, may be found in Mouffe 1988, especially p. 44. Compare Mouffe's views with Max Horkheimer and Theodor W. Adorno's still extremely powerful, but more pessimistic, approach (1989 [1944]).

6. Espiritu offers a model analysis of many of these points, focusing especially on the 1982 Vincent Chin case and its impact on various Asian American communities. On the anti-Asian violence of the 1992 Los Angeles riots, see Omi and Winant 1993).

7. When we focus political discussion on the problem of oppression, the question of subject positions arises at once. This is because oppression today is not only a matter of unjust rule or tyranny by those who hold power, but also has an extended sense: it is a *structure* that operates ordinarily and normally, that is, without malevolent intent, to limit not only the rights and freedoms but also the subjectivity of particular groups. Thus oppression/subjection is an unbreakable linkage. I derive these points chiefly from Iris M. Young 1990, from which I draw extensively in the conclusion to this chapter.

8. Speaking after participating in an all-night demonstration against racism in Paris on December 14, 1992, Fode Sylla, president of the group SOS-Racisme, said, "The problem in France is not immigration. This is only the mirror of profound socio-economic problems which affect the whole of French society. To attack the extreme right we must fight in the first place against misery and the creation of marginal ghettos. . . . It is indispensable that we stop demonizing Germany here in France — which was the case during the referendum campaign on Maastricht in September — as though the ultra-rightist attacks in Rostock were the only expression of racism in Europe. This is a big lie. The insistence on this anti-German discourse serves only to conceal our own miseries in matters of racism" (Institute for Global Communications 1992).

9. On November 21, 1992, a massive demonstration against racism took place in Spain to protest the racially motivated murder of Lucrecia Perez, a Dominican immigrant. About 100,000 Dominicans live in the Madrid area alone.

10. See Levinas 1986. Robert M. Young also makes use of Levinas, though in my view he "Derridizes" Levinas's contribution unduly; see R. Young 1990: 13-16.

11. This argument is extensively developed in West 1990. Thanks also to Lucius Outlaw for making me aware of some of these points.

8. Racial Formation and Hegemony: Global and Local Developments

1. This approach obviously involves an interpretation of Gramsci that cannot be spelled out within the limits of the present essay. For some beginning reference points, see Gramsci 1971, Hall 1986, and Mouffe and Laclau 1985.

2. When southern slaveholders sought to maintain illiteracy among the slaves, to ban all news about slave insurrections, and particularly to withhold news of the Haitian revolution, they exemplified this form of rule.

3. "To say that 'race' is a biological fiction is not to deny that it has real material effects in the world; nor is it to suggest that 'race' should disappear from our critical vocabularies. Clearly it is no more adequate to hold that 'race' is itself merely an empty effect than it is to suggest that 'race' is solely a matter of skin color. What is called for is a closer look at the production of racial subjects, at what forces organize, administer, and produce racial identities. What is called for is an approach which intervenes in the essentialist/constructivist polemic that has hitherto imprisoned 'race' in a rigidified and falsifying logic" (Fuss 1989: 92).

4. As I have noted, even Marx frequently legitimated such processes as the inevitable and ultimately beneficial birth pangs of classlessness — by way of the ceaselessly revolutionary bourgeoisie.

5. The two types of primitive accumulation detailed in Marx's *Capital* — the conquest al-

ready mentioned and the destruction of the English peasantry known as "enclosure"—clearly are not parallel in terms of their destructiveness and brutality. For all the miseries brought upon the nascent English working class by the onset of capitalism, enclosure cannot be described as genocidal. Conquest cannot be understood in any other way.

6. In 1989, U.S. blacks were almost three times as likely to be poor as whites. The median income of black families was 56 percent that of white families; 44 percent of black children lived in poverty, as compared to 16 percent of white children (U.S. Bureau of the Census 1990). Latino median income is about two-thirds that of whites, and Latinos are roughly twice as likely to be poor as whites, though this group is far more stratified than are blacks (Bean and Tienda 1987). Similar variations exist among Asians (O'Hare and Felt 1991: 7). Among Native Americans, poverty rates approach or exceed those of blacks: median family income in 1980 was $13,678, as compared to $19,917 for whites; native peoples were 2.5 times more likely than whites to be living in poverty (U.S. Bureau of the Census 1989).

7. Other cases present a great variety of possible race-class combinations. The great colonial powers Britain and France, with racially homogeneous internal populations, developed strong class conflicts at home and "exterior" models —themselves quite different—of racial hierarchy. Brazil, whose population at abolition (1888) was still quite dark, adopted a "whitening" ideology and policy (unrestricted European immigration) in an effort to develop as a capitalist society.

8. I concentrate here on stratification within the black community, but solely for reasons of space. Stratification of various types has deeply affected all racially defined minority communities since the late 1960s, for example by dividing new immigrants from established residents, undocumented from documented workers, and those who could take advantage of affirmative action and similar programs from those who could not.

9. For an early usage, see Rainwater 1969. On processes of "social dislocation" in the ghetto, see Wilson 1991. The general discussion provided here on the evolution of the "underclass" debate draws on Katz 1989: 195-209.

10. The extent of such practices was revealed in the hearings on the nomination of Clarence Thomas to the Supreme Court in October 1991

9. Rethinking Race in Brazil

1. See, for example, Pierson 1967 [1942]; Tannenbaum 1947; Freyre 1959. For reasons of space this essay focuses on contemporary issues of race. I do not consider the origins or history of racial dynamics or ideas in Brazil. For good sources on these topics see Skidmore 1974; Viotti da Costa 1977, 1982, and 1985, especially pp. 234-46.

2. Thales de Azevedo, Roger Bastide, Florestan Fernandes, Marvin Harris, and Charles Wagley, among others, were associated with the UNESCO project. Wagley 1963 is a convenient collection of papers from the rural phase of this research. The work of Bastide and Fernandes is the chief product of its urban phase. The importance of these studies for Brazilian social science, and more indirectly for Brazilian racial dynamics themselves, cannot be overestimated.

3. Azevedo presents the process of transition as a shift from racially identified status or prestige groups to classes. Formerly, whites were identified as a superior status group and blacks, conversely, as an inferior group. Race served as an indicator of status, but the deeper, more "objective" category of class is a matter of economics, not of color or prestige. Thus race becomes less salient as class formation proceeds: "From this structure of two levels social classes are beginning to emerge, which may be identified from an economic point of view by property differences, income levels, consumption patterns, levels of education and rules of behavior, and even by their incipient self-consciousness. The system of classes is organized in

part by the older status groups and is still very much shaped by the old order. Its three elements are an upper class or *elite*, a middle class, and a lower class or *the poor*" (Azevedo 1966: 34, emphasis original). This view thus combines class reductionism (what is ultimately important about race is how it fits people into the economic system) with an implicit optimism about its transcendence in and by an emerging class system.

4. These arguments led Eugene Genovese to defend the admittedly conservative Gilberto Freyre (as well as Frank Tannenbaum and others) from the admittedly radical and "materialist" attack of Harris. Genovese perceived in Freyre a far more complex and "totalizing" view of the meaning of race in Brazil than he found in Harris (Genovese, 1971: 41-43).

5. Thus the impoverished northeast—the traditional locus of Brazilian poverty and underdevelopment, and the focus of Harris's and Azevedo's studies—is also disproportionately black, while the urbanized and industrialized southeast is disproportionately white.

6. Campanha Censo 90 was announced in July 1990 by a broad coalition of Afro-Brazilian organizations of various political and cultural tendencies, and continued through 1991 as the Brazilian census proceeded. Its slogan was "Não deixe a sua cor passar em branco: responda com bom c/senso" (Don't let your color be passed off as white: respond with good sense—punning on sense/census/consensus).

7. This analysis has strong parallels with Pierre van den Berghe's views on Brazil; van den Berghe argues that in the early post-*abolição* period racial dynamics were "paternalistic," but later (as capitalism developed), became "competitive." In other words, there was a shift from a nonantagonistic pattern of racial inequality toward a more conflictual one. See van den Berghe 1967; Bastide and van den Berghe 1957.

8. This is close to Fernandes's argument, although his understanding of racism as a "survival" antagonistic to full capitalist development limits his appreciation of the point (see Fernandes 1969).

9. The Frente was the most significant Afro-Brazilian organization of the 1920s and 1930s. It was repressed by Getúlio Vargas in 1937 after transforming itself into a political party. See Fernandes 1978, vol. 2: 10-115.

10. The Movimento Negro Unificado Contra Discriminação Racial (later simply Movimento Negro Unificado, or MNU) was the most significant movement of the 1970s. See Gonzalez 1985; M. E. do Nascimento 1989.

11. The new social movements also descended in part from the ideas popularized by the Brazilian educator and activist Paulo Freire. Indeed, these primordial political experiences were in themselves acts of reinterpretation, of rearticulation.

12. Such as the Palmares group, *terreiros* of Candomblé, *afoxes* and *blocos africanos*, etc. Cultural and religious groups are entirely central in black organizational efforts in Brazil, and in recent years have more frequently linked their traditional vocations with political themes. For example, *afoxes* are groups of religious orientation, based in Candomblé. They dance and sing in African languages, and paricipate in *Carnaval*. Formerly outlawed, they were legalized in the late 1970s.

13. As in the United States and many other countries, black women play a crucial role in many social movements in Brazil (Carneiro and Santos 1985). They have challenged both sexism in the black movement and racism in the women's movement. The topic of Afro-Brazilian women and feminism has generated much movement debate and several significant studies. The MNU included antisexist points in its statement of principles, for example (Gonzalez 1985). On other aspects of these issues see Oliveira, Porcaro, and Araujo 1987; see also Barroso 1982.

14. The MNU was, however, riven by regional and ideological divisions, and was unable to maintain its cohesion at a national level (M. E. do Nascimento 1989).

15. In a campaign sharply polarized by issues of racism, "Bené" narrowly lost her bid to

become mayor of Rio de Janeiro in 1992. She often combines her antiracist polemic with defense of women's rights. See da Silva 1986.

16. In the United States, black movement successes were met with sophisticated state strategies that I have analyzed elsewhere in terms of "absorption" and "insulation" (Omi and Winant 1986: 81). Predictably, in Brazil there are big debates about the extent of service versus the degree of co-optation offered by such organizations. The state tendency to establish a bureaucracy when it is confronted by opposition is very strong.

10. "The Fact of Blackness" in Brazil

1. "Money whitens," a well-known Brazilian expression.

2. I employ the concept of *racial dualism* following W. E. B. Du Bois's notion of the "veil" that, Du Bois argued, divided the black psyche into "two warring souls." The concept expresses an enforced splitting or doubling of consciousness or identity. The veil was a line drawn *within* the black psyche in response to racism. It was a survival mechanism, a defense mechanism, that permitted the subordinated or subaltern to see her/himself not only from within, as a black person with a particular identity, but also allowed for an externalized self-recognition: to see her/himself *as the white does*. But the veil also and most obviously embodied the pain and internalized anger engendered by racism. The veil is a constant theme in Du Bois's enormous oeuvre, but it is most famously and succinctly framed in *The Souls of Black Folk* (1989 [1903]).

3. There is by now a fairly extensive literature on the process by which those who denounce racism are themselves accused of practicing it. See van Dijk 1992.

4. Of course, class questions enter into these relationships, as Fanon would recognize immediately. His essay "The Fact of Blackness" highlights the educated, professionally trained black man's (and in 1952, his focus is largely upon men) slow realization that his blackness outweighs all other factors in assigning him a low status, not only by marking him as forever outside the social and cultural order of France, but also by linking him with other blacks, Arabs, etc., "other others," no matter what their class. But elsewhere, for example, in *The Wretched of the Earth* (1963), Fanon deals with the peasant, the worker, the casbah resident (i.e., the *favelado*) in terms that frame the racial order as a unity across class lines.

5. "To be black is to have to be something more." "The black is more primitive, perhaps. Primitive in the sense of immediate, first of all: emotion comes before reason. Maybe racist discourse had something right in saying that the black is more emotional." "My grandfather used to say that the dark person, and above all the black, did not try too hard. If you see confusion, you should know that it's the black who is causing it; if you see a black running, he's a thief. One must marry a white person to clean out the womb." "To be black is to have to prove something—it is to encounter a series of obstacles and to show that you can attain a higher level, a different culture."

6. As a director of the Tieté Boating Club in São Paulo told Reid Andrews, "If we were to accept a colored member and he entered the pool, within an hour one hundred members would quit the club" (Andrews 1991: 173).

11. Democracy Reenvisioned, Difference Transformed: Comparing Contemporary Racial Politics in the United States and Brazil

1. Some key works in this tradition are Degler 1986 (1971); Hasenbalg 1979; Skidmore 1972; Wagley and Harris 1958.

2. The systematic nature of racial discrimination in the United States is often contrasted with the supposedly more benign and casual discrimination of Brazil. Recent historical re-

search, however, has now demonstrated the extent to which overt and systematic racial discrimination was practiced in postabolition Brazil. See Andrews 1991.

3. In a strict sense, racial violence has always existed in Brazil, especially in rural areas and in the northeast, where its primary logic has been the struggle over land (see, among a voluminous literature, Movimento dos Trabalhadores Sem Terra, 1986). However, this type of violence has been less explicitly racialized than the recent urban type. The prime example of the latter is the proliferating "death squads" whose primary targets are black street children in the many *favelas* encircling Brazilian cities. This seems to be a new type of racial violence, symptomatic of changing patterns of racism in Brazil. See Centro de Articulação de Populações Marginalizadas 1989.

4. Getulio Vargas suppressed the FNB in 1937, after determining that it was a political party in formation; see Fernandes 1978: vol. 1, 10-115. In 1975, President Ernesto Geisel intervened in a case of racial discrimination; see Mitchell 1985: 118-19. In general the military hewed to the line of "antiracist racism": to denounce discrimination was to give evidence of one's own racism, of which Brazil was not culpable, etc.

5. Most prominently, the Olodum Cultural Group. A 1992 statement by Olodum, "In Freedom's Rhythm," is reprinted in translation in Mills 1992: 14.

6. In 1990, a group of nongovernmental organizations concerned with racism in Brazil formed Campanha Censo 90 with the aim of convincing Afro-Brazilians to identify themselves accurately, rather than to "lighten" themselves, in the upcoming census. The census itself was later postponed to 1991. The campaign, whose slogan was "Não deixe a sua cor passar em branco: responda com bom c/senso" (Don't let your color pass for white: respond with good sense—punning on sense/census/consensus), achieved significant attention through its strategy of using the mass media to get the message out. See Domingues 1992a, 1992b.

7. The *locus classicus* of this position is Wilson 1980, but it is very widely argued today.

8. For a review of the continuing (and in some respects worsening) dynamics of racial stratification in the United States, see Hacker 1992. For a review of Brazilian conditions, see the various papers in Lovell 1991.

9. Such was the interiority of the veil, with which I am particularly concerned here. But the veil also partook of exteriority: it was the color line, the color bar, segregation, Jim Crow, the racialized social structure as a whole. It tantalized and tormented black people as a collectivity, permitting them to view, but not granting them the right to partake of, their social, political, and economic birthright. It constantly proffered and withdrew alternative strategies for dealing with racism: the possibility of separation, of return to Africa, of abandoning the hateful white world. Du Bois continued his engagement with the metaphor of the veil throughout his work. See Du Bois 1991 (1940): 130-32 for a treatment of the theme that focuses more extensively on segregation.

10. For example, in some industrial sectors, which since the late 1930s had undergone strenuous unionization drives led by the integrated CIO. Even there, however, internal labor markets were largely segregated.

11. "Money whitens," a familiar Brazilian expression.

12. "In Brazil there is no racism. The black man knows his place."

Bibliography

Alba, Richard D., *Ethnic Identity: The Transformation of White America* (New Haven, Conn.: Yale University Press, 1990).

Amenta, Edwin, and Theda Skocpol, "Redefining the New Deal: World War II and the Development of Social Provision in the United States," in Margaret Weir et al., eds., *The Politics of Social Policy in the United States* (Princeton, N. J.: Princeton University Press, 1988).

Anderson, Benedict, *Imagined Communities: Reflections on the Origins and Spread of Nationalism*, rev. ed. (New York: Verso, 1991 [1983]).

Andrews, George Reid, *Blacks and Whites in São Paulo, Brazil, 1888-1988* (Madison: University of Wisconsin Press, 1991).

Appiah, Kwame Anthony, "Racisms," in David Theo Goldberg, ed., *Anatomy of Racism* (Minneapolis: University of Minnesota Press, 1990).

_____, "The Uncompleted Argument: Du Bois and the Illusion of Race," in Henry Louis Gates, ed., *"Race," Writing, and Difference* (Chicago: University of Chicago Press, 1986).

Apple, R. W., Jr., "Riots and Ballots," *New York Times*, May 2, 1992.

Auletta, Ken, *The Underclass* (New York: Random House, 1982).

Azevedo, Celia Marinho de, *Onda Negra, Medo Branco: O Negro no Imaginário das Elites—Século XIX* (Rio de Janeiro: Paz e Terra, 1987).

Azevedo, Thales de, *Democracia Racial: Ideologia e Realidade* (Petropolis: Editora Vozes, 1975).

_____, *Cultura e Situação Racial no Brasil* (Rio de Janeiro: Editora Civilização Brasileira, 1966).

Balibar, Etienne, and Immanuel Wallerstein, *Race, Nation, Class: Ambiguous Identities*, trans. Chris Turner (New Tork: Verso, 1991).

Baraka, Imamu Amiri, *Raise, Race, Rays, Raze: Essays Since 1965* (New York: Vintage, 1972).

Barkan, Elazar, *The Retreat of Scientific Racism: Changing Concepts of Race in Britain and the United States Between the World Wars* (New York: Cambridge University Press, 1992).

Barroso, Carmen, ed., *Mulher, Sociedade, e Estado no Brasil* (São Paulo: Brasilense, 1982).

Bastide, Roger, *The African Religions of Brazil: Toward a Sociology of the Interpenetration of Civilizations* (Baltimore: Johns Hopkins University Press, 1978).

———, "A Imprensa Negra do Estado de São Paulo," in idem, *Estudos Afro-Brasileiros* (São Paulo: Editora Perspectiva, 1973).

———, "The Development of Race Relations in Brazil," in Guy Hunter, ed., *Industrialization and Race Relations: A Symposium* (New York: Oxford University Press, 1965).

Bastide, Roger, and Florestan Fernandes, *Brancos e Negros em São Paulo* (São Paulo: Companhia Editora Nacional, 1959).

Bastide, Roger, and Pierre L. van den Berghe, "Stereotypes, Norms, and Interracial Behavior in São Paulo, Brazil," *American Sociological Review* 22 (1957).

Bean, Frank D., and Marta Tienda, *The Hispanic Population of the United States* (New York: Russell Sage Foundation, 1987).

Bell, Derrick, *Faces at the Bottom of the Well: The Permanence of Racism* (New York: Basic Books, 1992).

Bhabha, Homi K., *The Location of Culture* (New York: Routledge, 1993).

———, "DissemiNation: Time, Narrative, and the Margins of the Modern Nation," in idem, ed., *Nation and Narration* (London: Routledge, 1990a).

———, "Interrogating Identity: The Postcolonial Prerogative," in David Theo Goldberg, ed., *Anatomy of Racism* (Minneapolis: University of Minnesota Press, 1990b).

———, ed., *Nation and Narration* (New York: Routledge, 1990c).

Blauner, Robert, *Racial Oppression in America* (New York: Harper & Row, 1972).

Boschi, Renato R., "Social Movements and the New Political Order in Brazil," in John Wirth et al., eds., *State and Stability in Brazil: Continuity and Change* (Boulder, Colo.: Westview, 1987).

Boston, Thomas D., *Race, Class, and Conservatism* (Boston: Unwin Hyman, 1988).

Braudel, Fernand, *The Structures of Everyday Life: The Limits of the Possible*, vol. I of Braudel, *Civilization and Capitalism, 15th-18th Century*, trans. Sian Reynolds (New York: Harper & Row, 1981).

Brooks, Roy L., *Rethinking America's Race Problem* (Berkeley: University of California Press, 1990).

Brownstein, Ronald, "Clinton: Parties Fail to Attack Race Divisions," *Los Angeles Times*, May 3, 1992.

Burleigh, Michael, and Wolfgang Wippermann, *The Racial State: Germany, 1933-1945* (New York: Cambridge University Press, 1992).

Bush, George, "Excerpts from Speech by Bush in Los Angeles," *New York Times*, May 9, 1992.

Carby, Hazel, "Policing the Black Woman's Body," *Critical Inquiry* 18, no. 4 (1992).

Cardoso, Ruth C. L., "Movimentos Sociais Urbanos: Balanço Crítico," in Sebastião Velazco e Cruz et al., eds., *Sociedade e Política no Brasil pos-64* (São Paulo: Brasilense, 1983).

Carmichael, Stokely, *Stokely Speaks: Black Power Back to Pan-Africanism* (New York: Vintage, 1971).

Carneiro, Sueli, and Thereza Santos, *Mulher Negra* (São Paulo: Nobel/Conselho Estadual da Condição Feminina, 1985).

Carson, Clayborn, *In Struggle: SNCC and the Black Awakening of the 1960s* (Cambridge, Mass.: Harvard University Press, 1981).

Centre for Contemporary Cultural Studies, *The Empire Strikes Back: Race and Racism in 70s Britain* (London: Hutchinson, 1982).

Centro de Articulação de Populaçoes Marginalizadas (CEAP), *Extermínio de Crianças e Adolescentes no Brasil* (Rio de Janeiro: CEAP, 1989).

Chang, Irene, and Greg Krikorian, "30,000 Show Support in Koreatown March," *Los Angeles Times*, May 3, 1992.

Chase, Allan, *The Legacy of Malthus: The Social Costs of the New Scientific Racism* (New York: Knopf, 1977).

Chung, L. A., "S.F. Includes Asian Indians in Minority Law," *San Francisco Chronicle*, June 25, 1991.

Coleman, Wanda, "Blacks, Immigrants, and America," *Nation*, February 15, 1993.

Collins, Patricia Hill, *Black Feminist Thought: Knowledge, Consciousness, and the Politics of Empowerment* (New York: Routledge, 1991).

Cone, James H., *Martin and Malcolm in America: A Dream or a Nightmare* (Maryknoll, N. Y.: Orbis, 1991).

Connolly, William E., *Identity \ Difference: Democratic Negotiations of Political Paradox* (Ithaca, N. Y: Cornell University Press, 1991).

Cooper, Marc, and Greg Goldin, "Some People Don't Count," *Village Voice*, May 12, 1992.

Cornell, Stephen, *The Return of the Native: American Indian Political Resurgence* (New York: Oxford University Press, 1988).

Costa, Manoel Augusto, ed., *O Segundo Brasil: Perspectivas Socio-Demográficas* (Rio de Janeiro: Ebano, 1983).

Cross, William E., Jr., *Shades of Black: Diversity in African-American Identity* (Philadelphia: Temple University Press, 1991).

Cruse, Harold, *Rebellion or Revolution?* (New York: Morrow, 1968).

da Silva, Benedita Souza, "A Identidade da Mulher Negra—A Identidade da Mulher India," unpublished paper presented at the Conferencia Nacional Saude e Direitos da Mulher, October 1986.

Daniels, Roger, and Harry H. L. Kitano, *American Racism: Exploration of the Theory of Prejudice* (Englewood Cliffs, N.J.: Prentice-Hall, 1970).

Darnton, Robert, "Reading a Riot," *New York Review of Books*, September 22, 1992.

Davis, David Brion, *The Problem of Slavery in the Age of Revolution, 1770-1823* (Ithaca, N.Y.: Cornell University Press, 1975).

Davis, F. James, *Who Is Black? One Nation's Definition* (University Park: Pennsylvania State University Press, 1991).

Davis, Mike, *City of Quartz: Excavating the Future in Los Angeles* (London: Verso, 1990).

Degler, Carl N., *Neither Black nor White: Slavery and Race Relations in Brazil and the United*

States (Madison: University of Wisconsin Press, 1986 [1971]).

Dent, David, "The New Black Suburbs," *New York Times Magazine*, June 14, 1992.

Derrida, Jacques, "White Mythology," in idem, *Margins—of Philosophy*, trans. Alan Bass (Chicago: University of Chicago Press, 1982).

de Souza, Amaury, "Raça e Política no Brasil Urbano," *Revista Administração de Empresas* 2, no. 4 (1971).

Dionne, E. J., *Why Americans Hate Politics* (New York: Simon & Schuster, 1991).

Domingues, Regina, "The Color of a Majority without Citizenship," *Conexoes* 4, no. 2 (November 1992a). *Conexoes* is available from the African Diaspora Research Project, Urban Affairs Programs, Michigan State University, East Lansing, MI 48824-1109.

———, "The Politics of Whitening and the Black Hole of Citizenship," *Contato* 5, nos. 7-8 (November 30, 1992b). *Contato* is available from the Brazil Network, 815 15th St. N.W., Suite 426, Washington, DC 20005.

dos Santos, Joel Rufino, *O Movimento Negro e a Crise Brasileira* (São Paulo: FESP, 1985). Mimeo.

dos Santos, Theotonio, "Crisis y Movimientos Sociales en Brasil," in Fernando Calderón Gutierrez, ed., *Los Movimientos Sociales ante la Crisis* (Buenos Aires: CLACSO/United Nations University, 1985).

Drake, St. Clair, and Horace Cayton, *Black Metropolis: A Study of Negro Life in a Northern City*, 2 vols., 2nd ed., (New York: Harper & Row, 1962).

Du Bois, W.E.B., *Dusk of Dawn: An Essay Toward an Autobiography of a Race Concept* (New Brunswick, N.J.: Transaction, 1991 [1940]).

———, *Black Reconstruction in America: An Essay Toward a History of the Part Which Black Folk Played in the Attempt to Reconstruct Democracy in America, 1860-1880* (New York: Atheneum, 1977 [1935]).

———, *The Souls of Black Folk* (New York: Penguin, 1989 [1903]).

———, *The Philadelphia Negro: A Social Study* (New York: Schocken, 1967 [1899]).

Dunne, John Gregory, "Law and Disorder in Los Angeles" (two parts), *New York Review of Books*, October 10 and 24, 1991.

Dzidzienyo, Anani, *The Position of Blacks in Brazilian Society* (London: Minority Rights Group, 1971).

Edsall, Thomas Byrne, with Mary Edsall, *Chain Reaction: The Impact of Race, Rights, and Taxes on American Politics*, rev. ed. (New York: Norton, 1992).

Edsall, Thomas Byrne, and Mary D. Edsall, "Race," *Atlantic Monthly*, May 1991.

Eric B. and Rakim, "The Ghetto," on idem, *Let the Rhythm Hit 'Em* (MCA Records, 1990).

Erickson, Frederick, "Gatekeeping and the Melting Pot: Interaction in Counseling Encounters," *Harvard Educational Review* 45 (1975).

Espiritu, Yen Le, *Asian American Panethnicity: Bridging Institutions and Identities* (Philadelphia: Temple University Press, 1992).

Essoyan, Susan, "Native Hawaiians Vote for Clout," *San Francisco Chronicle*, January 31, 1990.

Evans, Sara, *Personal Politics* (New York: Random House, 1980).

Ezorsky, Gertrude, *Racism and Justice: The Case for Affirmative Action* (Ithaca, N.Y.: Cornell University Press, 1991).

Fanon, Frantz, *The Wretched of the Earth*, trans. Constance Farrington (New York: Grove, 1963).

———, "The Fact of Blackness," in idem, *Black Skin, White Masks*, trans. Charles Lam Markmann (New York: Grove, 1967 [1952]).

Feagin, Joe R., "The Continuing Significance of Race: Antiblack Discrimination in Public Places," *American Sociological Review* 56 (1991).

Ferguson, Ann, *Sexual Democracy: Women, Oppression, and Revolution* (Boulder, Colo.: Westview, 1991).

Fernandes, Florestan, *A Integração do Negro na Sociedade de Classes*, 2 vols., 3rd ed. (São Paulo: Atica, 1978).

———, "The Weight of the Past," in J. H. Franklin, ed., *Color and Race* (Boston: Beacon, 1969).

Fields, Barbara Jeanne, "Slavery, Race and Ideology in the United States of America," *New Left Review* 181 (May/June 1990).

Fontaine, Pierre-Michel, ed., *Race, Class, and Power in Brazil* (Los Angeles: Afro-American Studies Center, UCLA, 1985).

Forbes, Jack D., "The Hispanic Spin: Party Politics and Governmental Manipulation of Ethnic Identity," in Martha Gimenez et al., eds., *Latin American Perspectives*, no. 75 (vol. 19, no. 4; Fall 1992), special issue on "The Politics of Ethnic Construction: Hispanic, Chicano, Latino?"

———, *Black Africans and Native Americans: Color, Race and Caste in the Evolution of Red-Black Peoples* (New York: Basil Blackwell, 1988).

Franklin, John Hope, *From Slavery to Freedom: A History of Negro Americans* (New York: Vintage, 1969).

Frazier, E. Franklin, *Black Bourgeoisie: The Rise of a New Middle Class in the United States* (New York: Free Press, 1957).

Fredrickson, George M., *The Black Image in the White Mind: The Debate on Afro-American Character and Destiny, 1817-1914* (Middletown, Conn.: Wesleyan University Press, 1987).

Freeman, Richard, *The Black Elite: The New Market for Highly Educated Black Americans* (New York: McGraw-Hill, 1976).

Freyre, Gilberto, *New World in the Tropics: The Culture of Modern Brazil* (New York: Knopf, 1959).

———, *O Mundo Que o Português Criou* (Rio de Janeiro: Jose Olimpio, 1940).

Fuss, Diana, *Essentially Speaking: Feminism, Nature, and Difference* (New York: Routledge, 1989).

Gans, Herbert J., "Symbolic Ethnicity: The Future of Ethnic Groups and Cultures in America," *Ethnic and Racial Studies* 2 (January 1979).

Garreau, Joel, "Competing Bonds of Race and Class," *Washington Post*, November 30, 1987.

Gates, Henry Louis, Jr., "What's in a Name? Some Meanings of Blackness," in idem, *Loose Canons: Notes on the Culture Wars* (New York: Oxford University Press, 1992).

———, "Fanon and Colonial Discourse Theory," paper presented at the 1989 meetings of the Modern Language Association.

———, "Editor's Introduction: Writing 'Race' and the Difference It Makes," in idem, ed., *"Race," Writing, and Difference* (Chicago: University of Chicago Press, 1986a).

———, ed., *"Race," Writing, and Difference* (Chicago: University of Chicago Press, 1986b).

Genovese, Eugene D., *In Red and Black: Marxian Explorations in Southern and Afro-American History* (New York: Pantheon, 1971).

Giddings, Paula, *When and Where I Enter: The Impact of Black Women on Race and Sex in America* (New York: Morrow, 1984).

Gilroy, Paul, *"There Ain't No Black in the Union Jack": The Cultural Politics of Race and Nation* (Chicago: University of Chicago Press, 1991).

Gimenez, Martha, et al., eds., *Latin American Perspectives*, no. 75 (vol. 19, no. 4; Fall 1992), special issue on "The Politics of Ethnic Construction: Hispanic, Chicano, Latino?"

Gonzalez, Leila, "The Unified Black Movement: A New Stage in Black Political Mobilization," in Pierre-Michel Fontaine, ed., *Race, Class, and Power in Brazil* (Los Angeles: Afro-American Studies Center, UCLA, 1985).

Gould, Stephen J., *The Mismeasure of Man* (New York: Norton, 1981).

Gramsci, Antonio, *Selections from the Prison Notebooks*, ed. Geoffrey Nowell-Smith and Quentin Hoare (New York: International Publishers, 1971).

Grasmuck, Sherri, and Patricia R. Pessar, *Between Two Islands: Dominican International Migration* (Berkeley: University of California Press, 1991).

Greenberg, Stanley B., *Report on Democratic Defection*, prepared for the Michigan House Democratic Campaign Committee (Washington, D.C.: Analysis Group, 1985).

———, *Race and State in Capitalist Development: Comparative Perspectives* (New Haven, Conn.: Yale University Press, 1980).

Guha, Ranajit, and Gayatri Chakravorty Spivak, eds., *Selected Subaltern Studies* (New York: Oxford University Press, 1988).

Hacker, Andrew, *Two Nations, Black and White, Separate, Hostile, Unequal* (New York: Scribner, 1992).

Hall, Stuart, "Gramsci's Relevance for the Study of Race and Ethnicity," *Journal of Communication Inquiry* 10, no. 2 (1986).

Hanchard, Michael, *Orpheus and Power: The Movimento Negro of Rio de Janeiro and São Paulo, Brazil, 1945-1988* (Princeton, N.J.: Princeton University Press, forthcoming).

———, "Taking Exception: Narratives of Racial Equality in Brazil, Mexico, and Cuba," presented at the 1992 meetings of the Latin American Studies Association in Los Angeles.

———, "Identity, Meaning, and the African-American," *Social Text* 24 (1990).

Harding, Sandra, *The Science Question in Feminism* (Ithaca, N.Y.: Cornell University Press, 1987).

Harding, Vincent, *There Is a River: The Black Struggle for Freedom in America* (New York: Vintage, 1981).

Harris, Marvin, *Patterns of Race in the Americas* (New York: Walker, 1964).

Hasenbalg, Carlos A., untitled presentation, *Estudos Afro-Asiaticos* 12 (Rio de Janeiro: Conjunto Universitario Candido Mendes, August 1986).

_____, *Raça e Desigualdades Socioeconomicas no Brasil* (Rio de Janeiro: IUPERJ, 1983).

_____, *Discriminação e Desigualdades Raciais no Brasil* (Rio de Janeiro: Graal, 1979).

Hobsbawm, Eric J., *The Age of Revolution: 1789-1848* (New York: New American Library, 1962).

Hoetink, Harry, " 'Race' and Color in the Caribbean," in Sidney Mintz and Sally Price, eds., *Caribbean Contours* (Baltimore: Johns Hopkins University Press, 1985).

_____, *The Two Variants in Caribbean Race Relations* (London: Oxford University Press, 1967).

hooks, bell, *Ain't I a Woman? Black Women and Feminism* (Boston: South End Press, 1981).

Horkheimer, Max, and Theodor W. Adorno, *Dialectic of Enlightenment*, trans. John Cumming (New York: Continuum, 1989 [1944]).

Hurtado, Aida, "Relating to Privilege: Seduction and Rejection in the Subordination of White Women and Women of Color," *Signs: Journal of Women in Culture and Society* 14, no. 4 (1989).

Institute for Global Communications, "Europe: Racism Increasing," December 15, 1992, IGC:Gen.Newsletter (computerized newsletter); available from 18 de Boom St., San Francisco, CA 94107).

Institute for the Study of Social Change, *The Diversity Project: An Interim Report to the Chancellor* (Berkeley: University of California, 1990).

Inter Press Service, "Sweden: Racial Tension Simmers as Neo-Nazis March through Capital," December 4, 1992. IGC:ips.englibrary (computerized newsletter); available from the Institute for Global Communications, 18 de Boom St., San Francisco, CA 94107.

Jaynes, Gerald D., and Robin M. Williams, Jr., *A Common Destiny: Blacks and American Society* (Washington, D.C.: National Academy Press, 1989).

Jencks, Christopher, *Rethinking Social Policy: Race, Poverty, and the Underclass* (Cambridge, Mass.: Harvard University Press, 1992).

Jordan, Winthrop, *White over Black: American Attitudes toward the Negro, 1550-1812* (New York: Norton, 1977 [1968]).

Katz, Michael B., *The Undeserving Poor: From the War on Poverty to the War on Welfare* (New York: Pantheon, 1989).

Kaus, Mickey, *The End of Equality* (New York: Basic Books, 1992).

Kevles, Daniel J., *In the Name of Eugenics: Genetics and the Uses of Human Heredity* (New York: Knopf, 1985).

Kilson, Martin, "Problems of Black Politics: Some Progress, Many Difficulties," *Dissent*, Fall 1989.

Kilson, Martin, and Clement Cottingham, "Thinking about Race Relations: How Far Are We Still from Integration?" *Dissent*, Fall 1991.

Kim, David D., and Jeff Yang, "Koreatown Abandoned," *Village Voice*, May 12, 1992.

Kovel, Joel, *White Racism: A Psychohistory*, 2nd ed. (New York: Columbia University Press, 1984).

Kuper, Leo, *Genocide* (New York: Penguin, 1981).

Lamounier, Bolivar, "Raça e Classe na Política Brasileira," *Cadernos Brasileiros* 47 (1968).

Landry, Bart, *The New Black Middle Class* (Berkeley: University of California Press, 1987).

Leary, Warren E., "Uneasy Doctors Add Race-Consciousness to Diagnostic Tools," *New York Times*, September 25, 1990.

Lechner, Norbert, *Los Patios Interiores de la Democracía: Subjetividad y Política* (Santiago: FLACSO, 1988).

Lemann, Nicholas, *The Promised Land: The Great Black Migration and How It Changed America* (New York: Knopf, 1991).

Levinas, Emmanuel, "The Trace of the Other," in Mark C. Taylor, *Deconstruction in Context* (Chicago: University of Chicago Press, 1986).

Lieberson, Stanley, and Mary C. Waters, *From Many Strands: Ethnic and Racial Groups in Contemporary America* (New York: Russell Sage Foundation, 1988).

Light, Ivan H., and Edna Bonacich, *Immigrant Entrepreneurs: Koreans in Los Angeles, 1965-1982* (Berkeley: University of California Press, 1988).

Lopez, David, and Yen Espiritu, "Panethnicity in the United States: A Theoretical Framework," *Ethnic and Racial Studies* 13 (1990).

Lovell, Peggy, ed., *Desigualdade Racial no Brasil Contemporáneo* (Belo Horizonte: CEDEPLAR/FASE/UFMG; MGSP Editores, 1991).

Los Angeles Times, "Voices," May 3, 1992.

Lyman, Stanford M., *The Asian in the West* (Reno and Las Vegas: University of Nevada Press, 1970).

McMillen, Neil R., *Dark Journey: Black Mississippians in the Age of Jim Crow* (Urbana and Chicago: University of Illinois Press, 1989).

Maggie, Yvonne, ed., *Catálogo: Centenário da Abolição* (Rio de Janeiro: CIEC/UFRJ, 1989).

Mainwaring, Scott, "Urban Popular Movements, Identity, and Democratization in Brazil," undated manuscript.

Marley, Bob, and the Wailers (lyrics based on a speech of Haile Selassie), "War," *Rastaman Vibration* (Island Records, 1976).

Marsh, Dave, et al., *You've Got a Right to Rock* (Los Angeles: August 1990; available from Box 341305, Los Angeles, CA 90034).

Marx, Karl, *Capital*, vol. I (New York: International Publishers, 1967).

Meier, August, and Elliot Rudwick, *CORE: A Study in the Civil Rights Movement, 1942-1968* (New York: Oxford University Press, 1973).

Miles, Jack, "Blacks vs. Browns," *Atlantic Monthly*, October 1992.

Mills, Gisele, ed., "The Black Movement Today," *Contato* 5, nos. 7-8 (November 30, 1992). *Contato* is available from the Brazil Network, 815 15th St. N.W., Suite 426, Washington, DC 20005.

Minow, Martha, *Making All the Difference: Inclusion, Exclusion, and American Law* (Ithaca, N.Y.: Cornell University Press, 1990).

Mitchell, Michael, "Blacks and the *Abertura Democrática*," in Pierre-Michel Fontaine, ed. *Race, Class, and Power in Brazil* (Los Angeles: Afro-American Studies Center, UCLA, 1985).

Montejano, David, *Anglos and Mexicans in the Making of Modern Texas, 1836-1986* (Austin: University of Texas Press, 1987).

Morris, Aldon D., *The Origins of the Civil Rights Movement: Black Communities Organizing for Change* (New York: Free Press, 1984).

Morrison, Toni, *Playing in the Dark: Whiteness and the Literary Imagination* (Cambridge, Mass.: Harvard University Press, 1992a).

———, ed., *Race-ing Justice, En-gendering Power: Essays on Anita Hill, Clarence Thomas, and the Construction of Social Reality* (New York: Pantheon, 1992b).

Mosse, George, *Toward the Final Solution: A History of European Racism* (New York: Howard Fertig, 1978).

Mouffe, Chantal, "Radical Democracy: Modern or Postmodern?" in Andrew Ross, ed., *Universal Abandon? The Politics of Postmodernism* (Minneapolis: University of Minnesota Press, 1988).

Mouffe, Chantal, and Ernesto Laclau, *Hegemony and Socialist Strategy: Towards a Radical Democratic Politics* (London: Verso, 1985).

Moura, Clovis, *Brasil: As Raizes do Protesto Negro* (São Paulo: Global Editora, 1983).

Movimento dos Trabalhadores Sem Terra, *Assassinato no Campo: Crime e Impunidade* (São Paulo: Sem Terra, 1986).

Moynihan, Daniel P., *Family and Nation* (New York: Harcourt Brace Jovanovich, 1986).

Mudimbe, V. Y., *The Invention of Africa: Gnosis, Philosophy, and the Order of Knowledge* (Bloomington: Indiana University Press, 1988).

Muñoz, Carlos, Jr., *Youth, Identity, Power: The Chicano Movement* (New York: Verso, 1989).

Murray, Charles, *Losing Ground: American Social Policy, 1950-1980* (New York: Basic Books, 1984).

Mydans, Seth, "Los Angeles Police Officers Acquitted in Taped Beatings," *New York Times*, April 30, 1992.

Nascimento, Abdias do, "Quilombismo: The African-Brazilian Road to Socialism," in Molefi Kete Asante and Kariamu Welsh Asante, eds., *African Culture: The Rhythms of Unity* (Westport, Conn.: Greenwood, 1985)

———, ed., *O Negro Revoltado* (Rio de Janeiro: Edicoes GRD, 1978a).

———, *O Genocídio do Negro Brasileiro: Processo de Um Racismo Mascarado* (Rio de Janeiro: Paz e Terra, 1978b).

Nascimento, Maria Ercilia do, *A Estratégia da Desigualdade: O Movimento Negro dos Anos 70*, master's dissertation, PUC-São Paulo, 1989.

Novak, Michael, *The Rise of the Unmeltable Ethnics* (New York: Macmillan, 1972).

O'Hare, William P., and Judy Felt, "Asian Americans: America's Fastest Growing Minority Group," Population Trends and Public Policy Occasional Papers no. 19 (Washington, D.C.: Population Reference Bureau, 1991).

Oboler, Suzanne, *Labeling Hispanics: The Dynamics of Race, Class, Language, and National Origins* (Minneapolis: University of Minnesota Press, forthcoming).

————, "The Politics of Labeling: Latino/a Cultural Identities of Self and Others," in Martha Gimenez et al., eds., *Latin American Perspectives*, no. 75 (vol. 19, no. 4; Fall 1992), special issue on "The Politics of Ethnic Construction: Hispanic, Chicano, Latino?"

Oliveira, Lucia Elena Garcia, Rosa Maria Porcaro, and Tereza Cristina Nascimento Araujo, *O Lugar do Negro na Força de Trabalho* (Rio de Janeiro: IBGE, 1985).

————, "Repensando o Lugar da Mulher Negra," *Estudos Afro-Asiaticos* 13 (Rio de Janeiro: Conjunto Universitário Candido Mendes, March 1987).

Omi, Michael, and Howard Winant, "Contesting the Meaning of Race in the Post-Civil Rights Period," in Sylvia Pedraza and Ruben Rumbaut, eds., *Immigration, Race and Ethnicity in America: Historical and Contemporary Perspectives* (Belmont, Calif.: Wadsworth, forthcoming).

————, "The Los Angeles 'Race Riot' and Contemporary U.S. Politics," in Robert Gooding-Williams, ed., *Reading Rodney King, Reading Urban Uprising* (New York: Routledge, 1993).

————, "Race and the Right: The Politics of Reaction," in John H. Stanfield II, ed., *Research in Social Policy: Historical and Contemporary Perspectives*, vol. 1 (Greenwich, Conn.: JAI Press, 1987).

————, *Racial Formation in the United States: From the 1960s to the 1980s* (New York: Routledge, 1986).

————, "By the Rivers of Babylon: Race in the United States," part II, *Socialist Review* 72 (November/December 1983).

Painter, Nell Irvin, "Hill, Thomas, and the Use of Racial Stereotype," in Toni Morrison, ed., *Race-ing Justice, En-gendering Power: Essays on Anita Hill, Clarence Thomas, and the Construction of Social Reality* (New York: Pantheon, 1992).

Patterson, Orlando, "The Black Community: Is There a Future?" in Seymour Martin Lipset, ed., *The Third Century: America as a Postindustrial Society* (Stanford, Calif.: Hoover Institution Press, 1979).

Perlman, Selig, *The History of Trade Unionism in the United States* (New York: Augustus Kelley, 1950).

Phillips, Kevin, *The Politics of Rich and Poor: Wealth and the American Electorate in the Reagan Aftermath* (New York: HarperCollins, 1991).

Pierson, Donald, *Negroes in Brazil: A Study of Race Contact in Bahia* (Carbondale: Southern Illinois University Press, 1967 [1942]).

Piven, Frances Fox, and Richard A. Cloward, *The New Class War: Reagan's Attack on Welfare and Its Consequences* (New York: Pantheon, 1982).

Polanyi, Karl, *The Great Transformation: The Political and Economic Origins of Our Time*, rev. ed. (Boston: Beacon, 1957 [1944]).

Portes, Alejandro, and Robert L. Bach, *Latin Journey: Cuban and Mexican Immigrants in the United States* (Berkeley: University of California Press, 1985).

Przeworski, Adam, "Some Problems in the Study of the Transition to Democracy," in Guillermo O'Donnell et al., eds., *Transitions from Authoritarian Rule: Comparative Perspectives* (Baltimore: Johns Hopkins University Press, 1986).

Rabinow, Paul, "Representations Are Social Facts: Modernity and Post-Modernity in Anthropology," in James Clifford and George E. Marcus, eds., *Writing Culture: The Poetics and Politics of Ethnography* (Berkeley: University of California Press, 1986).

Rainwater, Lee, "Looking Back and Looking Up," *Transaction* 6 (February 1969).

Reed, Adolph, Jr., "False Prophet I: The Rise of Louis Farrakhan," and "False Prophet II: All for One and None for All," *Nation*, January 21 and 28, 1991.

Reed, Julia, "His Brilliant Career," *New York Review of Books*, April 19, 1992.

Rodrigues da Silva, Carlos Benedito, "Black Soul: Aglutinação Espontánea ou Identidade Étnica: Uma Contribuição ao Estudo das Manifestaçoes Culturais no Meio Negro," paper presented at the fourth annual meeting of the Associação Nacional de Posgraduação e Pesquisas em Ciencias Sociais (ANPOCS), 1980.

Rodriguez, Clara E., "Racial Classification among Puerto Rican Men and Women in New York," *Hispanic Journal of Behavioral Sciences* 12, no. 4 (November 1990).

_____, *Puerto Ricans: Born in the USA* (Boston: Unwin Hyman, 1989).

Roediger, David R., *The Wages of Whiteness. Race and the Making of the American Working Class* (New York: Verso, 1991).

Rosenbaum, David E., "White House Speaking in Code on Riot's Cause," *New York Times*, May 6, 1992.

Rothmiller, Mike, and Ivan G. Goldman, *L.A. Secret Police: Inside the LAPD Elite Spy Network* (New York: Pocket Books, 1992).

Rutten, Tim, "A New Kind of Riot," *New York Review of Books*, June 11, 1992.

Said, Edward, *Orientalism* (New York: Pantheon, 1978).

Santos Souza, Neusa, *Tornar-Se Negro* (Rio de Janeiro: Graal, 1983).

Sartre, Jean-Paul, *Critique of Dialectical Reason I: Theory of Practical Ensembles*, trans. Alan Sheridan Smith (London: New Left Books, 1976).

Saxton, Alexander, *The Rise and Fall of the White Republic: Class Politics and Mass Culture in Nineteenth Century America* (New York: Verso, 1990).

_____, *The Indispensable Enemy: Labor and the Anti-Chinese Movement in California* (Berkeley: University of California Press, 1971).

Scherer-Warren, Ilse, and Paulo J. Krischke, eds., *Uma Revolução no Cotidiano? Os Movimentos Sociais na America do Sul* (São Paulo: Brasilense, 1987).

Schmink, Marianne, "Women in Brazilian Abertura Politics," *Signs: Journal of Women in Culture and Society* 7 (Autumn, 1981).

Schuman, Howard, et al., *Racial Attitudes in America: Trends and Interpretations* (Cambridge, Mass: Harvard University Press, 1985).

Scott, James, *Weapons of the Weak: Everyday Forms of Peasant Resistance* (New Haven, Conn.: Yale University Press, 1985).

Shklar, Judith N., *American Citizenship: The Quest for Inclusion* (Cambridge, Mass.: Harvard University Press, 1991).

Silva, Nelson do Valle, "Industrialization, Employment, and Stratification in Brazil," in John Wirth et al., eds., *State and Society in Brazil* (Boulder, Colo.: Westview, 1987).

_____, "Updating the Cost of Not Being White in Brazil," in Pierre-Michel Fontaine, ed.,

Race, Class, and Power in Brazil (Los Angeles: Afro-American Studies Center, UCLA, 1985).

———, "Cor e Processo de Realização Socioeconomica," *Dados* 24, no. 3 (1980).

Skidmore, Thomas E., "Race and Class in Brazil: Historical Perspectives," in Pierre-Michel Fontaine, ed. *Race, Class, and Power in Brazil* (Los Angeles: Afro-American Studies Center, UCLA, 1985).

———, *Black into White: Race and Nationality in Brazilian Thought* (New York: Oxford University Press, 1974).

———, "Toward a Comparative Analysis of Race Relations Since Abolition in Brazil and the United States," *Journal of Latin American Studies* 4, no. 1 (May 1972).

Skocpol, Theda, "The Limits of the New Deal System and the Roots of Contemporary Welfare Dilemmas," in Margaret Weir et al., eds., *The Politics of Social Policy in the United States* (Princeton, N.J.: Princeton University Press, 1988).

Sleeper, Jim, *The Closest of Strangers: Liberalism and the Politics of Race in New York* (New York: Norton, 1990).

Small, Stephen, " 'Racialised Relations' in Britain: An Introspective and International Perspective," unpublished paper, 1991.

Sodre, Muniz, *A Verdade Seduzida* (Rio de Janeiro: Francisco Alves, 1983).

Sombart, Werner, *Why Is There No Socialism in the United States?* trans. Patricia Hocking and C. T. Husbands (White Plains, N.Y.: International Arts and Sciences Press, 1976 [1896]).

Source, subscriptions available from 594 Broadway, New York, NY 10012.

Sowell, Thomas, *The Economics and Politics of Race: An International Perspective* (New York: Quill, 1983).

Spivak, Gayatri Chakravorty, "Can the Subaltern Speak?" in Cary Nelson and Lawrence Grossberg, eds., *Marxism and the Interpretation of Culture* (Urbana: University of Illinois Press, 1988).

Stepan, Alfred, *Rethinking Military Politics: Brazil and the Southern Cone* (Princeton, N.J.: Princeton University Press, 1988).

Stephens, Thomas M., *Dictionary of Latin American Racial and Ethnic Terminology* (Gainesville: University of Florida Press, 1989).

Takagi, Dana Y., *The Retreat from Race: Asian Admissions and Racial Politics* (New Brunswick, N.J.: Rutgers University Press, 1993).

Takaki, Ronald, *Strangers from a Distant Shore: A History of Asian Americans* (New York: Penguin, 1990).

Tannenbaum, Frank, *Slave and Citizen: The Negro in the Americas* (New York: Vintage, 1947).

Terkel, Studs, *Race: How Blacks and Whites Think and Feel about the American Obsession* (New York: New Press, 1992).

Thomas, W. I., and Dorothy Swaine Thomas, *The Child in America* (New York: Knopf, 1928).

Tikkum, "Roundtable: Domestic Social Policy after the L.A. Uprising," vol. 7, no. 4 (July/August 1992).

Todorov, Tsvetan, *The Conquest of America: The Question of the Other*, trans. Richard Howard (New York: Harper & Row, 1985).

Turner, J. Michael, "Brown into Black: Changing Racial Attitudes of Afro-Brazilian University Students," in Pierre-Michel Fontaine, ed., *Race, Class, and Power in Brazil* (Los Angeles: Afro-American Studies Center, UCLA, 1985).

U.S. Bureau of the Census, *Money Income and Poverty Status in the United States* (Washington, D.C.: Government Printing Office, 1990).

_____, Current Population Reports, P-60, no. 168 (Washington, D.C.: Government Printing Office, 1989).

Valente, Ana Lucia E. F., *Política e Relações Raciais: Os Negros e as Eleições Paulistas de 1982* (São Paulo: USP, Faculdade de Filosofia, Letras, e Ciencias Humanas, 1986).

Van Deburg, William L., *New Day in Babylon: The Black Power Movement and American Culture, 1965-1975* (Chicago: University of Chicago Press, 1992).

van den Berghe, Pierre, *Race and Racism: A Comparative Perspective* (New York: Wiley, 1967).

van Dijk, Teun, "Discourse and the Denial of Racism," *Discourse and Society* 3, no. 1 (1992).

Viotti da Costa, Emilia, *The Brazilian Empire: Myths and Histories* (Chicago: University of Chicago Press, 1985).

_____, *Da Senzala a Colónia*, 2nd ed. (São Paulo: Diffusão Europeia, 1982).

_____, *Da Monarquia a República: Momentos Decisivos* (São Paulo, Grijalbo, 1977).

Wagley, Charles, ed., *Race and Class in Rural Brazil* (New York: Columbia University Press, 1963).

Wagley, Charles, and Marvin Harris, *Minorities in the New World: Six Case Studies* (New York: Columbia University Press, 1958).

Walters, Ronald, "White Racial Nationalism in the United States," *Without Prejudice* I 1 (Fall 1987).

Waters, Mary C., *Ethnic Options: Choosing Identities in America* (Berkeley: University of California Press, 1990).

West, Cornel, "Black Leadership and the Pitfalls of Racial Reasoning," in Toni Morrison, ed., *Race-ing Justice, En-gendering Power: Essays on Anita Hill, Clarence Thomas, and the Construction of Social Reality* (New York: Pantheon, 1992).

_____, "Nihilism in Black America," *Dissent*, Spring 1991.

_____, *The American Evasion of Philosophy: A Genealogy of Pragmatism* (Madison: University of Wisconsin Press, 1990).

_____, "Race and Social Theory: Towards a Genealogical Materialist Analysis," in Mike Davis et al., eds., *The Year Left 2* (London: Verso, 1987).

Wilkerson, Isabel, "Separate Senior Proms Reveal an Unspanned Racial Divide," *New York Times*, May 5, 1991.

Williams, Lena, "When Blacks Shop, Bias Often Accompanies Sale," *New York Times*, April 30, 1991.

Wilson, William Julius, "The Right Message," *New York Times*, March 17, 1992.

_____, "Studying Inner-City Social Dislocations," *American Sociological Review* 56, no. 1 (1991).

_____, *The Truly Disadvantaged: The Inner City, the Underclass, and Public Policy* (Chicago: University of Chicago Press, 1987).

————, *The Declining Significance of Race: Blacks and Changing American Institutions*, 2nd. ed. (Chicago: University of Chicago Press, 1980).

Winant, Howard, "Race: Theory, Culture, and Politics in the United States Today," in Marcy Darnovsky, Barbara Epstein, and Richard Flacks, eds., *Social Movements and Cultural Politics* (Philadelphia: Temple University Press, forthcoming).

————, "Postmodern Racial Politics: Difference and Inequality," *Socialist Review* 90, no. 1 (January/March 1990).

Wolf, Eric, *Europe and the People without History* (Berkeley: University of California Press, 1982).

Wood, Charles H., and Jose Alberto Magno de Carvalho, *The Demography of Inequality in Brazil* (New York: Cambridge University Press, 1988).

Young, Iris Marion, *Justice and the Politics of Difference* (Princeton, N.J.: Princeton University Press, 1990).

Young, Robert M., *White Mythologies: Writing History and the West* (New York: Routledge, 1990).

Index

Compiled by Robin Jackson

Howard Winant teaches in the sociology department and the Latin American studies program at Temple University in Philadelphia. He is the coauthor of *Racial Formation in the United States* (second edition, 1994) and has also written *Stalemate: Political Economic Origins of Supply-Side Policy* (1988).

epistemology
anathema
fungible
ossify

970 - 349 - 2262

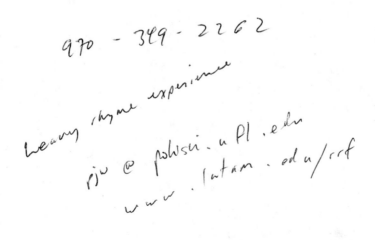

heavy thyme experience

rju @ polisci.uPl.edu
www.lutam.edu/rrf